Merrymeeting Merry Eating

A collection of recipes gathered in Maine

Regional Memorial Hospital Auxiliary Brunswick, Maine 04011

Dedication

Dedicated to the 250th Anniversary of Incorporation,
Town of Brunswick, Maine 1739-1989

The Cookbook Committee

Co-chairmen
Audrey Parkinson
Millie Stewart

Marie Almy
Mary Brown
Timmy Browne
Kay Charles
Lindsay Crosby
Honour Edgerton
Lea Favreau
Betty Fitzjarrald
Debbie Gleason

Betty Hentz
Kay Haggerty
Jan Harris
Helen Hunter
McGee Kanwit
Harriet Paris
Pat Robinson
Debbie Schall
Marilyn Scott
Marge West
Barbara Whitney
Lois Widmer
Doris Williams

Special thanks to Stephen Harris for the many hours
he has spent at his word processor preparing the recipes for
this book.

A Note About the Recipe Testing

Our dedicated committee has gathered this collection of over 400 recipes and each one has been tested in a kitchen of the Brunswick region. Every effort has been made to insure that the ingredients are obtainable and that directions and quantities are correct. Refinements were made where necessary to provide the cook with simple, logical steps.

Wherever possible, salt has been reduced to a minimum. Today we are more conscious than ever of foods which might cause problems for our bodies. Adapt the recipes to individual needs. Unless specified, all eggs in the recipes are large, all sugar is white and granulated, all flour is all-purpose white, and all milk is whole. Brand names of ingredients are used only if a recipe specified no substitutions. For best results, use fresh ingredients.

Table of Contents

BRUNSWICK

Scale: 240 Rods to the inch.

Introduction

On the coast of Maine, at the confluence of the Abaga-
dusset, Androscoggin, Cathance, Kennebec and Muddy
Rivers, there lies a body of water with a charming name—
Merrymeeting Bay. The bay is rich with wildlife, beauty and
history. It is as lovely today as it was to our native
Americans centuries ago.

The rivers meander past historic towns. Indians and early
settlers lived along the shores of this bay and these rivers.
Thomas Purchase was the first settler to live in Brunswick,
coming in 1628 to seek adventure in a free land. He was a
hunter, trapper, fisherman and trader. The Androscoggin
River and Merrymeeting Bay were then known as among the
best fishing grounds in New England. Now, with environ-
mental programs cleaning up our rivers, pollution has been
halted and fish have returned.

Merrymeeting Merry Eating, is published in honor of the
250th anniversary of the incorporation of the town of
Brunswick. A population center as it was 250 years ago,
Brunswick represents a diverse and wonderful mix of people.
Here we have Bowdoin College, Brunswick Naval Air
Station, the French Canadians who came in the mid 19th
century, the Scotch Irish who were the first permanent
settlers, and others who have come to enjoy the amenities of
the town.

Along with all peoples of the world, the rites of passage of
life in Maine are accompanied by ceremony, good food and
drink. These merry meetings make for merry eating.

The cookbook has been two years in planning by members
of Brunswick's Regional Memorial Hospital Auxiliary. It
represents the kind of community we are, bringing together
our kitchens, our cultures and travels experienced by our
cooks. Our lives are enriched by sharing these recipes.

We heartily acknowledge and thank the many friends and employees of the hospital, members of the Auxiliary and volunteers who contributed to the book by sharing their ideas and recipes. It has been a remarkable community project and represents thousands of volunteer hours. All proceeds will benefit Regional Memorial Hospital.

Welcome to *Merrymeeting Merry Eating*! Enjoy the bounty of the good earth, prepared by good people and good cooks—with good intentions.

Appetizers

Blue Cheese Log

1 Log

Ingredients

4 ounces blue cheese
8 ounces cream cheese, softened
¼ cup margarine, softened
1 tablespoon sweet vermouth or sherry
¼ cup chopped ripe olives
1 tablespoon chopped chives or green onions
4 ounces almonds, chopped fine

Preparation

Work cheeses and margarine together until creamy. Add other ingredients, except nuts, and shape into long cylinder (or two smaller ones). Roll in almonds and chill. May be stored in refrigerator for a week.

"Boursin" Cheese in Snow Peas

1 cup

Ingredients

8 ounces cream cheese, softened
¼ cup margarine or butter. softened
2 teaspoons milk
½ teaspoon oregano
¼ teaspoon each: thyme, basil, dill weed, marjoram
¼ teaspoon garlic powder
1½ pounds fresh snow peas, strings removed

Preparation

Cream cheese and margarine and add other ingredients, blending until smooth. Refrigerate several hours to blend flavors. Blanch peas in boiling water for 10 seconds. Chill in cold water immediately. Gently open and fill with cheese.

Brie Cheese in Pastry

20 servings

Wonderful warm cheese

Ingredients

1   17½-ounce package frozen puff pastry, thawed
1   36-ounce wheel of Brie cheese
1   egg
1   teaspoon water

Preparation

Roll pastry into two circles, large enough to fit the wheel of cheese. Place one circle on baking pan and place cheese on top. Place other circle on top and pinch edges of pastry together. Beat egg and water together and brush onto pastry. Bake in preheated 400° oven for 25 minutes. Allow to cool 10 minutes before transferring to a large serving platter which has a rim. Serve with crackers.

Cheese Crispies

5 dozen

Oldies, but goodies

Ingredients

1   cup butter or margarine, softened
2   cups grated sharp Cheddar cheese
2   scant cups flour
⅛   teaspoon salt
⅛   teaspoon ground hot pepper
⅛   teaspoon Tabasco sauce
2   cups Rice Krispies

Preparation

Work butter and cheese together with hands. Add flour and seasonings. Mix well. Add Rice Krispies. Roll into small balls and place on ungreased cookie sheet. Flatten with fork. Bake in preheated 350° oven 12 to 15 minutes. These wafers freeze well.

Pineapple Chutney Cheese Canapé

10 servings

Pretty for a party

Ingredients

½ small fresh pineapple
¼ cup chutney, cut into small pieces
¼ teaspoon dry mustard
1 teaspoon curry powder
8 ounces cream cheese
2 tablespoons chopped candied ginger, optional
¼ cup chopped walnuts or pecans

Preparation

Cut pineapple in half lengthwise, leaving on some of green stem. Remove most of pineapple from shell. Mix chutney, mustard, curry powder, cheese and ginger. Pack into pineapple shell. Sprinkle with nuts. Serve with crackers. Cut pineapple removed from shell into chunks, spear with toothpicks, and serve on tray with canapé.

Sherry Cheese Pie

15 to 20 servings

Ingredients

4 ounces blue cheese, crumbled
8 ounces cream cheese, softened
8 ounces sharp Cheddar cheese, grated
1 teaspoon curry powder
2 tablespoons dry sherry
½ cup Major Grey's chutney
1 bunch scallions, chopped

Preparation

Mix cheeses, curry powder and sherry. Lightly grease a 9-inch glass pie plate and spread mixture evenly on bottom. Chill until 3 hours before serving. Cover entire top with chutney and top with scallions. Serve with large corn chips or crackers.

Very Special Cheese Ring 12 to 15 servings

Unique, delicious combination!

Ingredients
1 pound New York sharp Cheddar cheese, grated
1 cup chopped pecans
1 cup mayonnaise
1 small onion, grated
cracked pepper to taste
dash of cayenne pepper
1 pound jar strawberry preserves

Preparation
Mix all ingredients, except preserves, adding seasonings last. Mold mixture in hands into a long, sausage-like shape and place on serving dish in a circle. Cover with plastic wrap and refrigerate until thoroughly chilled. When ready to serve, fill the center with strawberry preserves. Serve with crackers.

Hot Sausage Canapés 30 to 40 balls

Ingredients
1 pound hot Italian sausage, casings removed
3 cups Bisquick
10 ounces sharp Cheddar cheese, grated

Preparation
Mix sausage meat and Bisquick by hand. Melt cheese in double boiler and pour over sausage mix. Knead well. Make into small balls and bake on ungreased cookie sheet in preheated 350° oven for 20 minutes. Serve hot. Balls may also be frozen and baked as needed after thawing.

Sweet and Sour Meatballs

12 servings

So good!

Ingredients

2 pounds lean ground beef
2 eggs
1 envelope dehydrated onion soup
⅔ cup fresh bread crumbs
1¼ cups water (that's right!)
¼ teaspoon pepper
¼ teaspoon garlic powder

Sauce:
16 ounces Hunt's tomato sauce
⅓ cup brown sugar
juice of 1 lemon
1 teaspoon Worcestershire sauce

Preparation

Mix ingredients for meatballs lightly and form into 1-inch balls. Brown these in a little butter or under broiler. Cool and store until ready to use, or freeze. Heat sauce and add meatballs. Serve warm in chafing dish. May also be served as a luncheon dish with rice or noodles.

Curry Dip

1 cup

Ingredients

½ cup Hellman's mayonnaise
½ cup sour cream
½ teaspoon curry powder
1 tablespoon Major Grey's Chutney (or more to taste)
paprika or finely chopped parsley, for garnish

Preparation

Mix ingredients well. Garnish with dusting of paprika or finely chopped parsley. Serve with assorted raw vegetables.

M. Ying's Fried Walnuts

4 cups

Ingredients

4   cups walnuts (halves and quarters)
½   cup sugar
½   teaspoon salt
    peanut oil

Preparation

Bring 6 cups water to a boil, add nuts and boil 1 minute. Rinse under warm running water. Drain well. Toss walnuts in sugar. Heat 1-inch of oil in electric skillet at 350°. Add half the walnuts and fry 5 minutes, or until golden, stirring often. Place walnuts in sieve over bowl to drain. Sprinkle with salt and toss lightly to keep from sticking together. Transfer to brown paper to drain and cool. Repeat process with second half of walnuts. Store in tightly covered container.

Spiced Pecans

1 pound

Ingredients

1   large egg white
1   tablespoon water
1   pound pecan halves
¾ to 1 cup sugar
1   teaspoon cinnamon
½   teaspoon salt

Preparation

Beat egg white and water until frothy. Add pecan halves. Mix sugar, cinnamon and salt and stir into nuts. Spread on buttered baking sheet. Bake in preheated 225° oven for 1 hour, stirring every 15 minutes.

Creamy Horseradish Mold

2 cups

Serve with cold meats

Ingredients

3 ounces lemon-flavored gelatin
½ cup boiling water
1 tablespoon unflavored gelatin
2 tablespoons cold water
1 scant cup mayonnaise
5 ounces prepared horseradish
1 cup sour cream

Preparation

Dissolve lemon gelatin in boiling water. Soften unflavored gelatin in cold water. Add to lemon gelatin and stir in remaining ingredients. Pour into 2-cup oiled mold and refrigerate. Especially good with ham and biscuits, instead of mustard.

Chicken Liver Mold

2 cups

Ingredients

¼ cup butter
1 pound chicken livers
1 small onion, chopped
1 cup cream sherry
½ teaspoon marjoram
  dash pepper
1 slice toast, made into crumbs in blender
4 slices crisp bacon, crumbled

Preparation

Melt butter and sauté chicken livers until no longer pink in center. Remove from pan and cook onion until transparent. Remove from pan. Add sherry and cook a few minutes, stirring to incorporate brown bits. Pour into blender and add onions and livers with spices. Blend until smooth. Turn into bowl and add bread crumbs and bacon. Pour into greased 2-cup mold, cover and chill at least 2 hours until firm. Serve with Melba toast. Freezes well.

Green Chili Cheese Bites   25 to 30 servings

Ingredients

10   ounces chopped green chilies, drained
20   ounces Monterey Jack cheese, shredded
6   eggs, beaten
12   Ritz crackers, crushed
1   cup sour cream

Preparation

Mix ingredients and pour into buttered 9 x 13-inch casserole dish. Bake in preheated 350° oven for 60 minutes, or until knife comes out clean. Remove from oven and cool 10 minutes. Cut into 1-inch squares and serve warm.

Hot Chili Spread   12 servings

Ingredients

8   ounces cream cheese, softened
16   ounces chili without beans
8   ounces Cheddar cheese, grated
¼   cup onion, finely chopped
½   cup black olives, sliced

Preparation

Lightly grease quiche dish or 9-inch glass pie plate. Spread cream cheese over bottom. Cover cream cheese with chili. Sprinkle Cheddar over chili as evenly as possible. Sprinkle onions and olives over top. Bake in preheated 375° oven for 15 minutes or until mixture bubbles. Serve with corn or tortilla chips.

Tex-Mex Layered Dip

24 servings

Great for a crowd!

Ingredients

1½ pounds ground beef
1 medium onion, chopped
12 ounces refried beans
7 ounces chopped green chilies, mild or hot, your choice
3 to 5 cups grated Monterey Jack cheese
2½ to 3 cups guacamole
1 pint sour cream
4 scallions, chopped
1 small can black olives, sliced
1 large tomato, seeded and chopped
1 large bag tortilla chips

Guacamole:
3 to 4 ripe avocados
salt to taste
juice of 2 lemons
dash of Tabasco sauce

Preparation

Sauté meat and onion, drain. Add beans and chilies and spread on 9 x 13-inch ovenproof platter. Sprinkle cheese over mixture and warm in preheated 250° oven until cheese melts. Spread guacamole dip over cheese, top with sour cream. Arrange scallions, olives and tomato over sour cream. Serve with tortilla chips.

For dip, cut and scoop pulp from avocados. Mash with fork. Add other ingredients. To maintain green color, leave an avocado seed in dip until ready to use.

Calliope Crab

4 cups

Ingredients

10½ ounces cream of mushroom soup
8   ounces cream cheese
2   tablespoons unflavored gelatin, dissolved in 3
     tablespoons cold water
½   cup chopped celery
½   cup chopped onion
1   cup mayonnaise
1   cup crabmeat
     fresh parsley

Preparation

Heat soup, add cream cheese and stir until melted. Add gelatin and rest of ingredients, except parsley. Pour into 4 cup mold. Refrigerate several hours or overnight. Unmold onto plate and decorate with parsley. Serve with crackers.

Crabby Dip

4 cups

Ingredients

½   cup butter, melted
¼   cup onion, chopped
2   tablespoons chopped parsley
¼   cup chopped celery
8   ounces cream cheese, softened
⅛   teaspoon garlic powder
¼   teaspoon Tabasco sauce
½   teaspoon salt
1   tablespoon Worcestershire sauce
1   pound crabmeat

Preparation

Sauté onions, parsley and celery in butter. Stir in cream cheese. Add seasonings and mix well. Fold in crabmeat gently. Place in 2-quart baking dish and bake in preheated 350° oven for 15 minutes, or microwave on high for 4 minutes. Serve with crackers or chips.

Lobster Dip

2 cups

One lobster will do it!

Ingredients

8   ounces cream cheese, softened
1   medium garlic clove, chopped fine
1   tablespoon lemon juice, heated
2   tablespoons cocktail sauce
1   teaspoon Worcestershire sauce
    salt and pepper to taste
1   tablespoon mayonnaise
¼   cup milk
1   cup chopped lobster
½   cup sliced almonds

Preparation

Combine all ingredients except lobster and almonds, beating well. Fold in lobster and place in 2 cup casserole. Top with almonds. Bake in preheated 350° oven for 15 to 20 minutes. Serve with crackers.

Mussels Divine

25 servings

Make a day ahead

Ingredients

2   pounds mussels, in shells
¼   cup dry white wine
1   onion, chopped
¼   cup olive oil
2   garlic cloves, minced
1   teaspoon ground cumin
1   pound tomatoes, chopped, or 35-ounce can Italian plum tomatoes, chopped and drained
1   4-inch fresh green hot chili pepper, minced
2   tablespoons chopped scallions
2   teaspoons dried coriander

Preparation   Steam mussels in wine until shells open. Strain and reserve
½ cup liquid. Discard top shells. Loosen mussels and leave
in bottom shells. Chill. Sauté onion in olive oil until soft,
add garlic and cumin, ½ cup reserved liquid and tomatoes.
Simmer 10 minutes. Stir in chopped chili pepper, scallions,
salt and pepper to taste. Let cool. Stir in coriander and
spoon sauce over mussels. Serve cold.

Mussels in Garlic Butter   24 servings

Ingredients   24   fresh mussels in shells
½   cup softened butter or margarine
1   tablespoon finely chopped fresh parsley
1   tablespoon fresh lemon juice
1   shallot, minced
3   large garlic cloves, minced
1   slice uncooked bacon, minced
salt and pepper to taste

Preparation   Clean mussels and put into pot with ½ cup water. Cover
and steam 5 to 7 minutes on high heat until shells are wide
open. Remove mussels and discard half the shells.

Blend butter and remaining ingredients thoroughly. Put dab
in each of 24 shells, place mussel on top and cover with
more butter mixture. Place shells in shallow baking dish and
bake in preheated 400° oven for 15 to 20 minutes, until very
hot and bubbly. Serve sizzling hot with cocktail forks or
picks. These mussels may be prepared ahead, frozen, and
baked at last minute.

Saffron Scallops

20 servings

Ingredients

1 pound sea scallops, cut horizontally into rounds
⅓-inch thick
1 tablespoon olive oil

Saffron Mayonnaise:
⅛ teaspoon crumbled saffron threads
1 large egg, at room temperature
5 teaspoons fresh lemon juice
1 teaspoon Dijon mustard
¼ teaspoon salt
¼ teaspoon white pepper
1 cup olive oil
chopped chives for garnish

Preparation

In large skillet, sauté scallops in 1 tablespoon olive oil, covered, until opaque, 2 to 3 minutes. Place in bowl, cover loosely and allow to cool.

For saffron mayonnaise, combine saffron with 2 teaspoons hot water in small bowl. Mix egg and seasonings in blender and, with motor running, add 1 cup oil in slow stream until emulsified. Stir in saffron mix and adjust seasonings to taste. Place in large bowl. Dry scallops and put into saffron mayonnaise, coating well. Chill in refrigerator. When ready, to serve place each scallop on round of melba toast. Garnish with chopped chives.

Shrimp Cranberry Puffs

40 servings

Ingredients

10 slices firm white bread
1 cup Hellman's mayonnaise
⅓ cup grated sharp Cheddar cheese
¼ cup chopped fresh cranberries
1 pound cooked Maine shrimp or 2 cans medium shrimp, rinsed
extra cranberries, halved

Preparation Toast bread slices lightly and make 40 1½-inch rounds. Mix mayonnaise, cheese and chopped cranberries. Place one shrimp on each toast round and frost generously with mayonnaise mixture. Top with ½ cranberry. Broil just until golden and puffy, 2 to 3 minutes.

Artichoke Squares

24 squares

Ingredients
- 12 ounces marinated artichoke hearts
- 1 small onion, finely chopped
- ¼ cup dried fine bread crumbs
- 2 cups grated sharp Cheddar cheese
- 4 eggs, beaten
- ¼ teaspoon salt
- ⅛ teaspoon pepper
- ⅛ teaspoon dried oregano
- 2 tablespoons minced fresh parsley
- ⅛ teaspoon Tabasco sauce

Preparation Use liquid from 1 jar artichokes to sauté onion. Chop artichoke hearts and mix with onion, bread crumbs and liquid. Add eggs, cheese and seasonings. Pour into buttered 7 x 11-inch pan. Bake in preheated 325° oven for 30 minutes. Cool slightly and cut into squares.

Asparagus with Crêpes

32 servings

Ingredients

10 stalks asparagus, cut into 3-inch pieces
mayonnaise

Crepes:
½ cup cold water
½ cup cold milk
2 eggs
1 cup flour
2 tablespoons butter or margarine, melted
¼ teaspoon salt

Preparation

Blanch asparagus in boiling water 1½ to 2 minutes. Chill immediately in cold water. Drain well.

Make crêpes by combining ingredients in blender and blending 1 minute. Scrape down sides and blend another minute. Refrigerate 2 hours or more. Heat and oil crêpe pan. For each crêpe, add 1 tablespoon batter, swirl to about 3 inches and cook until top is almost dry and bottom is slightly brown. Reserve on wax paper. Repeat with remaining batter. Crêpes may be made ahead and frozen between layers of wax paper. Thaw at room temperature.

To assemble, spread crêpe with mayonnaise and place piece of asparagus on top. Roll up.

Caponata

2½ cups

Ingredients

1 pound whole eggplant, pricked several times with fork
½ cup chopped onion
1 large tomato, seeded and quartered
¼ cup chopped fresh parsley
3 garlic cloves, minced
2 tablespoons tomato paste
1 teaspoon salt
¼ teaspoon freshly ground black pepper
2 tablespoons good quality olive oil
2 teaspoons fresh lemon juice

Preparation

Place eggplant on double thickness of paper toweling in microwave, uncovered, and cook at 100 percent for 12 minutes. Remove and cool. When eggplant is cool enough to handle, cut in half lengthwise and scoop out meat.

Place eggplant, onion, tomato, parsley, garlic, tomato paste, salt and pepper in food processor and process just until mixture is coarsely chopped. Stir in oil and lemon juice. Serve at room temperature with warm pita bread or raw vegetables.

Cucumbers and Cherry Tomatoes with Salmon

60 servings

Ingredients

1	cup flaked cooked salmon
3	hard boiled eggs
¼	cup mayonnaise
1	tablespoon freshly grated horseradish
1	tablespoon minced celery
1	teaspoon tomato paste
1	teaspoon lemon juice
	salt and pepper to taste
12	cherry tomatoes
4	4-inch pickling cucumbers
	fresh dill for garnish

Preparation

Purée salmon, eggs, mayonnaise, horseradish, celery, tomato paste, lemon juice, salt and pepper in food processor or blender.

Remove thin slice from top of each tomato, reserving slice to use as lid. Remove pulp and seeds. Sprinkle with salt and invert on paper towels to drain. Half cucumbers lengthwise and scoop out seeds. Sprinkle with salt and also invert on paper towels to drain.

Fill tomatoes and cucumbers with salmon mixture. Replace lids on tomatoes and decorate with sprig of dill. Sprinkle dill on cucumbers. Slice each cucumber into 6 slices.

Marinated Mushrooms
8 servings

Ingredients

⅔ cup tarragon vinegar
½ cup vegetable oil
1 garlic clove, minced
1½ teaspoons salt
1½ teaspoons pepper
1 tablespoon sugar
2 tablespoons water
3 dashes Tabasco sauce
3 small sliced onions
24 ounces button mushrooms, fresh or canned

Preparation

Mix ingredients in non-metal bowl with lid and refrigerate. Best after several days.

Onion Pesto Tart
40 servings

Ingredients

Pesto:
2 large garlic cloves
3 ounces freshly grated Parmesan cheese
¼ cup pine nuts
2 cups fresh basil leaves
½ teaspoon salt
⅓ cup good quality olive oil

10 medium onions, 2¼ pounds, sliced in ¼-inch slices
3 tablespoons good quality olive oil
1 tablespoon sugar
3 tablespoons Dijon mustard
8½ ounce sheet puff pastry
20 Greek olives, pitted and halved

Preparation

For pesto, finely mince garlic, cheese, nuts, basil and salt in food processor or blender. Add oil and mix well. Reserve.

Add onions to heated oil in large skillet. Sprinkle with sugar. Cook gently until onions are very soft, about 20 minutes. Do not brown. Roll out puff pastry on floured board into 13 x 17-inch rectangle. Place on ungreased cookie sheet. Brush mustard over rolled dough, spread pesto sauce on top and evenly distribute onions. Space 8 olive halves, cut side down, along long sides of pan and 5 along short sides. Fill rows in with remaining olive halves.

Bake in preheated 350° oven for about 25 minutes, or until pastry is well browned. Remove from oven, cool 5 minutes and cut into 2-inch squares with olive in center of each. Serve hot or at room temperature. Tart may be made in advance and reheated in cold oven at 350°. Bake until heated through, about 15 minutes.

Stuffed Mushroom Caps 30 servings

From The Bowdoin Steakhouse in Brunswick

Ingredients

½   small onion, chopped
3   stalks celery, chopped
1   tablespoon butter
¼   cup dry sherry
1   pound breakfast sausage
1   teaspoon Dijon mustard
1   teaspoon thyme
1   teaspoon basil
½   cup bread crumbs
1   egg
30 mushroom caps and stems
    grated cheese for topping

Preparation

Sauté onion and celery in butter until onion is translucent. Add sherry and cook until reduced by half. Set aside. Cook sausage. Drain well. Chop mushroom stems. Mix all ingredients, except mushroom caps. Stuff caps and top with cheese. Place on shallow, buttered baking pan and bake in preheated 350° oven for 20 minutes.

Tomato Cheese Tart

40 servings

Ingredients

¾ cup fresh parsley, minced
2 teaspoons dried oregano
3 large garlic cloves, minced
1 jalapeno pepper, seeded and minced
1 cup good quality olive oil
1 teaspoon salt
    freshly ground black pepper to taste
16 small plum tomatoes, cored and sliced ⅜-inch thick
8½ ounce sheet puff pastry
⅓ cup Dijon mustard
1 pound Monterey Jack cheese, shredded

Preparation

Mix parsley, oregano, garlic and pepper with oil, salt and pepper. Transfer to large plastic bag. Add tomato slices to bag, seal tightly and refrigerate 4 hours or overnight.

Roll out puff pastry on floured board into 13 x 17-inch rectangle. Place on ungreased cookie sheet. Brush pastry with mustard and sprinkle with cheese. Remove tomatoes from marinade. Arrange in overlapping rows along width of dough. Bake in preheated 375° oven for about 25 minutes, or until pastry is well browned. Remove from oven, cool 5 minutes, and cut into 2-inch squares. Serve hot or at room temperature. Tart may be made several hours in advance and held at room temperature. To reheat, place in cold oven at 350°. Bake until heated through, about 15 minutes.

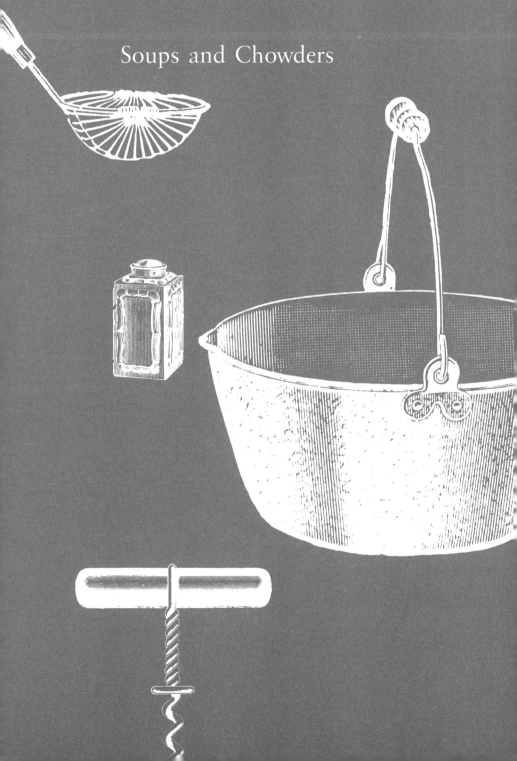

Soups and Chowders

Al's Mom's Borscht

10 to 12 servings

From Poland

Ingredients

2 to 3 pounds pork shoulder, butt or country ribs, trimmed
    of excess fat
4   quarts water
1   tablespoon peppercorns
3   bay leaves
2 to 3 bunches beets, stems removed and well washed
1   cup flour
1   pint sour cream
    salt to taste
½   cup white vinegar
10 to 12 boiled potatoes

Preparation

Combine pork, water, peppercorns and bay leaves in large saucepan. Bring to a boil, skim surface, cover and simmer 1½ to 2 hours. Remove pork, cool and reserve. Strain broth and return to pan. Bring to a boil, add whole beets, cover and simmer 1 hour. Shred pork from bones, using fingers for best texture. Remove beets from broth, cool, peel and shred on coarse grater. Reserve.

Mix flour and sour cream thoroughly and gradually add to broth. Whisk briskly to combine. Return to a boil. Simmer for ½ hour more. Add pork, beets, salt and vinegar. Place boiled potatoes in soup bowls and ladle borscht over them.

The goal is to achieve a tangy, robust flavor. This is done by the perfect balance of salt and vinegar. Do not be afraid to add more vinegar or salt if soup tastes too bland.

Avgolemono Soup

6 servings

Greek lemon soup from an Auxilary June luncheon

Ingredients

4½ cups chicken broth
3½ tablespoons uncooked rice
2   small eggs, beaten
⅜   cup lemon juice
     salt and pepper to taste
6   lemon slices for garnish

Preparation

Bring broth to a boil and add rice, boiling for 15 minutes. Beat eggs with wire whisk. Add ¾ cup boiling broth to lemon juice. Slowly add lemon broth to beaten eggs, beating constantly.

Turn off heat under broth-rice mixture and slowly beat hot broth, little by little, into lemon-egg mixture.

Garnish with lemon slices. Serve hot or very cold.

Best Ever Cream of Summer Squash Soup

4 servings

Ingredients

2   tablespoons butter or margarine
1   pound yellow crook neck squash, thinly sliced
2   tablespoons chopped shallots or onions
2   tablespoons water
½   teaspoon curry powder
14   ounces chicken broth
½   cup heavy cream or small can evaporated milk
     salt and pepper to taste

Preparation

Heat butter, add squash, shallots or onions and water. Cover and simmer gently for 10 minutes. Do not let squash brown. Cool. Transfer mixture to blender or food processor, add curry powder, chicken broth and cream. Blend until smooth. Return to saucepan and reheat to serving temperature. If too thick, dilute with more broth. Zucchini squash may be substituted but a very different flavor results.

Billi Bi (Mussel Soup)

4 servings

A real taste treat

Ingredients

2   pounds mussels
2   green onions, chopped
2   small onions, quartered
1   cup dry white wine
¼   cup fresh parsley, chopped
1   bay leaf
½   teaspoon thyme
2   tablespoons butter or margarine
     salt and pepper to taste
2   cups half and half or light cream
1   egg yolk, beaten

Preparation

Scrub mussels to clean. Put in large saucepan with green onions, small onion quarters, wine, parsley, bay leaf, thyme, butter, salt and pepper. Cover and bring to a boil. Cook 5 to 10 minutes or until mussels open. Discard any mussels that do not open. Strain liquid at least twice through double thickness of cheesecloth to remove all sand. Remove mussels from shells, cut large ones in half, set aside.

Bring liquid to a boil, add cream and return to a boil. Remove from heat, add egg yolk and mussels. Return to heat, but do not boil. Serve hot or cold.

Black Bean Soup

6 servings

Ingredients

1   cup black (turtle) beans
     water
½   teaspoon salt
1   ham bone or 2 smoked hocks
4   bay leaves
4   whole cloves
¼   teaspoon celery seed
2   celery stalks with leaves, chopped
1   large red onion, chopped
1   garlic clove, minced
1   tablespoon butter or vegetable oil

¼ teaspoon dry mustard
1 teaspoon chili powder
2 dashes Tabasco sauce
6 teaspoons sherry, divided
12 slices hard cooked egg and 6 slices lemon or lime for garnish

Preparation Soak beans overnight in enough water to more than cover them. Remove beans, measure water and add enough to make 1 quart. Add salt, ham bone or hocks, bay leaves, cloves, celery seed and celery to beans and liquid. Sauté onion and garlic in butter or oil until tender. Add to beans. Also add mustard, chili powder and Tabasco sauce. Bring to a simmer and cook until beans are tender, about 1 hour. Discard bay leaves and bones. Purée in blender or food processor until smooth. Reheat. Add 1 teaspoon sherry to each serving and garnish with 2 slices hard cooked egg and 1 slice lemon or lime. Serve hot.

Bowdoin College Celery Apple Soup

10 to 12 servings

An original from the Wentworth Hall cooking staff

Ingredients 5½ cups peeled, cored and coarsely chopped apples
6 cups coarsely chopped celery, including leaves
8 tablespoons butter or margarine
½ cup flour
8 cups chicken broth
1½ cups heavy cream
salt and pepper to taste
finely chopped dark green celery leaves or parsley for garnish

Preparation Sauté apples and celery in butter or margarine until celery is very tender. Slowly add flour to make a roux. Cook roux 2 to 3 minutes. Add broth and blend well. Remove from heat. Purée mixture in blender or food processor with ½ cup of cream. Return mixture to saucepan, add remaining cream, salt and pepper. Reheat but do not boil. If soup is too thick, add more chicken broth or cream. Serve hot or cold garnished with chopped celery leaves.

Butternut Squash Soup

6 servings

A delicious and unusual soup from Pennsylvania

Ingredients

4 cups chicken broth
1 cup chopped onion
2 slices bread, cubed, crusts removed
2 tart apples, cored and coarsely chopped
1 pound butternut squash, washed, halved lengthwise and seeded
1½ teaspoons salt
¼ teaspoon marjoram
¼ teaspoon rosemary
¼ teaspoon pepper
2 large egg yolks
¼ cup heavy cream

Preparation

Combine stock, onion, bread, apples, squash and seasonings. Bring to a boil, reduce heat and simmer 15 minutes. Remove from heat. Remove squash and scoop out flesh, returning to broth mixture. Discard skin. Purée soup in batches in food processor or blender, transferring to a saucepan when it is smooth.

Beat egg yolks and cream together. Stir a little soup into cream mixture and then stir cream mixture into rest of soup. Heat over moderate heat until hot, but do not boil.

Carrot Bisque

4 to 6 servings

Don't omit the coriander!

Ingredients

2 tablespoons butter or margarine
3 whole cloves
¼ teaspoon ground coriander
¼ teaspoon salt
¼ teaspoon sugar
white pepper to taste

1½ pounds carrots, sliced
2½ cups chicken broth
1   cup half and half
     chopped fresh chives, and parsley or grated nutmeg for
     garnish

Preparation Melt butter or margarine. Add all seasonings and gently
sauté for 1 minute. Add carrots and mix thoroughly. Add
broth, bring to a boil, reduce heat and simmer until carrots
are very tender. Purée in blender or food processor. Stir in
half and half. May be served hot or cold.

Cream of Carrot with Dill Soup

12 servings

Hot in winter; cold in summer

Ingredients
2   pounds carrots
4   tablespoons butter or margarine
1¾ cups finely chopped onion
4   cups chicken broth
1   cup heavy cream
1   cup milk
2   tablespoons finely chopped fresh dill
¼   teaspoon cayenne pepper
     salt to taste
     sour cream for garnish, optional

Preparation Cut carrots into ¾ inch rounds. Heat butter, add onions
and sauté until tender. Add carrots and broth, bring to a
boil and simmer 20 minutes or until carrots are soft. Pour
into blender or food processor and purée. Return to
saucepan, add cream, milk, dill, pepper and salt. Serve hot
or very cold with dollop of sour cream, if desired.

Creamy Crab Soup
4 servings

Ingredients

2   tablespoons butter or margarine
1   tablespoon finely chopped onion
1   tablespoon finely chopped fresh parsley
1½   cups crabmeat
2   tablespoons flour
2   cups chicken broth
2   cups light cream
     cayenne pepper and salt to taste

Preparation

Melt butter, add onion, and sauté until golden. Add parsley
and crabmeat. Stirring often, sauté another 5 minutes. Add
flour, stir and sauté 3 minutes. Add chicken broth and
simmer 20 minutes with cover on. Add cream and
seasonings and heat through.

Cream of Mushroom Soup with Brie
4 servings

Ingredients

¼   cup unsalted butter
1   pound fresh mushrooms, chopped
1   shallot, chopped
½   medium onion, chopped
1½   cups chicken broth
¾   cup port
1   cup heavy cream
     freshly grated nutmeg
     freshly ground black pepper
     salt
4   ounces firm Brie

Preparation

Melt butter, add mushrooms, shallot and onion. Sauté over
medium heat until mushrooms begin to wilt and onion starts
to turn translucent. Add stock and wine, bring to a boil and
cook 2 minutes, stirring until thickened and smooth. Reduce
heat and simmer 15 minutes. Add cream and seasonings to
taste. Stir until well blended. Cut Brie into 4 slices. Place on
top of soup and let heat of soup melt cheese. Serve immediately.

Cream of Cauliflower Soup

6 to 8 servings

An easy harvest soup

Ingredients

1	large onion, sliced
2	tablespoons butter or margarine, melted
28	ounces chicken broth
2	medium carrots, sliced
1	medium head cauliflower, trimmed and cut into small pieces
1	cup half and half
½	teaspoon nutmeg
	salt and pepper to taste
2	tablespoons dry sherry
¼	cup fresh parsley sprigs, finely chopped, and 6 slices cooked carrot for garnish

Preparation

Sauté onion slices in butter for 5 minutes. Pour in chicken broth. Bring to a boil, adding carrots and cauliflower. Cover and simmer until vegetables are tender. Purée soup in blender or food processor until smooth. Return to soup pot. Add cream, nutmeg, salt, pepper and sherry. Heat to simmering. Garnish with parsley and carrot slices.

Curried Cream of Celery Soup

6 servings

Curry makes the difference

Ingredients

6 large celery ribs with leaves, sliced
2 cups chopped onion
2 tablespoon butter or margarine
2 teaspoons curry powder
1 quart beef stock
2 cups heavy cream
   salt and pepper to taste

Preparation

Sauté celery and onions in butter. Stir in curry. Add stock and simmer 40 minutes. Purée vegetables in blender or food processor and return to broth. Add cream, salt and pepper. Heat thoroughly but do not boil.

Curried Cream of Rice Soup with Apples

10 servings

Hearty cold weather soup from Scotland

Ingredients

1½ cups chopped onion
1   cup chopped celery
1   teaspoon minced garlic
4   tablespoons butter or margarine, melted
2   tablespoons curry powder
3   cups canned or fresh tomatoes
1   bay leaf
½   teaspoon dried thyme
1   cup rice
7   cups chicken broth
½   cup heavy cream
    salt and pepper to taste
1½ cups peeled and cored apples, cut into ¼-inch cubes

Preparation Sauté onion, celery and garlic in melted butter, until wilted. Add curry powder and sauté, stirring, 1 minute more. Add tomatoes, bay leaf, thyme and rice. Bring to a boil and add chicken broth. Return to a boil and simmer 30 minutes, or until rice is tender. Remove bay leaf. Add cream, salt and pepper and apple cubes. Serve hot.

If smooth soup is preferred, after removing bay leaf, purée soup in food processor or blender. Add more hot chicken broth if soup is too thick. Then add cream, salt and pepper and apples.

Corn and Carrot Soup   6 servings

A quick lunch for a busy day

Ingredients
1 cup chopped onions
2 tablespoons butter or margarine
1 cup chopped cooked carrots
1 16-ounce can cream style corn
1 10½-ounce can cream of mushroom soup
2 cups milk
   salt and pepper to taste
6 small pats butter

Preparation Sauté onions in butter until golden. Add carrots, corn, mushroom soup, milk, salt and pepper. Heat to boiling. Put small pat of butter in each bowl before filling with soup.

French Onion Soup

8 servings

From an Australian in Nova Scotia

Ingredients

2   pounds onions, thinly sliced
1   garlic clove, crushed
3   tablespoons butter or margarine
1   tablespoon flour
1   teaspoon sugar
30 ounces beef consommé
3   cups water
    salt and pepper to taste
⅓ cup dry red wine
1   tablespoon dry sherry
1   loaf French bread
4   tablespoons butter or margarine
1   garlic clove, crushed
8   ounces Swiss cheese, grated
½ cup grated Parmesan cheese

Preparation

Sauté onions and garlic in 3 tablespoons butter until onions are deep golden brown. Add flour and stir 1 minute. Add sugar, consomme, water, salt, pepper and red wine. Stir until combined. Bring to a boil, reduce heat and simmer, covered for 45 minutes, stirring occasionally. Add sherry and simmer 5 minutes.

About 15 minutes before serving, cut bread into ½ inch slices. Melt 4 tablespoons butter, add garlic. Brush bread slices on both sides with butter-garlic mixture. Brown 1 side of bread under broiler. Pour soup into individual, ovenproof bowls, top with slice of bread, toasted side down. Combine cheeses and sprinkle over bread. Place bowls under broiler until cheeses are melted and golden brown.

Fresh Strawberry Soup

6 servings

A welcome to summer!

Ingredients

2 tablespoons cornstarch
⅓ cup white sugar
⅛ teaspoon salt
1 cup red or rosé wine
1 cup water
4 cups fresh strawberries, puréed
1 cup sour cream
6 whole strawberries, sliced, and 6 sprigs fresh mint for garnish

Preparation

Combine cornstarch, sugar, salt, wine and water. Cook over medium heat, stirring constantly until thick and clear. Remove from heat. Chill well. Add puréed strawberries and sour cream. Blend until evenly mixed. Chill until serving time. Serve in glass bowls with slices of fresh strawberries floating on top and sprig of fresh mint as garnish.

Fresh Tomato Soup

6 to 8 servings

Concocted by neighbors when gardens were brimming with ripe tomatoes

Ingredients

2   medium onions, coarsely chopped
2   garlic cloves, minced
¼   cup butter or margarine
4   pounds very ripe tomatoes, peeled, seeded and chopped
6   cups chicken broth
4   tablespoons tomato paste
1½   teaspoons salt
½   teaspoon pepper
⅓   cup fresh basil, chopped, or 2 tablespoons dried basil
croutons or cucumber slices for garnish

Preparation

Sauté onions and garlic in butter until onion is tender. Add tomatoes, broth, tomato paste, salt and pepper. Simmer, stirring occasionally, for 15 minutes, or until slightly thickened. Remove from heat, cool slightly and purée in blender or food processor. Return to pan. Stir in basil and heat gently. Serve with croutons, or chill and serve with sliced cucumbers.

Grand Central Station Oyster Bar Oyster Stew

1 serving

Clam broth makes the difference

Ingredients

1   teaspoon Worcestershire sauce
¼   teaspoon paprika
¼   teaspoon celery salt
2   tablespoons butter, divided
7   freshly opened oysters
½   cup clam broth
1   cup milk

Preparation   Bring Worcestershire sauce, paprika, celery salt and 1
tablespoon butter to a boil. Add oysters and clam broth and
cook until edges of oysters curl. Add milk and bring just to
a boil. Pour into soup bowl and top with 1 tablespoon
butter and a dash of paprika. Bulk oysters may be used. Do
not freeze.

J. Hathaway's Italian Sausage Soup

6 servings

Make a day in advance

Ingredients   6 to 8 sweet Italian sausage links
1   tablespoon butter or margarine
1   large onion, sliced vertically into crescents
6   cups water
1   tablespoon beef bouillon granules or 3 cubes
28   ounces canned crushed tomatoes or 3½ cups fresh
     tomatoes, crushed
¼   green pepper, diced
¼   teaspoon oregano
¼   teaspoon basil
⅛   teaspoon pepper
2   small zucchini, cubed
2   ounces linguine, broken into 2-inch pieces
2   tablespoons grated Parmesan cheese

Preparation   Fully cook sausage, pierce skin and drain on absorbent
paper. When cool, cut into ½ inch rounds and set aside.
Melt margarine and sauté onion until slightly soft. Add
water, bouillon granules or cubes, tomatoes, green pepper,
oregano, basil and pepper. Bring to a full boil then add
sausage, zucchini, linguine and Parmesan cheese. Cover and
continue to cook until soup is simmering, stirring
occasionally to prevent pasta from sticking. Remove from
heat, still covered and allow to cool. Refrigerate and reheat
as needed.

Jambalaya Soup

6 servings

Shrimp and okra make for a hearty one-dish meal

Ingredients

1 ham bone or 2 ham hocks
1 slice onion
1 cup celery leaves
¼ teaspoon ground hot red pepper
5 cups water
1 cup chopped celery
½ cup chopped onion
1 garlic clove, minced
2 tablespoons butter or margarine
1 cup tomato sauce
¼ cup catsup
½ cup long grain rice
1 10-ounce package frozen okra
½ pound shelled Maine shrimp
salt and pepper to taste

Preparation

Bring ham bone, onion, celery leaves, red pepper and 5 cups of water to a boil. Reduce heat, cover and simmer 30 to 45 minutes. Remove bone. Let cool. Remove meat from bone and chop it. Discard bone. Strain broth if desired. Sauté celery, onion and garlic in butter until tender. Stir in broth, ham, tomato sauce, catsup and rice. Bring to a boil, reduce heat, cover and simmer 15 minutes. Add okra and shrimp, simmer 5 minutes or until shrimp are cooked. If you prefer a 'hot' soup, add hot pepper to taste. Do not overcook or reheat okra because it gets stringy.

Joshua's Cream of Broccoli Soup

6 servings

A good, basic broccoli soup

Ingredients

1 pound fresh broccoli, cut into small pieces
2 cups water
¼ cup butter or margarine
1 cup chopped onions

1   garlic clove, minced
2   tablespoons flour
2   chicken bouillon cubes
2   cups half and half
    salt and pepper to taste

Preparation Cook broccoli in water until tender. Purée water and broccoli in blender or food processor. Melt butter, sauté onion until transparent. Add garlic and flour. Stir until paste forms. Add vegetable purée. Stir well. Add bouillon cubes and simmer 10 minute. Just before serving, add half and half, salt and pepper. Heat but do not boil.

Lentil Soup

4 to 6 servings

A warming lunch on a cold winter day

Ingredients
1   cup lentils
½   teaspoon salt
6   cups water
¾   cup sliced onion
1   garlic clove, crushed
2   ribs celery, diced
1   tablespoon chopped parsley
¼   cup olive oil
1   cup canned Italian tomatoes
      salt and pepper to taste
1   teaspoon chopped dried basil
      chopped fresh parsley and Parmesan cheese for garnish

Preparation Add lentils and salt to water and simmer, covered, 20 to 30 minutes until soft but not mushy. Sauté onion, garlic, celery and parsley in olive oil until slightly browned. Add tomatoes and simmer 15 minutes. Combine with lentils and simmer for another 15 minutes. Add salt, pepper and basil. Serve hot, garnished with parsley and Parmesan cheese.

Lobster Bisque

5 to 6 servings

For a family Christmas Eve celebration

Ingredients

1   quart milk
1   rib celery, sliced
1   onion, sliced
3   tablespoons butter
2   tablespoons flour
1   teaspoon salt
1   teaspoon paprika
     meat from 5 1-pound lobsters, or 2 6½-ounce cans
     lobster meat
1   cup sour cream, optional
     finely minced fresh chives for garnish

Preparation

Scald milk with celery and onion. Strain and discard vegetables. Melt butter, stir in flour, salt and paprika. Gradually blend in milk and cook, while stirring, until soup thickens slightly. Stir in lobster meat and sour cream and heat almost to boiling. To serve, garnish with fresh chives.

Bisque is best made day in advance, with sour cream added when being reheated for serving.

Minestre (Pepperoni Soup)   12 servings

Created by a 95-year old Italian New Yorker

Ingredients

1	ham bone or slice of ham
3	quarts water
2	cups onions, sliced in half-moons
1	stick pepperoni, cut into ¼ -inch pieces
2	ribs celery, chopped
2	cans white navy beans, or white kidney beans, undrained
	meatballs (recipe follows)
¼	teaspoon garlic powder
½	cup chopped fresh parsley
½	teaspoon dried oregano
	salt and pepper to taste
1	pound fresh spinach, chopped, or 2 10-ounce packages frozen chopped spinach, thawed

Meatballs:

1	pound hamburger
2	eggs
¼	cup freshly grated Parmesan cheese
¼	cup chopped fresh parsley
⅛	teaspoon garlic powder
½	teaspoon dried basil
½	teaspoon dried oregano
	salt and pepper to taste
¼	cup bread crumbs

Preparation

Boil ham in water for 30 minutes. Remove, cut ham into bite-size pieces and set aside. Discard bone. Add onions, pepperoni and celery to stock and simmer until vegetables are soft. Add beans, meatballs, garlic powder, parsley, oregano, salt and pepper. Simmer 15 minutes or until meatballs are cooked through. Add spinach and cook 5 minutes longer. Add diced ham.

For meatballs, combine all ingredients and shape into balls size of quarter. Makes 46 to 48 meatballs.

Minted Cucumber Soup

4 servings

Serve hot or cold.

Ingredients

2 tablespoons butter or margarine
2 medium onions, thinly sliced
2 tablespoons flour
2 cups chicken broth
1 to 1½ pounds cucumbers, peeled, seeded and cut into
   ½ inch cubes
1 sprig fresh mint
   salt and white pepper to taste
½ cup cream
   chopped fresh mint or chopped fresh parsley for garnish

Preparation

Melt butter, add onion, cover and cook 10 minutes. Do not
brown. Stir in flour, then add broth and stir until it boils.
Add cucumbers, sprig of mint, salt and pepper. Cover and
simmer until cucumbers are tender. Remove mint, discard,
and purée soup in blender or food processor. Can be stored
in refrigerator at this point up to 48 hours, covered. Five
minutes before serving, stir in cream. If serving hot, do not
boil. Garnish with mint or parsley.

Mushroom Pumpkin Soup

6 servings

Ingredients

½ pound fresh mushrooms, sliced, or chopped if large
1 small onion, grated
2 tablespoons vegetable oil or butter
2 tablespoons flour
1 tablespoon curry powder
3 cups chicken broth
2 cups cooked pumpkin purée
1 tablespoon honey
   dash freshly grated nutmeg
   salt and white pepper to taste
1 cup evaporated milk
   yogurt or sour cream for garnish

Preparation | Sauté mushrooms and onions in oil or butter until fully cooked but not browned. Add flour and curry powder. Stir to blend, then gradually add broth. Add pumpkin, honey, nutmeg, salt and pepper. Cook, stirring occasionally, for 10 to 15 minutes. Add evaporated milk and heat through without boiling. Top with dollop of yogurt or sour cream.

Peg's Lobster Stew
6 servings

Great anytime

Ingredients

meat of 7 1-pound cooked lobsters
8 tablespoons butter
2 quarts milk
salt and pepper to taste

Preparation | Sauté lobster and butter for about 1½ to 2 hours very slowly until all butter is absorbed. Slowly add milk and season. Allow to "age" overnight, if possible. Serve hot, but do not boil.

Quick Mulligatawny Soup
4 servings

Something new has been added — raisins!

Ingredients

2   tablespoons vegetable oil
½   cup chopped onion
2   teaspoons curry powder
2   cups chicken broth
1½ cups water
⅓   cup uncooked long-grain white rice
½   teaspoon salt
⅛   teaspoon pepper
2   cups bite-sized chunks cooked chicken
1   cup unsweetened applesauce
⅛   cup chopped fresh parsley
½   cup heavy cream
½   cup raisins, soaked in warm water for 5 minutes,
    drained and patted dry

Preparation

Heat oil, add onion and curry powder. Stir over medium-low heat 3 minutes or until onion is translucent. Add chicken broth, water, rice, salt and pepper. Bring to a boil, reduce heat, cover and simmer for 20 minutes or until rice is cooked. Stir in chicken, applesauce and parsley. Cover and simmer 5 minutes or until soup is hot. Remove from heat and stir in cream and raisins. Serve immediately.

Portuguese Caldo Verde
6 servings

From a cooking class in Portugal

Ingredients

2   pounds potatoes, peeled and cut into 1-inch pieces
1   onion, at least 4 ounces in weight, sliced
1   pound Italian hot sausage, sliced ¼-inch thick
1   pound kale, stems discarded
½   cup olive oil
    water
    salt and pepper to taste

Preparation | Boil potatoes, onion, sausage and ¼ cup olive oil in water to cover until potatoes are soft, about 20 minutes. Meanwhile, shred kale very finely. Boil kale in water to cover for about 10 minutes. Use uncovered saucepan to keep it bright green. Drain potatoes and onions, reserving liquid and sausage. Purée potatoes and onions in blender or food processor. Drain kale and pour ¼ cup olive oil over it and mix with potato purée and sausage. Add enough reserved liquid to make soup desired consistency. Season with salt and pepper to taste and reheat.

Portuguese Vegetable Soup 6 to 8 servings

Improves with reheating

Ingredients
½   pound linguica
1½   tablespoons olive oil
½   cup chopped onion
1   garlic clove, minced
2½   cups diced potatoes
5   cups chicken broth
28   ounces canned crushed tomatoes or 3½ cups fresh crushed tomatoes
16   ounces canned red kidney beans, undrained
1   cup chopped celery leaves and celery
     salt and pepper to taste

Preparation | Simmer sausage in 3 cups water for 20 minutes. Remove sausage and chop. Reserve 1 cup of liquid. Heat oil, add onion and garlic, and sauté until onion is tender, but not brown. Add chicken broth and potatoes to reserved liquid and bring to a boil, simmering until potatoes are tender. Purée potatoes and stock in blender or food processor. Return to pan, add onion mixture, sausage, tomatoes and beans. Simmer 10 minutes. Add celery and leaves, salt and pepper to taste.

Swiss and Veggie Soup

6 to 8 servings

Looks as good as it tastes

Ingredients

4   tablespoons butter or margarine
4   tablespoons flour
4   cups chicken broth
1   cup coarsely chopped broccoli and/or cauliflower
1   cup chopped celery with leaves
1   cup sliced or diced carrots
½   cup chopped onion
½   cup sliced fresh mushrooms
1   large garlic clove, minced
1   pint cream or half and half
1   egg yolk
¼   teaspoon dried thyme
2   tablespoons chopped fresh parsley
⅛   teaspoon fresh ground pepper
2   teaspoons chopped fresh chives
1½ to 2 cups shredded Swiss cheese

Preparation

Melt butter, add flour and cook several minutes, stirring. Remove from heat and add broth. Bring to a boil, stirring. Add vegetables. Cover and simmer till barely tender. Blend cream and egg yolk in bowl. Gradually blend several tablespoons soup into cream and egg mixture, then blend into soup. Add herbs and spices. Cook until thickened. Blend in cheese and stir until melted. Do not boil.

Velvet Cheese Soup
8 servings

Ingredients

8 tablespoons butter or margarine
½ cup finely chopped carrots
½ cup chopped onion
½ cup chopped celery
⅓ cup flour
4 cups chicken broth
2 cups milk
3 cups freshly grated Cheddar cheese
½ teaspoon Dijon mustard
½ teaspoon Worcestershire sauce
6 slices bacon, cooked, drained and crumbled for garnish

Preparation

Melt butter. Sauté carrots, onion and celery until soft but not brown. Add flour. Cook and stir 2 minutes or until blended. Slowly add 3 cups broth, stirring with wire whisk until mixture comes to a boil and thickens. Purée until smooth in blender or food processor. Return to pan and stir in remaining cup of broth and milk. Stir in cheese, mustard and Worcestershire sauce. Simmer until soup is hot and cheese is melted, but do not boil. Garnish with bacon.

Zucchini Tomato Bisque
3 servings

Ingredients

2 cups chopped zucchini
1 cup water
½ cup tomato juice
1 tablespoon chopped onion
1 chicken bouillon cube
⅛ teaspoon dried basil
8 ounces cream cheese

Preparation

Combine all ingredients except cream cheese. Cover and simmer 20 minutes. Pour into blender or food processor, add cream cheese and purée until smooth. Serve hot or cold. If freezing, do so before adding cream cheese. Add cream cheese when reheating.

Zucchini Soup with Variations

4 servings

Ingredients

1 cup chopped onion
2 tablespoons butter or margarine
14 ounces chicken broth
4 cups diced young zucchini, unpeeled
¼ teaspoon salt
⅛ teaspoon garlic powder
⅛ teaspoon celery salt
   pepper to taste
¼ cup fresh parsley, chopped

Preparation

Sauté onion in butter until soft, but not brown. Add remaining ingredients, except parsley, and cook until zucchini is soft. Pour into blender or food processor, add parsley and process until smooth. Serve hot or cold. May be frozen.

Variations:

1. Substitute ½ cup dry white wine for ½ cup broth

2. Add 8 ounces cream cheese, or 1 cup sour cream, or 1 cup heavy cream for richer soup. Do not freeze this one.

3. Add ½ to 1 teaspoon curry powder.

Elegant Scallop Chowder

4 to 6 servings

Ingredients

3 medium potatoes, peeled and diced
1 medium carrot, chopped
2 ribs celery, chopped
1 medium onion, chopped
2 cups chicken stock

½ teaspoon salt
¼ teaspoon pepper
½ bay leaf
½ teaspoon thyme, crumbled
½ pound fresh mushrooms, sliced
1½ tablespoons butter or margarine
1 pound fresh sea scallops, cut into pieces
½ cup dry white wine
1 cup light cream
2 tablespoons chopped parsley and paprika for garnish

Preparation Cover potatoes, carrot, celery and onion with chicken stock and bring to a boil. Add salt, pepper, bay leaf and thyme. Simmer, covered, until vegetables are tender. Remove bay leaf. Transfer mixture to food processor or blender, and process until smooth. Sauté mushrooms in butter. Add scallops and wine. Cook for 1 minute. Stir in cream. Combine this mixture with puréed vegetables and broth. Heat slowly without boiling and serve hot with parsley and paprika.

Georgetown Clam Chowder   4 servings

Ingredients
⅛ pound salt pork, diced
1 medium onion, diced
2 large potatoes, peeled and diced
   salt and pepper to taste
1 pint clams and liquid
12 ounces evaporated milk
1 cup whole milk

Preparation Sauté salt pork until crisp. Reserve pork cubes for garnish. Add onion to fat and sauté until golden. Add potatoes and enough water to cover. Season with salt and pepper and cover. Simmer until potatoes are just tender. Add clams and simmer just 2 minutes more. Heat evaporated milk and whole milk together and add to clam mixture. Check seasonings. Serve very hot with salt pork garnish.

Heart Smart Fish Stew 5 to 6 servings

Ingredients

1   tablespoon corn oil
1   cup sliced celery
1   cup sliced carrot
½   cup chopped onion
½   cup chopped green pepper
2   garlic cloves, minced
16 ounces canned tomatoes in juice, chopped, or 2 cups fresh, chopped
1   cup chicken broth
¼   cup dry white wine
½   teaspoon dill weed
1   bay leaf
1   cup water
6½ ounces canned chopped clams and juice, optional
1 to 1½ pounds white fish (cod, haddock, halibut, etc.) cut into 1-inch pieces
    salt and pepper to taste

Preparation

Heat oil and sauté celery, carrots, onion, green pepper and garlic about 10 minutes or until tender-crisp. Add tomatoes in juice, broth, wine and seasonings. Bring to a boil. Cover and simmer about 20 minutes. Add water and clams. Place fish on top of mixture and cook 10 minutes or until fish flakes when tested with fork. Stir together gently. Remove bay leaf, season and serve.

Maine Fish Chowder 4 to 5 servings

Ingredients

⅛   pound salt pork, diced
1   onion, sliced thin
3 to 4 potatoes, peeled and cubed
1   pound haddock
12 ounces evaporated milk
1 to 2 cups whole milk
2   tablespoons butter or margarine
    salt, pepper and thyme to taste

Preparation   Sauté salt pork until crisp. Reserve pork cubes for garnish.
Sauté onion in fat until tender. Add potatoes. Stir and add
water, barely to cover. Simmer until potatoes are tender. Add
fish and simmer until fish flakes. Add evaporated milk and
enough whole milk to give plenty of broth. Add butter and
seasonings. Remove from heat. Refrigerate when cool. Reheat
and sprinkle each serving with pork cubes. It is best if
chowder can "set" for several hours to a day. Recipe may be
easily doubled.

If using whole fish, cook separately. Reserve liquid and use
for cooking potatoes instead of water. Remove skin and
bones from fish before adding to chowder. Whole fish is
usually cheaper and gives more flavor than fillets.

Oven Fish Chowder   6 to 8 servings

Ingredients   4   large potatoes, peeled and diced
               salt and pepper to taste
          2   pounds white fish (haddock, hake, cod, etc.)
          ⅓   cup chopped celery leaves or parsley
          3   medium onions, thinly sliced
          4   tablespoons butter or margarine
          1   bay leaf
          2   cups boiling water
          ½   cup dry white wine or vermouth
          1½   cups light cream or half and half, heated
               paprika, chopped fresh dill or parsley for garnish

Preparation   Layer half the potatoes in large casserole. Lightly salt and
pepper. Add fish and season. Add celery and onions. Cover
with remaining potatoes. Dot with butter. Add bay leaf.
Pour 2 cups boiling water over top. Add wine. Cover tightly.
Bake in preheated 375° oven for 1 hour. Add cream and stir
to mix. Check seasonings. Sprinkle with paprika, dill or
parsley.

Salmon Chowder

6 servings

Ingredients

2 to 3 tablespoons butter or margarine
1 onion, sliced
3 to 4 potatoes, peeled and cubed
1 package dried chicken broth
generous pinch of dry mustard, thyme and parsley
15½ounces canned salmon with juice, skin and bones removed
12 ounces evaporated milk
salt and pepper to taste

Preparation

Sauté onion in butter. Add potato. Barely cover with water and simmer until tender. Add dried chicken broth, seasonings and salmon. Add evaporated milk. Continue to add more milk or water to provide sufficient broth. Season with salt and pepper. Serve hot.

Breads

Sherried Apple Raisin Bread

1 loaf

Best saved for the second day

Ingredients

1 cup brown sugar, firmly packed
½ cup vegetable oil
2 tablespoons cream sherry
1 teaspoon vanilla
1 cup raisins
½ cup chopped walnuts
2 cups coarsely grated, peeled raw apples
2 teaspoons baking soda
2 cups flour
½ teaspoon salt
½ teaspoon cinnamon
¼ teaspoon nutmeg

Preparation

Mix brown sugar, oil, sherry and vanilla. Stir in raisins and walnuts. Mix soda with apples. Combine with sugar-raisin mixture. Stir in dry ingredients and blend thoroughly. Spread in greased and floured 9 x 5-inch loaf pan. Bake in preheated 350° oven for about 1 hour, 25 minutes or until tests done. Allow to cool. Wrap in plastic and refrigerate for one day before slicing.

Carrot Bread

1 loaf

Ingredients

1 cup sugar
¾ cup vegetable oil
1½ cups flour
1 teaspoon baking powder
¼ teaspoon salt
1 teaspoon cinnamon
1 teaspoon baking soda
2 eggs
1 cup grated carrot
½ cup chopped nuts

Preparation   Mix sugar and oil, and add dry ingredients. Add eggs, one
               at a time, beating well after each addition. Stir in carrot and
               nuts. Pour into greased and floured 9 x 5 x 3-inch loaf pan.
               Bake in preheated 350° oven for 50 to 60 minutes.

Delicious Biscuits   14 biscuits

Ingredients   2   cups flour
               1   tablespoon baking powder
               ½   teaspoon salt
               3   tablespoons lard or vegetable shortening
               1   cup milk

Preparation   Mix flour, baking powder, salt and shortening with hands
               until shortening has been absorbed into flour. Add milk and
               mix. Add up to ½ cup more of flour, if necessary, to make
               the dough easy to handle, keeping the dough as moist as
               possible. Place dough on heavily floured waxed paper.
               Flatten with palm of hand to about ½ inch thick. Cut with
               biscuit cutter and place on lightly greased baking sheet.
               Prick tops with fork several times. Bake in preheated 550°
               oven for 10 minutes or until center is done.

Variation: Whole Wheat Biscuits
               Substitute 1 cup whole wheat flour for 1 cup white flour
               and add 1 teaspoon sugar, when mixing with shortening.
               After pricking with fork, moisten tops slightly with water.
               Bake as directed.

Good Morning Bread

1 loaf

Ingredients

½ cup margarine, softened
½ cup sugar
2 eggs
1 tablespoon grated orange rind
1 cup orange juice
2 cups flour
1 teaspoon salt
3 teaspoons baking powder
1½ cups flaked cereal, such as corn, bran or grapenut flakes
½ cup chopped nuts
½ cup raisins

Preparation

Beat margarine and sugar until light. Add eggs and orange rind and beat well. Stir in orange juice. Add flour, salt, and baking powder, stirring only to combine. Crush cereal to ¾ cup and stir in with nuts and raisins. Pour into well-greased 9 x 5-inch loaf pan and bake in preheated 350° oven for 1 hour. Cool 10 minutes before removing from pan. This recipe may be doubled and baked in a 10-inch tube pan.

Lemon Poppy Seed Bread

1 loaf

From the Lord and Taylor tea room

Ingredients

1   lemon
1   cup flour
¾   cup sugar
⅓   cup poppy seeds
1½   teaspoons baking powder
1   egg
⅔   cup milk
⅓   cup vegetable oil
½   teaspoon vanilla extract

Preparation

Grate lemon rind and squeeze out juice. Set aside. Combine flour, ½ cup sugar, poppy seeds and baking powder. Combine egg, milk, oil, vanilla and half the lemon rind. Add to dry ingredients and mix until smooth. Pour into greased and floured 9 x 5-inch loaf pan. Bake in preheated 350° oven for 50 minutes. Combine lemon juice and remaining rind with ¼ cup sugar. Stir to dissolve. Pour over hot baked loaf before removing from pan to cool. Make in miniature loaves to give as holiday gifts.

Nova Scotia Oat Cakes

6½ dozen

Ingredients

3   cups flour
3   cups rolled oats
2   cups sugar
2   teaspoons salt
1   teaspoon baking soda
2   cups margarine
¾   cup cold water

Preparation

Mix dry ingredients. Cut in margarine with pastry blender. Moisten with water to make dough. Roll dough ½-inch thick on floured board. Cut into squares of desired size. Bake on cookie sheet in preheated 350° oven for 15 minutes.

Sesame Seed Bread 1 loaf

Ingredients

2 cups flour
1 cup graham or whole wheat flour
3 teaspoons baking powder
1 cup sesame seeds
1 teaspoon salt
1 cup sugar
1 egg, well beaten
1 cup milk

Preparation

Mix dry ingredients. Mix egg and milk together and gradually add to dry ingredients. Beat well. Pour into oiled 9 x 5-inch loaf pan and let stand for 20 minutes. Bake in preheated 350° oven for about 40 minutes or until tests done. Good toasted. Sesame seeds may be purchased inexpensively at health food stores.

Spicy Pumpkin Bread 2 loaves

Spicier the second day!

Ingredients

¾ cup butter or margarine, softened
2½ cups sugar
4 eggs
2 cups pureed pumpkin, fresh or canned
⅔ cup water
3½ cups flour
2 teaspoons baking soda
1½ teaspoons salt
1½ teaspoons baking powder
1 teaspoon cinnamon
1 teaspoon ground cloves
⅔ cup chopped nuts
½ cup maraschino cherries, chopped, or
½ cup mini-chocolate chips, optional

Preparation   Cream butter and sugar. Add eggs, one at a time, beating well. Mix in pumpkin and water. Sift dry ingredients and stir into pumpkin mixture, a little at a time. Thoroughly blend the batter. Fold in nuts and cherries or chocolate chips. Pour batter into 2 greased and floured 9 x 5-inch loaf pans. Bake in preheated 350° oven for about 1 hour and 10 minutes, or until tests done. Cool for 10 minutes and remove from pan. Winter squash may be substituted for the pumpkin.

Spinach Spoon Bread   6 servings

An unusual combination of ingredients

Ingredients
10   ounces frozen onions in cream sauce
10   ounces frozen chopped spinach
2   eggs, slightly beaten
1   cup sour cream
½   cup butter or margarine, melted
¼   teaspoon salt
8½   ounces corn muffin mix
½   cup Swiss cheese, shredded

Preparation   Prepare onions and spinach according to package directions. Drain spinach well. Combine onions, spinach, eggs, sour cream, butter and salt. Stir in corn muffin mix. Pour into well-greased 6 x 10-inch glass baking dish. Bake in preheated 350° oven for 30 minutes. Sprinkle top of bread with shredded cheese and return to oven for 2 minutes or until cheese is melted. Serve warm.

Almond Rhubarb Coffee Cake

15 servings

Ingredients

2   cups flour
3   teaspoons baking powder
2   tablespoons sugar
      dash of salt
⅓   cup butter or margarine
1   cup packed brown sugar
1   egg
1   cup milk
1   teaspoon vanilla extract
1½   cups finely chopped fresh rhubarb
½   cup sliced almonds

Topping:
½   cup sugar
1   tablespoon butter or margarine
½   cup sliced almonds

Preparation

Combine flour, baking powder, sugar and salt. Cut in margarine until mixture is grainy and has lumps the size of peas. Add brown sugar, egg, milk and vanilla. Beat hard until well-mixed. Stir in rhubarb and ½ cup almonds. Pour into greased 9 x 13-inch baking pan. Combine topping ingredients and sprinkle over batter. Bake in preheated 350° oven for about 30 minutes.

Apricot Almond Coffee Cake

14 servings

Ingredients

1   cup butter or margarine, softened
2   cups sugar
2   eggs
1   cup sour cream
1   teaspoon almond extract
2   cups flour
1   teaspoon baking powder

¼ teaspoon salt
1 cup sliced almonds
10 ounces apricot preserves

Preparation   Cream butter and sugar until very fluffy. Beat in eggs well, one at a time. Fold in sour cream and extract, then fold in sifted flour, baking powder and salt. Fill a greased and floured 10-inch tube or bundt pan with about ⅓ of the mixture. Sprinkle ½ almonds and ½ preserves over the batter. Spoon on rest of batter. Add remaining preserves and top with remaining almonds. Bake in preheated 350° oven for 1 hour or until done. Cool on rack.

Christmas Cranberry Coffee Cake

12 servings

Pretty for the holidays but delicious anytime

Ingredients   2 cups flour
1 teaspoon baking powder
1 teaspoon soda
⅛ teaspoon salt
1 cup sugar
½ cup butter or margarine, softened
2 large eggs
1 teaspoon almond extract
1 cup sour cream
8 ounces whole cranberry sauce
½ cup chopped almonds
confectioners' sugar

Preparation   Combine flour, baking powder, soda and salt. Cream sugar and butter well. Beat eggs and extract into the creamed mixture. Mix in dry ingredients alternately with sour cream, blending well. Spoon half the batter into well-greased 10-inch tube or bundt pan. Spread half of cranberry sauce on top and swirl slightly through the batter. Add remaining batter and remaining cranberry sauce. Sprinkle almonds on top. Bake in preheated 350° oven for about 1 hour. Cool in pan for 15 minutes, turn out and sprinkle lightly with confectioners' sugar. Best when served warm.

General Lyon Inn Sour Cream Coffee Cake

10 servings

A church fair favorite

Ingredients

½ cup butter or margarine
1 cup sugar
2 eggs, well beaten
2 cups flour
1 teaspoon baking powder
1 teaspoon baking soda
¼ teaspoon salt
1 cup sour cream
1 teaspoon vanilla extract
½ cup chopped nuts
1 teaspoon cinnamon
¼ cup sugar

Preparation

Cream margarine and sugar and beat in eggs. Sift flour, baking powder, baking soda and salt. Add to creamed mixture alternately with sour cream and vanilla. Combine nuts, cinnamon and sugar for topping. Spoon half the batter into greased and floured 10-inch tube pan. Sprinkle with half the topping. Repeat batter and topping. Bake in preheated 350° oven about 40 minutes. Serve warm or cold.

Apple Bran Muffins

1 dozen

Good with soup on a winter's night

Ingredients

1½ cups all-bran cereal
1¼ cups skim milk
1¼ cups flour
1 tablespoon baking powder
2 teaspoons cinnamon
¼ teaspoon nutmeg

¼   teaspoon ground cloves
1   egg
¼   cup corn oil
⅓   cup brown sugar
2   medium apples, peeled, cored and coarsely grated
⅔   cup raisins, optional

Preparation   Add cereal to milk and let stand while preparing rest of ingredients. Mix flour, baking powder and spices. Beat egg, oil and sugar with wire whisk. Add cereal mixture, apples and raisins to egg mixture and stir well. Add flour mixture all at once and stir only until barely blended. Fill 12 greased muffin tins and bake in preheated 400° oven for 18 minutes. These freeze well.

Grammy's Banana Muffins   1 dozen

A "best banana" muffin from Lisbon, Maine

Ingredients   2   cups flour
1¼   cups sugar
1   teaspoon baking powder
1   teaspoon baking soda
⅓   cup butter or margarine
½   cup buttermilk
1   teaspoon vanilla extract
1   cup mashed banana
1   egg
½   cup chopped walnuts

Preparation   Mix dry ingredients. Cut in margarine, then add the buttermilk, vanilla, banana and egg. Fold in walnuts. Fill 12 greased muffin tins and bake in preheated 375° oven for 20 to 25 minutes.

Jordan Marsh Blueberry Muffins

1 dozen

Ingredients

½ cup butter, margarine or vegetable oil
1 cup sugar
2 eggs
2 cups flour
2 teaspoons baking powder
½ teaspoon salt
½ teaspoon cinnamon
1 teaspoon vanilla extract
½ cup milk
2 cups blueberries, fresh or frozen
2 teaspoons sugar

Preparation

Cream shortening and sugar. Add eggs, one at a time and mix until blended. Fold in dry ingredients, vanilla, blueberries and milk. Grease 12 muffin tins or use cupcake liners. Pile muffin batter high in tins. Sprinkle sugar on tops. Bake in preheated 375° oven for 25 to 30 minutes.

Variation:

Raspberry Muffins
Omit blueberries and cinnamon and add 2 cups fresh raspberries.

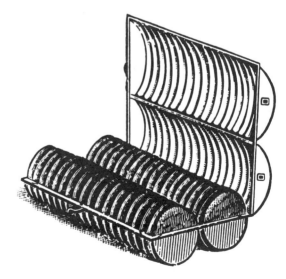

Miss Nason's Johnny Muffins 2 dozen

An old New Hampshire recipe

Ingredients

1 cup corn meal
2 cups flour
4 teaspoons baking powder
½ teaspoon salt
1 cup sugar
1 egg
2 cups milk

Preparation

Mix corn meal, flour, baking powder, salt and sugar. Add egg and milk. Mixture should be quite soft. Bake in hot, greased muffin tins in a preheated 400° oven for 20 minutes, or until a delicate brown.

Sourdough Bran Muffins 4 dozen

May be refrigerated for two months

Ingredients

2 cups boiling water
6 cups 100 percent bran cereal
1 cup margarine or vegetable oil
1 cup sugar
4 eggs
1 cup molasses
1 quart buttermilk
5 cups flour
5 teaspoons baking soda
1 teaspoon salt

Preparation

Pour boiling water over bran and let stand to absorb moisture. Cream margarine or oil and sugar together. Add eggs. Add remaining ingredients, with bran added last. Mix may be stored covered in a gallon glass jar for up to 2 months in the refrigerator. When ready to use, raisins, nuts, or fresh or frozen blueberries may be added. Fill greased muffin tins ⅔ full. Bake in preheated 400° oven for 20 minutes. Note: May use commercial powdered buttermilk now available in supermarkets.

Zucchini Dill Muffins

15 muffins

Delicious with a soup and salad luncheon

Ingredients

¾ cup butter or margarine
4 tablespoons sugar
2 eggs
2 cups flour
5 teaspoons baking powder
½ teaspoon baking soda
1 teaspoon celery salt
2 tablespoons dried onion flakes
1½ cups grated zucchini
½ cup sour milk
2 cups oatmeal
2 tablespoons chopped dill or
½ teaspoon dried dillweed
2 tablespoons chopped fresh parsley

Preparation

Cream margarine, sugar and eggs, beating well. Combine dry ingredients. Moisten onion flakes in zucchini. Mix zucchini and milk alternately with dry ingredients into margarine mixture. Add oatmeal, dill and parsley. Put into lightly greased muffin tins with an ice cream scoop, which will make tops round. Bake in preheated 375° oven for about 25 minutes.

Anne's French Bread 4 baguettes

Ingredients

2½ cups warm water
1 package dry yeast
2 tablespoons sugar
1 tablespoon salt
7 cups flour
1 egg white, beaten

Preparation

Combine water, yeast, sugar and salt, stirring until dissolved. Add flour and when well mixed, turn onto floured board. Knead 10 minutes. Place dough in oiled bowl, turning to coat. Let rise in warm place until doubled in bulk. Punch dough down and knead 3 to 4 times to remove air. Divide into 4 equal parts. Shape into long loaves and place in well-greased baguette pans or on baking pans. Slash tops on the diagonal several times. Brush with beaten egg white. Let rise again until almost double in bulk. Bake in a preheated 450° oven for 15 minutes, then at 350° for 30 more minutes. Remove from pans and cool.

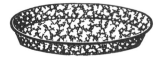

Whole Wheat Bread

2 large loaves

A big seller at the RMH Gift Shop Christmas fair

Ingredients

½ cup milk
½ cup brown sugar
½ cup shortening
4 teaspoons salt
1¾ cups lukewarm water
2 teaspoons sugar
2 packages dry yeast
4 cups whole wheat flour
2 cups white flour
melted butter

Preparation

Warm milk, brown sugar, shortening and salt, stirring constantly until shortening melts. Cool to lukewarm. Combine water and sugar and sprinkle yeast on top. Let stand 7 to 10 minutes. Stir in milk mixture. Combine whole wheat and white flours, making a well in the center. Pour in yeast-milk mixture. Work flours into yeast, a little at a time. Mix well and turn out onto lightly floured board, kneading until smooth and elastic, about 5 minutes. Place in greased bowl, turning to coat, cover and let rise until double in bulk, about 1 hour. Punch down, divide and shape into two loaves. Place in greased 9 x 5-inch loaf pans and brush tops with melted butter. Cover and let rise until center of dough is slightly higher than edge of pans, about 45 minutes. Bake in preheated 375° oven for 40 to 50 minutes. Remove from pans immediately and cool on wire racks.

Crusty Italian Bread 4 large loaves

Ingredients

1 teaspoon sugar
2 packages dry yeast
1 cup warm water
3 cups water
1 tablespoon salt
2 tablespoons oil
12 cups flour
1 egg white

Preparation

Dissolve sugar and yeast in 1 cup warm water and let stand 5 minutes. Combine 3 cups water, salt and oil. Add yeast and stir. Add 6 cups flour and beat well. Add the remaining 6 cups flour and turn onto a floured board. Knead, adding more flour if necessary. Knead for 10 minutes or until smooth and glossy. Place in greased bowl, turning to coat sides, and cover. Let dough rise for 2 hours. Punch down and let rise again for 1 hour. Shape into 4 large or 6 small loaves. Place on greased baking pan. Brush with cold water. Let rise for 1 hour, slash loaves crosswise and brush tops with egg white beaten with a little water. Bake in preheated 425° oven for 20 minutes. Brush tops again with egg white and continue baking about 10 more minutes, or until golden brown.

Danish Pastry

3 dozen

Ingredients

3   packages dry yeast
1   teaspoon sugar
½   cup warm water
1   egg, beaten
½   cup sugar
1   teaspoon salt
¾   cup milk, warmed
4   cups flour
2½   sticks margarine, softened
     jams for filling

Icing:
1   cup confectioners' sugar
     orange juice

Preparation

Dissolve yeast and 1 teaspoon sugar in warm water. Mix egg, sugar, salt and milk. Stir in yeast mixture. Add 2 cups flour and beat well. Add remaining 2 cups. Dough will be stiff. Turn dough onto floured board and knead 2 minutes. Roll dough into 12 x 18-inch rectangle. Spread 1 stick of margarine over middle and right thirds of dough. Fold left third over middle and fold right third over. Turn dough and roll into 12 x 18-inch shape again. Repeat procedure twice for remaining 1½ sticks margarine. Roll fourth time.

Cut dough in half horizontally and each half into 18 strips. Twist each strip several times, carefully tie a knot and tuck ends under to form rosette. Place on 2 large ungreased cookie sheets. Let rise until double in bulk and light. Very gently, press center of each with tip of teaspoon dipped in flour. Fill centers with teaspoon of jam. Bake in preheated 400° oven for about 8 minutes. Make icing and while pastry is still warm, drizzle a bit of icing over the tops.

Dill Casserole Bread

1 loaf

Adapted for contemporary times from an old German recipe

Ingredients

1   cup creamed cottage cheese
¼   cup water
1   tablespoon butter or margarine
3   cups flour
2   tablespoons sugar
1   tablespoon minced onion
2   tablespoons dill seed
1   teaspoon salt
½   teaspoon baking soda
1   package dry yeast
1   egg

Preparation

Warm cottage cheese, water and butter until butter is melted. Combine 1 cup flour, sugar, onion, dill seed, salt, soda and yeast. Add cheese mixture and egg to flour mixture. Blend on low speed until moistened, then beat at medium speed for 3 minutes. Stir in remaining flour by hand to form stiff dough. Cover and let rise until doubled, about 1 hour. Stir down. Turn into well-greased 1½-quart casserole. Cover and let rise again, 30 to 45 minutes. Bake in preheated 350° oven 30 minutes, or until golden brown. Brush top with melted margarine. May be served warm or cold.

East Brunswick Cinnamon Rolls

2 dozen

Ingredients

Dough:
2 packages dry yeast
½ cup warm water
1½ cups milk, warmed
½ cup sugar
2 eggs
2 teaspoons salt
½ cup vegetable oil
6 to 7 cups flour

Filling:
½ cup butter or margarine, melted
1 cup white sugar
½ cup raisins
3 tablespoons cinnamon

Frosting:
2 cups confectioners' sugar
1 teaspoon vanilla
   milk
1 cup sliced almonds

Preparation — Dissolve yeast in warm water. Add milk, sugar, eggs, oil, salt and 3 cups flour. Beat well. Gradually add 3 or more cups flour until a soft dough forms. Turn dough onto floured board and knead until smooth, about 5 minutes. Place dough in oiled bowl, turn to coat, cover and let rise in warm place until double in bulk. Punch down, turn onto floured board and roll into a 12 x 24-inch rectangle. Spread melted butter over dough, sprinkle with sugar, raisins and cinnamon. Roll dough up and carefully cut into 24 slices. Place slices flat side down in 2 greased 9 x 13-inch baking pans and let rise again until light. Bake in preheated 400° oven for about 15 minutes, checking frequently. Blend confectioners' sugar and vanilla with just enough milk to spread easily over pans of warm rolls. Sprinkle almonds over tops. At Christmas, decorate with red and green candied cherries for festive touch.

Variation: Sticky Buns

Syrup:
2   cups brown sugar
½   teaspoon cinnamon
6   tablespoons butter or margarine
½   cup light Karo
1   cup pecan halves

Preparation — Follow cinnamon roll recipe to point of slicing dough into 24 pieces. Then combine ingredients for "sticky" syrup and bring to a boil. Spread evenly between 2 9 x 13-inch baking pans. Arrange ½ cup pecans, rounded side down, in each pan. Arrange 12 rolls of dough in each pan over "sticky" syrup. Let rise until light. Bake in a preheated 400° oven for about 15 minutes. To serve immediately, let cool slightly, then turn over carefully onto tray, letting syrup run down over sides. Decorate each bun with a candied cherry, if desired. For freezing, let cool in pan and wrap. Reheat at serving time and turn onto tray.

Finnish Cheese Buns

2 dozen

Ingredients

1 package dry yeast
½ cup warm water
1 cup milk, scalded and cooled
1 teaspoon salt
½ cup sugar
2 eggs, well beaten
5 cups flour
½ cup margarine, melted
1 beaten egg, to brush on dough

Filling:
2 eggs
½ cup sugar
½ cup sour cream
1 8-ounce package cream cheese
1 tablespoon lemon juice
1 tablespoon grated lemon rind

Preparation

Dissolve yeast in warm water. Stir in milk, salt, sugar and eggs. Add 2 cups flour to yeast mixture and beat until smooth. Add melted margarine and combine well. Add enough flour to make a stiff dough, cover and let rest 15 minutes. Knead on floured board until smooth. Let rise in greased bowl, covered, until double in bulk. Divide dough in 24 pieces and shape into slightly flattened balls. Place on two greased cookie sheets 3 inches apart. Let rise until puffy. Flatten and let rise again.

Beat filling ingredients together until thick and smooth. Flatten centers of rounds gently with teaspoon leaving edges higher. Brush with beaten egg and fill centers with 2 tablespoons of filling. Bake in preheated 375° oven for 12 to 15 minutes, or until filling is set. Serve warm.

German Rye Bread

2 round loaves

Especially good for sliced turkey sandwiches!

Ingredients

3 cups medium rye flour
3 cups white flour, more or less
¼ cup cocoa
1 tablespoon sugar
1 tablespoon salt
1 tablespoon caraway seeds
2 packages dry yeast
⅓ cup molasses
2 tablespoons margarine, softened
2 cups hot tap water
oil

Preparation

Combine 1 cup rye flour, 1 cup white flour, cocoa, sugar, salt, caraway seeds and yeast. Add molasses, margarine and tap water. Beat 2 minutes at medium speed with mixer. Add 1 cup rye flour. Beat at high speed for 2 minutes. Stir in remaining 1 cup rye flour and enough white flour to make a stiff dough. Turn onto floured board and knead, about 8 to 10 minutes. Place in greased bowl and turn. Cover and let rise until double in bulk, about 1 hour. Punch down and shape into two balls. Flatten tops slightly. Place on greased baking sheet, cover and let rise again until doubled. Slash tops with knife. Bake in preheated 400° oven for 25 minutes or until done. Brush with oil.

Greenery Honey Grapenut Bread

2 loaves

Ingredients

2 packages dry yeast
2 cups warm water
½ cup honey
1 cup grapenuts
6 cups high gluten flour
¼ cup vegetable oil
1 tablespoon salt
1 egg beaten with 1 tablespoon water

Preparation

Soften yeast in ½ cup warm water mixed with ¼ cup of honey. Set aside for 10 minutes. Soften grapenuts in water to cover. Mix flour, oil, salt and rest of honey. Add grapenuts and yeast mixture. Slowly add rest of warm water, mixing dough well. Add only enough water so that dough pulls away from bowl. Turn onto floured board and knead well. Let rise in oiled bowl, turning to coat, covered, until doubled in bulk. Divide dough in half, cover and let rise 1 more hour. Punch down, shape into 2 loaves and place in oiled 9 x 5-inch loaf pans. Cover and let rise again. Brush egg wash on tops of loaves. Bake in preheated 400° oven for 10 minutes. Turn down to 350° and bake 45 to 50 minutes. Remove from pans and cool. Makes nice toast.

Harpswell Anadama Bread

2 loaves

Ingredients

5 cups white flour
2 packages dry yeast
2 cups water
½ cup yellow corn meal
1 tablespoon salt
2 tablespoons wheat germ
½ cup molasses
¼ cup margarine
1 cup old-fashioned oats
2 eggs

Preparation   In large bowl, combine 2 cups of flour and yeast. In saucepan, bring water to a boil. Remove from heat and stir in cornmeal, salt and wheat germ. Cook mixture, stirring, 2 minutes over low heat. Add molasses, margarine and oats and cook 3 minutes. Cool. Add eggs to cooled mixture, beating well after each addition. Combine with flour and yeast and beat 2 minutes. Add remaining 3 cups of flour or enough to make soft dough which can be handled easily. Turn onto floured board and knead until smooth, about 5 minutes. Place in oiled bowl, turning to coat and cover. Let rise in warm place until doubled in bulk, about 1 hour. Punch down, cut into half and shape into 2 loaves. Place in lightly oiled 8½ x 4½-inch bread pans. Let rise again until double in bulk. Bake in preheated 375° oven for about 40 minutes. Remove from pans and cool.

Harvest Buns   2 dozen

Ingredients   1   package dry yeast
               ¼   cup warm water
               ⅔   cup milk, warmed
               1   cup cooked and mashed squash, pumpkin or carrots
               1   teaspoon grated orange rind
               ⅓   cup brown sugar
               1   teaspoon salt
               ⅓   cup margarine, melted
               4 to 5 cups flour

Preparation   Dissolve yeast in warm water. Combine milk, vegetable, rind, sugar, salt and margarine, blending well. Add yeast and 2 cups flour. Beat well and gradually add more flour until dough is stiff enough to knead. Turn onto floured board and knead 3 to 5 minutes. Place in greased bowl. Turn to coat, cover and let rise until double in bulk. Punch down and shape into 24 rolls of desired shape. Place in greased baking pan and let rise again until doubled. Bake in preheated 400° oven for 10 to 12 minutes, or until done. Brush tops with more melted margarine while warm.

Moravian Sugar Cake

Ingredients

2   packages dry yeast
1   cup warm water
1   cup sugar
1   cup hot mashed potato
¾   cup butter or margarine, melted
1   teaspoon salt
2   eggs, beaten slightly
4 to 5 cups flour
½   cup each butter or margarine and brown sugar
      cinnamon, if desired
      confectioners' sugar

Preparation

Dissolve yeast in warm water. Stir sugar into potatoes and add to yeast mixture. Add ¾ cup shortening and salt. Stir in beaten eggs and add flour, mixing well. Cover and let rise until double in bulk. Punch down and spread evenly in greased 9 x 13-inch baking pan or 2 8-inch pans. Let rise for 1 hour. Make holes evenly spaced in rows. Place bit of butter and teaspoon of brown sugar in each hole. Sprinkle dough with cinnamon. Bake in preheated 350° oven for 25 to 30 minutes. Confectioners' sugar may be dusted over top. Serve warm.

Northern Maine Oatmeal Bread

2 large loaves

A five-generation recipe

Ingredients

2   cups boiling water
1   tablespoon butter or margarine
1   cup rolled oats
1   package dry yeast
½   cup warm water
½   cup molasses
2   teaspoons salt
5   cups flour

Preparation

Combine boiling water, butter and oats and let stand 1 hour, or 30 minutes if using "quick" oatmeal. Dissolve yeast in ½ cup warm water. Add yeast, molasses, salt and flour to oats and mix thoroughly. Knead dough for 8 to 10 minutes, adding more flour if necessary to form smooth dough. Let rise in oiled bowl, covered with damp cloth, in warm place until double in bulk. Punch dough down and shape into 2 loaves. Place in 2 oiled 9 x 5-inch loaf pans and let rise again until almost double in bulk. Bake in preheated 375° oven 40 to 50 minutes. After removing from pans to cool, butter tops to soften crust.

One Loaf Oatmeal Bread

1 loaf

Maine's foremost cookbook author, Marjorie Holbrook Standish, grew up in the New Meadows section of East Brunswick. In fact, her ancestor Alister Coombs, arrived there about 1675. This oatmeal bread is from Alma "Allie" Holbrook who was Marjorie's mother's best friend. Alma was noted for years for the good food she served to the public at 36 Federal St., Brunswick, and later at 16 School St. Marjorie's books are "Cooking Down East" and " Keep Cooking the Maine Way".

Ingredients

1	package dry yeast
¼	cup warm water
¾	cup boiling water
¼	cup molasses
½	cup rolled oats
⅓	cup shortening
1½	teaspoons salt
1	egg
2¾	cups flour

Preparation

Dissolve dry yeast in warm water. Stir boiling water, molasses, oatmeal, shortening and salt together. Cool. When lukewarm, stir in yeast mixture. Beat egg slightly and add, beating with spoon. Stir in flour gradually. Knead for few minutes and place in lightly oiled bowl. Cover and refrigerate for 2 hours. Remove dough, punch down, and shape into one loaf, using small amount of extra flour. Place in oiled 9 x 5-inch loaf pan, cover and allow to rise until double in bulk, about 2 hours. Bake in preheated 350° oven 1 hour. Remove from pan to cool. While still warm, butter top to soften crust.

Orange Coconut Coffee Cake

24 servings

Ingredients

1   package dry yeast
¼   cup warm water
1   cup sugar
1   teaspoon salt
2   eggs
½   cup sour cream
8   tablespoons margarine, melted
2¾ to 3 cups flour
1   cup sweetened flaked coconut
2   tablespoons grated orange rind
½   cup chopped pecans

Orange glaze:
¾   cup sugar
½   cup sour cream
2   tablespoons orange juice
¼   cup margarine

Preparation

Soften yeast in warm water. Stir in ¼ cup sugar, salt, eggs, sour cream and 6 tablespoons margarine. Gradually add flour to form stiff dough, beating well after each addition. Cover and let rise until light and doubled, about 2 hours.

Combine ¾ cup sugar, ¾ cup coconut, orange rind and pecans. Knead dough about 15 times on floured board and divide in half. Roll each half into 12-inch circle. Brush each with 1 tablespoon margarine and spread with half the sugar mixture. Cut each circle into 12 wedges. Roll up starting with wide end. Place rolls, point side down, in 3 rows in greased 9 x 13-inch baking pan. Cover and let rise in warm place until doubled in bulk, about 1 hour.

Bake in preheated 350° oven for about 25 minutes. For glaze, combine sugar, sour cream, orange juice and margarine and boil 3 minutes. Stir occasionally. Pour glaze over hot coffee cake and sprinkle with remaining ¼ cup coconut. Best served warm.

Pizza Dough

2 14 to 16-inch pizzas

Ingredients

1 package dry yeast
⅓ cup warm water
3¾ cups flour (may use ½ whole wheat flour)
1 teaspoon salt
1¼ cups water
3 tablespoons olive oil

Preparation

Dissolve yeast in ⅓ cup water. Mix all other ingredients with yeast. Knead until smooth and shiny. Let rise until triple in bulk. Divide dough in half. Roll each half into circle and let rest, covered with towel, for about 2 minutes. Roll out again and let dough rest. Continue process until dough is desired size. It will take about 10 minutes. Transfer dough to oiled pizza pan and top with favorite pizza sauce and toppings. Bake in preheated 450° oven for 12 to 15 minutes, or until bottom of crust is browned.

Refrigerator Rolls

2 dozen

Ingredients

2 packages dry yeast
½ cup lukewarm water
1½ cups milk, scalded
½ cup sugar
2 teaspoons salt
¼ cup shortening
1 egg, beaten
6 to 7 cups flour

Preparation Dissolve yeast in lukewarm water. Add sugar, salt and shortening to milk. Cool to lukewarm. Add yeast, egg and 2 cups flour, and beat well. Add remaining flour to make soft dough. Knead on lightly floured board until dough is smooth. Place in oiled bowl, turn to coat, cover and refrigerate overnight.

For rolls, remove dough from refrigerator and punch down. Shape as desired. Place in greased pans and let rise until doubled, about 1½ hours. Bake in preheated 375° oven for 10 minutes or until nicely browned.

Sourdough English Muffins 2 dozen

Powdered starter is available at L.L. Bean Inc.

Ingredients
2 packages dry yeast
2 cups warm water
1 cup starter
½ cup dry milk
1 tablespoon sugar
½ cup oil
2 teaspoons salt
6 cups flour
cornmeal

Preparation Dissolve yeast in water. Add starter, milk, sugar, salt, oil and 2 cups flour. Beat 2 minutes. Add rest of flour and mix. Knead for a few minutes and let rise, covered, in oiled bowl for 1½ hours. Punch down and let rise ½ hour. Roll dough to ½-inch thick and cut in desired diameter. Let rise ½ hour. Preheat electric skillet at 350° and sprinkle with cornmeal. Bake covered in skillet for 5 minutes on each side.

Springtime Hot Cross Buns   2 dozen

Ingredients

3¾ to 4 cups flour
2   packages dry yeast
1   teaspoon cinnamon
¾   cup milk
½   cup vegetable oil
⅓   cup sugar
¾   teaspoon salt
3   eggs
⅔   cup dried currants
½   cup finely chopped candied fruit
1   egg white, slightly beaten

Frosting:
egg white
¼   teaspoon vanilla extract
dash of salt
¾ to 1¼ cups confectioners' sugar

Preparation

Thoroughly stir together 1½ cups flour, yeast and cinnamon. Combine milk, oil, sugar and salt and heat just until warm. Add to dry mixture and add eggs. Beat at low speed on electric mixer for 30 seconds, scraping sides of bowl constantly. Beat 3 minutes on high speed. By hand, stir in currants, candied fruit and enough flour to make a soft dough. Cover and let rise until double in bulk, about 1 to 1½ hours.

Stir dough down. Shape into 24 round buns and place on greased baking sheet. Cover and let rise until almost double, 30 to 45 minutes. Brush tops with slightly beaten egg white, being careful not to spill any onto baking sheet. Bake in preheated 375° oven for 12 to 15 minutes. Cool, then with pastry tube pipe frosting crosses onto buns. For frosting, combine remainder of egg white with vanilla, salt and confectioners' sugar to make moderately stiff frosting.

Salads and Dressings

Amy's Dutch Lettuce

4 servings

A nice change from tossed salad

Ingredients

4 cups lettuce, washed and torn into bite-size pieces
¼ cup green or red onions, chopped
4 slices bacon, cut in small pieces
¼ cup cider vinegar
¼ cup water
3 tablespoons sugar
1 egg
   salt and pepper to taste

Preparation

Place lettuce and onions in salad bowl and refrigerate. Fry bacon crisp, leaving pieces and fat in skillet. Mix vinegar, water and sugar and add to skillet. Just before serving, heat bacon mixture to boil—drop raw egg into it and move it around with a fork enough to break yolk and firm egg. Pour over lettuce hot, toss and serve.

Broccoli Celery Salad

8 servings

Ingredients

2 large bunches broccoli
2 cups sliced celery
2 tablespoons minced onion
4 tablespoons pimiento, diced
2 teaspoons celery seed
2 tablespoons lemon juice
1 cup mayonnaise
¼ cup sour cream
   freshly ground pepper

Preparation

Cut broccoli into 1-inch pieces. Cook in small amount of boiling water about 5 minutes, just until tender-crisp. Drain and cool. Add next 5 ingredients. Combine mayonnaise and sour cream and pour over broccoli mixture. Add pepper and toss gently. Refrigerate 4 to 6 hours or overnight.

Chermoula

6 to 8 servings

Great dish for antipasto

Ingredients

3	large sweet peppers (colorful to use 1 green, 1 red, 1 yellow)
4	large whole garlic cloves
¼	teaspoon salt
⅛	teaspoon paprika
1	cup fine olive oil
¼	cup vinegar
2	pinches ground coriander

Preparation

Wash, seed, de-vein and cut each pepper into 8 to 10 strips. Mix remaining ingredients, add peppers and cook slowly about 15 minutes or until done. If using different colored peppers, cook separately in order to keep colors clear. Spoon into clean glass jar, cool and store in refrigerator. Remove garlic before serving. (Leftover oil makes good salad oil.)

Egg Olive Rice Salad

8 servings

Ingredients

¼	cup vegetable oil
2	tablespoons vinegar
2	tablespoons dry mustard
1½	teaspoons salt
⅛	teaspoons pepper
4½	cups hot, cooked rice
1	cup sliced ripe olives
2	hard-cooked eggs, diced
1½	cups sliced celery
¼	cup chopped dill pickles
¼	cup chopped pimiento
1	small onion, grated
½	cup mayonnaise

Preparation

Blend oil, vinegar, mustard, salt and pepper. Add to hot rice. Add remaining ingredients and chill.

Eight Layer Salad
10 to 12 servings

All done the night before

Ingredients

10 ounces fresh spinach, washed, dried and torn into pieces
½ pound bacon, cooked until crisp, drained and crumbled
6 hard-cooked eggs, chopped
1 head romaine or iceberg lettuce, washed, dried and torn into pieces
1 10-ounce package frozen peas, thawed and drained
1 cup sliced sweet onion
2 teaspoons sugar
  salt and pepper to taste
2 cups mayonnaise
1 cup sour cream
1 cup coarsely grated Swiss cheese

Preparation

In large glass salad bowl, arrange spinach seasoned with salt, pepper and 1 teaspoon sugar. Press down. Add layers of bacon, eggs and lettuce. Press down. Season again with salt, pepper and 1 teaspoon sugar. Add layers of peas and onion. Combine mayonnaise and sour cream and completely cover salad. Top with cheese. Cover and refrigerate overnight. Toss just before serving.

Florentine Citrus Salad
8 servings

Ingredients

2½ quarts assorted greens
1 medium Bermuda onion, sliced and separated into rings
½ cup orange sections
½ cup grapefruit sections
½ cup celery slices
½ cup walnut halves
⅔ cup French dressing
⅓ cup blue or feta cheese crumbs
2 teaspoons celery seeds

Preparation

Tear greens into bite-size pieces. Add onions, orange and grapefruit sections, celery and walnuts. Toss lightly. Combine dressing, cheese and celery seeds. Serve with salad.

Hot Potato Salad

8 servings

Ingredients

3 pounds potatoes, boiled until tender
¾ cup diced bacon
¾ cup minced scallions or onion
¼ cup chopped celery
¾ cup chicken broth
½ cup white wine vinegar
1 tablespoon sugar
salt and pepper to taste
¼ cup minced parsley
½ teaspoon celery seed

Preparation

Drain potatoes, peel and slice while still warm. Place in serving bowl. Sauté bacon until almost crisp. Add scallions or onions and celery, and sauté another minute. Add broth and vinegar, stirring in brown bits around sides of pan. Season dressing with sugar, salt and pepper to taste. Pour dressing over potatoes, add parsley and celery seed. Toss gently and serve.

Peas with Pizazz

8 servings

Ingredients

20 ounces frozen petite peas
1 cup sour cream
2 green onions, chopped
½ cup diced celery
7 slices bacon, cooked and crumbled
½ teaspoon salt
freshly ground pepper to taste

Preparation

Thaw peas and drain. Toss with remaining ingredients. Serve on lettuce.

Pennsylvania Dutch Pepper Cabbage

4 to 6 servings

Ingredients

1   medium head cabbage, finely chopped
1   medium green pepper, finely chopped
1   small onion, grated
1   medium carrot, grated

Dressing:
¼   cup sugar
½   teaspoon salt
½   cup light cream
⅓   cup tarragon vinegar

Preparation

Combine vegetables. Combine dressing ingredients and add to cabbage mixture. Refrigerate.

Red Cole Slaw

10 to 12 servings

Improves with age

Ingredients

1   cup sugar
1   cup warm vinegar
4   cups chopped, cooked beets
4   cups shredded cabbage
½   cup horseradish
1   teaspoon salt

Preparation

Dissolve sugar in vinegar. Add rest of ingredients and mix well. Chill.

Sauerkraut Salad

4 to 6 servings

Ingredients

2 cups sauerkraut
½ cup chopped celery
½ cup chopped onion
½ cup chopped green pepper
½ cup chopped carrot
½ small jar undrained pimiento, chopped
¼ cup vinegar
2 tablespoons vegetable oil
⅓ cup sugar.

Preparation

Add undrained sauerkraut to celery, onion, green pepper, carrots and pimiento. Mix vinegar, oil and sugar. Pour over vegetables and mix well. Cover and refrigerate overnight.

Sliced Tomatoes With Gorgonzola

6 servings

Ingredients

¼ pound firm Gorgonzola or Stilton Cheese, frozen for 30 minutes
6 garden fresh tomatoes, thinly sliced
¼ cup minced fresh parsley
3 tablespoons sliced shallot
2 tablespoons minced fresh or 2 teaspoons dried basil

Dressing:
2 tablespoons lemon juice
2 teaspoons Dijon mustard
⅓ to ½ cup olive oil
salt and pepper to taste

Preparation

Grate frozen cheese. Arrange tomatoes, overlapping slightly on large platter. Combine cheese, parsley, shallots and basil. Sprinkle over tomatoes.

Combine lemon juice and mustard. Add olive oil in a stream, whisking. Season with salt and pepper. Pour dressing over tomatoes.

Sesame Spinach Salad

4 servings

Ingredients

5 slices bacon, cooked until crisp, reserving fat
½ pound spinach, cleaned and torn into pieces
pepper to taste
sesame seeds

Dressing:
fat from bacon
1 teaspoon sugar
¼ cup malt, Japanese or raspberry vinegar
1 garlic clove, crushed
1 teaspoon catsup
¼ teaspoon hot sesame oil

Preparation

Crumble bacon over spinach, add pepper and sprinkle with sesame speeds. For dressing, combine fat, sugar, vinegar, garlic and catsup. Bring just to boil, add sesame oil and serve immediately over spinach.

Vegetable Pasta Salad

6 to 8 servings

Ingredients

8 ounces macaroni twists, cooked and drained
½ bunch broccoli, broken into florets
½ medium head cauliflower, broken in florets
½ cup grated Parmesan cheese
1 medium red onion, sliced paper thin
Best Salad Dressing (page 111)
12 cherry tomatoes, halved, for garnish

Preparation

Cook broccoli and cauliflower just until tender. Immediately rinse with cold water. Drain until dry. Mix macaroni, broccoli, cauliflower, cheese and onion. Chill at least 2 hours. Toss with Best Salad Dressing just before serving. Garnish with tomato halves.

Broccoli Chicken Salad

6 servings

Ingredients

2   chicken breasts, cooked, boned and cut into chunks
2   cups fresh broccoli, florets only, cooked briefly
4 to 5 green onions, thinly sliced
¼   cup chopped parsley
1   teaspoon dill weed

Dressing:
½   cup cottage cheese
½   cup mayonnaise
⅓   cup milk
1   tablespoon olive oil
1   garlic clove, minced·
2   tablespoons white wine vinegar or lemon juice
     pinch of sugar
½   teaspoon salt
     freshly ground pepper to taste

Preparation

Mix chicken, broccoli, onions, parsley and dill. Combine dressing ingredients and toss with chicken. Chill 2 hours before serving.

Exotic Chicken Chutney Salad

12 servings

Ingredients

8	cups diced cooked chicken
2	cups pineapple tidbits, drained, fresh or canned
8	ounces water chestnuts, sliced
2	cups sliced celery
½	cup sliced green onion
2	pounds seedless green grapes, halved
2	cups sliced almonds
3	cups mayonnaise
½	cup chopped chutney
2	teaspoons grated lime rind
2	tablespoons lime juice
1	tablespoon curry powder
1	teaspoon salt
	lettuce, seasonal fresh fruit and paprika for garnish

Preparation

Combine chicken, pineapple, water chestnuts, celery, onion, grapes and almonds. Mix mayonnaise, chutney, lime rind and juice, curry powder and salt. Add to chicken mixture. Serve on lettuce and garnish with fruit in season. Sprinkle with paprika if desired.

Mother's Lemon Ginger Chicken Salad

4 to 6 servings

Ingredients

½	cup mayonnaise
¼	cup sour cream or yogurt
1	tablespoon sugar
½	teaspoon grated lemon rind
½	teaspoon ginger
¼	teaspoon salt
2	cups diced cooked chicken
1	cup white grapes
1	cup celery, cut fine
	toasted slivered almonds for garnish

Preparation   Stir together first 6 ingredients. Add chicken, grapes and
celery and toss lightly to coat. Chill several hours. Sprinkle
with almonds.

Molded Salmon Salad   6 to 8 servings

Ingredients

1   teaspoon unflavored gelatin
¼   cup cold water
½   tablespoon flour
1   teaspoon dry mustard
    few grains cayenne pepper
2   egg yolks
1½ tablespoons melted butter
¾   cup milk
½   teaspoon salt
¼   cup vinegar
2   cups freshly poached flaked salmon

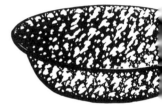

Cucumber dressing:
1   cup heavy cream
¼   teaspoon salt
    few grains cayenne pepper
3   tablespoons vinegar
1   medium cucumber, peeled, seeded, chopped and drained
    caviar, hard cooked eggs and tomatoes for garnish

Preparation   Prepare salmon. Dissolve gelatin in cold water. Mix flour,
mustard, cayenne pepper, egg yolks, butter, milk and salt.
Cook over boiling water to thicken. As it begins to thicken,
add vinegar. Remove from heat. Add gelatin to hot mixture
and blend well. Add flaked salmon and pour into 4-cup
mold. Chill until firm. Unmold onto serving dish.

For dressing, beat cream until stiff, slowly adding salt,
pepper and vinegar. Add cucumber just before serving.
Garnish salad with caviar, hard-cooked eggs and tomatoes.

Polynesian Salad

10 to 12 servings

Ingredients

14 ounces hearts of palm, cut into ¼ -inch slices
8 ounces bamboo shoots
8 ounces water chestnuts, sliced
14 ounces artichoke hearts, quartered
½ pound fresh bean sprouts, blanched
½ pound cherry tomatoes, halved
½ pound fresh mushrooms, sliced
½ pound freshly cooked gulf shrimp, cut into bite-size pieces
1½ cups cubed cooked chicken
½ pound bacon, fried crisp and crumbled

Dressing:
1 cup mayonnaise
4 tablespoons lemon juice
4 tablespoons soy sauce
½ teaspoon salt
½ teaspoon sugar
parsley for garnish

Preparation

Drain hearts of palm, bamboo shoots, chestnuts, artichoke hearts and bean sprouts. Pat dry on paper towels. Combine in salad bowl with tomatoes, mushrooms, shrimp, chicken and bacon.

Combine dressing ingredients, mixing well. Pour over salad and toss. Garnish with sprigs of parsley around edge of salad bowl.

Taco Salad

6 servings

Ingredients

1	pound ground beef
2	tablespoons chili powder
1	teaspoon ground cumin
¾	teaspoon salt
1	avocado, cut in ¼ inch cubes
2	tablespoons lemon juice
4	cups finely shredded lettuce
1½	cups finely sliced green onions
1½	cups shredded sharp Cheddar cheese
1	cup cherry tomatoes, quartered
½	cup sour cream
2	cups tortilla chips

Dressing:

3	4-ounce cans taco sauce
¼	cup chopped green chilies
2	tablespoons vegetable oil
½	teaspoon ground cumin

Preparation

Sauté beef until brown, stirring to break up meat. Drain and stir in chili powder, cumin and ½ teaspoon salt. Cook over low heat, stirring, 3 minutes. Cool. Sprinkle avocado with lemon juice and ¼ teaspoon salt.

Combine ingredients for dressing. To serve, arrange in concentric circles: lettuce, green onions, meat, cheese, avocado and tomatoes. Serve immediately with dressing, a dollop of sour cream and chips.

Tortellini Salad

4 to 6 servings

Ingredients

1½   pounds meat-filled tortellini
6   ounces sliced baked ham, cut into julienne strips
2   red peppers, cut into julienne strips
½   cup thinly sliced scallions
⅓   cup pine nuts, toasted
1½   tablespoons freshly grated Parmesan cheese

Dressing:
⅓   cup red wine vinegar
1½   teaspoons Dijon mustard
     salt and pepper to taste
1⅓   cups olive oil (or half olive and half vegetable oil)
1   tablespoon minced fresh parsley
1   tablespoon snipped fresh dill
2   teaspoons dried basil

Preparation

Cook tortellini according to package directions, or until al dente. Drain pasta and refresh under running cold water. Drain well.

In large serving bowl, combine vinegar, mustard, salt and pepper. Add oil in stream, beating dressing until well-combined. Stir in parsley, dill and basil. Add pasta, ham, peppers, scallion, pine nuts and Parmesan cheese. Toss gently. Chill salad, covered, for at least 1 hour.

Four Fruit Frozen Salad

6 to 8 servings

Ingredients

1   cup Miracle Whip
8   ounces cream cheese
2   tablespoons confectioners' sugar
15   ounces apricots, drained
16   ounces dark sweet cherries, drained
11   ounces mandarin oranges, drained
8   ounces cut pineapple, drained
1   cup small marshmallows

Preparation   Blend together first 3 ingredients and beat until soft and
               creamy. Add fruit and marshmallows, folding well. Turn into
               large loaf pan and freeze. To serve, thaw enough to remove
               from container and slice. Serve on lettuce and garnish as
               desired.

Cranberry Port Salad   12 servings

Ingredients   6   ounces raspberry-flavored gelatin
               2   cups boiling water
               16   ounces whole cranberry sauce
               8¾   ounces canned crushed pineapple, undrained
               ½   cup chopped walnuts
               ¾   cup port

Preparation   Dissolve gelatin in boiling water. Stir in cranberry sauce and
               pineapple. Fold in nuts and wine. Pour into 6-cup mold.
               Chill until firm. Unmold before serving. Recipe may be
               halved and cranberry juice may be used instead of port.

Molded Avocado Salad   6 servings

Ingredients   1   envelope unflavored gelatin
               ¾   cup water
               1   large avocado, peeled and mashed (1 cup)
               2   tablespoons lemon juice
               ½   cup sour cream
               ½   cup mayonnaise
               ⅛   teaspoon Tabasco sauce
               ½   teaspoon salt
               1   tablespoon onion juice
               1½   tablespoons sugar

Preparation   Sprinkle gelatin on water to soften. Stir over low heat until
               gelatin is dissolved. Chill until lightly thickened. Mix
               avocado with remaining ingredients. Stir in gelatin and pour
               into 4-cup mold. Chill until firm. Unmold before serving.

Pineapple Banana Frozen Salad

14 servings

Ingredients

2 cups sour cream
¾ cup sugar
2 tablespoons lemon juice
1 cup canned, crushed pineapple, drained
¼ cup cut maraschino cherries
¼ cup chopped nut meats
1 banana, sliced

Preparation

Mix all ingredients. Freeze in paper liners in muffin pans. When well-frozen, remove from muffin pans. Place in plastic bag and store in freezer for use when sweet salad is appropriate.

Strawberry Layered Salad

10 to 12 servings

Ingredients

6 ounces of strawberry-flavored gelatin
1 cup boiling water
20 ounces frozen sliced strawberries
16 ounces canned crushed pineapple, undrained
3 medium-sized bananas, mashed
1 cup chopped walnuts
1 pint sour cream, room temperature

Preparation

Combine gelatin with boiling water. Stir until dissolved. Stir in strawberries with their juice. Add undrained pineapple, bananas and half the walnuts. Put half the mixture in 12 x 8-inch baking dish as the first layer. Refrigerate 2 hours. Spread sour cream gently over that layer and spoon rest of mixture on top. Sprinkle rest of walnuts on top. Refrigerate until firmly set. Unmold before serving.

Tart Rhubarb Salad

6 to 8 servings

First taste of spring

Ingredients

4   cups diced rhubarb
1   cup cold water
¾   cup sugar
¼   teaspoon salt
6   ounces strawberry-flavored gelatin
1¾   cups cold water
¼   cup lemon juice
1   cup chopped celery
22   ounces mandarin oranges, drained

Preparation

Combine first 4 ingredients and bring to boil. Reduce heat and simmer until fruit is soft. Add gelatin and stir. Add cold water and lemon juice. Chill until slightly set. Add celery and oranges and pour into 10-cup mold. Chill until firm. Unmold before serving.

Cheesy Cucumber Ring
8 servings

Ingredients

1   envelope unflavored gelatin
½   cup cold water
½   teaspoon salt
1   medium cucumber, peeled, halved and seeded
½   small onion, grated and drained
2   ribs celery, cut up
3   cups cream-style cottage cheese
8   ounces cream cheese, softened
½   cup mayonnaise
⅔   cup finely chopped celery
⅓   cup broken walnuts, toasted

Preparation

Soak gelatin in water. Add salt. Heat until gelatin dissolves. Grate by hand or in food processor cucumber, onion and celery. Beat cheeses until blended. Stir in gelatin. Add vegetables and remaining ingredients. Pour into 6-cup ring mold and chill until firm.

Unmold and serve with cucumber slices, radishes, tomatoes, and cold cuts, or fill center with seafood.

Cranberry Borscht Salad
8 servings

Ingredients

16   ounces pickled beets
¾   cup cold water
2   cups cranberry juice
½   teaspoon salt
⅛   teaspoon pepper
1   small bay leaf
6   ounces lemon-flavored gelatin
2   tablespoons lemon juice
3   tablespoons finely chopped celery
2   tablespoons minced green onion

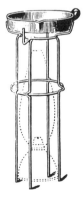

Horseradish dressing:
1   cup sour cream
2   tablespoons milk
1   tablespoon prepared horseradish
¼   teaspoon salt
1   teaspoon sugar

Preparation   Drain beets, reserving liquid. Dice beets. Add water,
cranberry juice, salt, pepper and bay leaf to beet juices. Heat
to boiling point, remove from heat and remove bay leaf. Stir
in gelatin until dissolved. Add lemon juice. Chill until
syrupy. Stir in beets, celery and onion. Pour into 6-cup
mold. Chill until firm. Unmold and serve on lettuce with
horseradish dressing.

For dressing, combine ingredients and stir until well-blended.
Plain yogurt may be substituted for sour cream.

San Francisco Tomato Aspic   8 servings

Ingredients   3   tablespoons unflavored gelatin
¾   cup cold tomato juice
2¼ cups hot tomato juice
1   cup undiluted consomme
4   tablespoons sugar
3   tablespoons lemon juice
½   teaspoon salt
    few drops hot pepper sauce

Preparation   Sprinkle gelatin on cold tomato juice. Heat remaining
ingredients. Stir in gelatin until dissolved. Pour into 4-cup
ring mold. Add asparagus or other vegetables if desired.
Chill until firm. Unmold before serving.

Tomato Mousse

6 to 8 servings

Ingredients

2   envelopes unflavored gelatin
½   cup cold water
10¾ounces canned tomato soup
6   ounces cream cheese, softened
1   cup mayonnaise
1   cup chopped celery
½   cup chopped green pepper
¼   cup finely chopped onion
¼   cup sliced olives

Preparation

Soften gelatin in cold water. Add soup and heat until gelatin is dissolved. Mix cream cheese with mayonnaise and add to soup mixture. Stir in remaining vegetables. Pour into 6-cup ring mold and chill until firm. Unmold and fill center of ring with shrimp, crab or lobster meat.

V-8 Lemon Aspic

5 to 6 servings

Ingredients

1¾ cups V-8 juice
3   ounces lemon-flavored gelatin
1   tablespoon lemon juice
1   teaspoon Worcestershire sauce
1   tablespoon catsup
1   tablespoon cider or tarragon vinegar
½   cup chopped celery
½   cup chopped green pepper
2   tablespoons chopped onion
¼   cup sliced green olives

Preparation

Bring V-8 juice to boil and add gelatin. Whisk until dissolved. Add other ingredients, except vegetables, and partially set. Add vegetables and pour into 4-cup mold. Chill until firm. Unmold before serving.

Best Salad Dressing

2 cups

Excellent for a pasta salad

Ingredients

1   egg
1   egg yolk
1   tablespoon vinegar
1   tablespoon plus 1 teaspoon Dijon mustard
1   cup vegetable oil
2   teaspoons dried oregano
3   teaspoons chopped fresh parsley
2   garlic cloves, minced
¾   teaspoon salt
½   teaspoon pepper

Preparation

Combine all ingredients in blender and blend 1 minute. Store in refrigerator in airtight container. Shake well before using.

Celery Seed Dressing

2 cups

Sweet and tasty—especially good for fruit

Ingredients

⅔   cup sugar
1   teaspoon dry mustard
1   teaspoon paprika
1   teaspoon celery seed
¼   teaspoon salt
⅓   cup honey
⅓   cup vinegar
1   tablespoon lemon juice
½   teaspoon grated onion
1   cup vegetable oil

Preparation

Combine first 5 ingredients. Add next 4. Beat with electric mixer to blend thoroughly. Gradually add oil in slow stream, beating until dressing is thick.

The Corsican Curried Mustard Dressing

2 cups

Ingredients

1 cup vegetable oil
½ cup vinegar
¼ cup vermouth
¼ cup soy sauce
1 teaspoon dry mustard
1 teaspoon curry powder
1 teaspoon garlic powder
½ teaspoon salt
½ teaspoon black pepper

Preparation

Place in blender and blend until thick and emulsified. Good on spinach salad.

Creamy Mustard Dressing

3 cups

Good on greens or mixed vegetable salad

Ingredients

½ cup sour cream
1½ cups mayonnaise
½ cup prepared mustard
¼ cup cider vinegar
2 tablespoons sugar
salt and pepper to taste

Preparation

Combine all ingredients and mix well. Season to taste.

Green Goddess Dressing

2½ cups

Ingredients

2   ounces anchovies, chopped
3   tablespoons chopped fresh chives
1   tablespoon lemon juice
3   tablespoons tarragon vinegar
1   cup sour cream
1   cup mayonnaise
½   cup chopped fresh parsley
½   teaspoon salt
    freshly ground pepper to taste

Preparation

Combine ingredients in blender and blend 2 seconds.

Low Sodium French Dressing

2 cups

Ingredients

10½ ounces Campbell's Low Sodium Tomato Soup (with tomato pieces)
1   small onion, cut fine
¼   cup sugar
⅔   cup vegetable oil
⅓   cup vinegar
½   teaspoon paprika
½   teaspoon pepper
2   dashes Worchestershire sauce if diet allows

Preparation

Combine ingredients and shake vigorously. Refrigerate.

Poppy Seed Dressing

2⅔ cups

For fruit salads, especially those with grapefruit

Ingredients

1 cup sugar
2 teaspoons dry mustard
2 teaspoons salt
⅔ cup vinegar
3 tablespoons onion juice
2 cups vegetable oil
3 tablespoons poppy seeds

Preparation

Combine sugar, mustard, salt and vinegar in blender. Add onion juice and blend thoroughly. Add oil slowly, blending constantly, and continue to blend until thick. Add poppy seeds and blend another 2 minutes. Store in refrigerator.

Vegetables

Asparagus Casserole

6 to 8 servings

Ingredients

30 ounces frozen asparagus spears
1⅓ cups cornflake crumbs
8 tablespoons butter or margarine
½ cup parsley flakes
½ teaspoon salt
¼ teaspoon pepper
2 tablespoons sherry
1 cup shredded mozzarella cheese

Preparation

Cook asparagus for only 2 minutes and drain. Brown cornflake crumbs in butter. Add parsley, salt, pepper and sherry. Cook until ingredients are dry. Butter 9 x 13-inch baking dish. Layer asparagus, crumbs and cheese. Repeat once more. Cover and bake in preheated 325° oven for 15 minutes. Uncover and bake an additional 15 to 20 minutes.

Baked Lima Beans

4 to 6 servings

Ingredients

1 pound dry lima beans
¼ to ½ cup molasses
¼ pound salt pork
2 tablespoons dry mustard
1 medium onion
salt and pepper to taste

Preparation

Soak beans overnight. Drain and add more water to cover. Parboil until partially cooked. Place undrained beans in crockpot with remaining ingredients and cook on high for 1 hour. Reduce heat to low and continue cooking 3 to 4 hours more.

Bar-B-Q Beans
8 to 10 servings

Ingredients

½ cup butter or margarine
3 medium onions, chopped
½ cup vinegar
1 cup catsup
1 teaspoon salt
½ cup brown sugar
15 ounces canned lima beans, drained
15 ounces canned kidney beans, drained
15 ounces canned baked beans, undrained

Preparation

Melt butter and sauté onions until transparent. Combine remaining ingredients. Add onions and stir well. Pour into greased 2-quart casserole. Bake in preheated 350° oven for 35 minutes.

Boston Baked Beans
6 to 8 servings

Ingredients

2 cups dry beans; use a mixture of 3 kinds or more such as yellow-eye, cattle, pea or kidney
¼ pound salt pork, halved or quartered
2 heaping tablespoons brown sugar
2 tablespoons molasses
1 teaspoon salt
¼ teaspoon dry mustard

Preparation

Soak beans overnight in water to cover. Drain and add more water to cover. Parboil 20 to 30 minutes or until skins begin to split. Add pinch of soda, drain and rinse with cold water. Stir in sugar, molasses, salt and mustard. Place in bean pot or heavy casserole with salt pork on top. Cover with hot water and bake, uncovered, in preheated 275° oven until beans are almost dry. Add more water as needed but not to cover. Bake until brown on top. Total cooking is 6 to 7 hours.

Green Beans in Horseradish Sauce

6 servings

Ingredients

4 tablespoons butter or margarine
2 tablespoons minced onion
4 tablespoons flour
½ teaspoon salt
2 tablespoons horseradish
⅛ teaspoon pepper
2 cups milk
2 pounds green beans, cooked and drained

Preparation

Melt butter in top of double boiler. Add onion and cook until tender. Add flour, salt, horseradish and pepper. Stir until smooth. Add milk, place over boiling water and cook, stirring constantly, until thick. Cover and cook 10 minutes. Add green beans, heat well and serve.

Chinese Beets

12 servings

Equally delicious hot or cold

Ingredients

6 cups canned or cooked fresh beets, sliced
1½ cups beet liquid
1 cup sugar
1 cup vinegar
2 tablespoons cornstarch
24 whole cloves
3 tablespoons catsup
1 teaspoon vanilla
3 tablespoons corn oil

Preparation

Mix all ingredients, except beets. Bring to a boil, stirring constantly. Add beets and cook for 3 minutes, stirring occasionally. Let cool, then store in refrigerator.

Broccoli Casserole

6 servings

Ingredients

20 ounces frozen, chopped broccoli, cooked and drained, or equal amount of fresh broccoli
10¾ ounces cream of mushroom soup
¾ cup mayonnaise
2 eggs, beaten
5 ounces sharp Cheddar cheese, grated
1 small onion, finely chopped

Topping:
½ cup Ritz cracker crumbs
2 tablespoons melted butter or margarine

Preparation

Mix all ingredients together, except topping, and place in buttered 2-quart casserole. Toss crumbs and butter and sprinkle over top. Bake in preheated 350° oven for 30 minutes.

Rotkohl (Red Cabbage)

6 servings

From the German Chef at Brunwick's Stowe House

Ingredients

1½ tablespoons butter or oil
1 medium onion, chopped
2 pounds red cabbage, finely shredded
2 bay leaves
8 whole cloves
2 tablespoons vinegar
½ to 1 teaspoon sugar depending on tartness of apples
⅔ cup water
2 medium apples, peeled and sliced ¼ inch thick
½ teaspoon salt
1 teaspoon cornstarch mixed with a little water

Preparation

Melt shortening in large pot and lightly brown onion. Add cabbage and stir until onion and shortening are well mixed. Add bay leaves, cloves, vinegar, sugar and water. Simmer, covered, for ½ hour. Add apples and salt and simmer, covered, for another ½ hour. Mix cornstarch with a little water and add to pot, stirring until slightly thickened. Remove bay leaves and serve.

Apricot-Glazed Carrots

4 to 6 servings

Ingredients

2 pounds fresh carrots, sliced on the diagonal
3 tablespoons butter or margarine
1/3 cup apricot jam
1/8 teaspoon ground nutmeg
1/4 teaspoon salt
1 teaspoon freshly grated orange rind
2 teaspoons lemon juice

Preparation

Cook carrots until tender-crisp, about 8 to 10 minutes. Drain well. In same saucepan, melt butter and stir in preserves until blended. Add remaining ingredients. Toss carrots in mixture until well-coated. Serve while hot.

Guess Again Carrots

6 servings

Ingredients

2 pounds carrots
2 tablespoons butter or margarine
1 medium onion, grated
8 ounces sharp Cheddar cheese, grated
1/2 teaspoon salt
1/8 teaspoon pepper

Preparation

Butter 2-quart casserole. Peel, slice and cook carrots until tender. Mash well or purée in food processor. Add remaining ingredients and place in casserole. Bake in preheated 350° oven for 40 minutes, or until hot and bubbly.

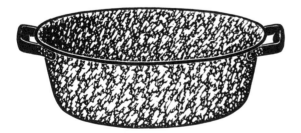

Corn Pudding

4 to 5 servings

Ingredients

17   ounces canned cream-style corn
2   eggs, lightly beaten
½   cup milk
     salt and pepper to taste
2   tablespoons melted butter or margarine
2   tablespoons each of chopped green or red pepper and onion
15   Ritz crackers, crushed

Preparation

Mix all ingredients except ¼ cup crushed crackers. Pour into buttered 1½-quart casserole. Sprinkle with reserved cracker crumbs. Bake in preheated 350° oven for about 1 hour or until center is firm.

Eggplant Casserole

6 servings

A wonderful aroma while baking

Ingredients

4   cups eggplant, diced
2   medium onions, chopped
3   tablespoons butter or margarine
1   teaspoon sugar
     salt and pepper to taste
16   ounces peeled tomatoes, cut into quarters
5   ounces sharp Cheddar cheese, grated

Preparation

Sauté eggplant and onion in butter or margarine until partially browned and softened, about 8 to 10 minutes. Place in buttered 2-quart casserole. Add sugar, salt and pepper to tomatoes and pour over eggplant. Sprinkle with cheese. Bake in a preheated 350° oven for about 1 hour.

Mushroom Casserole

8 to 10 servings

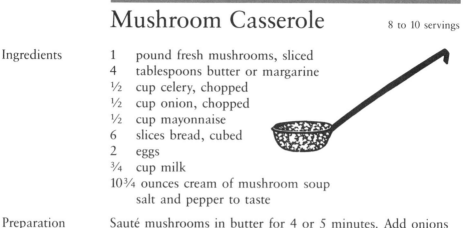

Ingredients

1   pound fresh mushrooms, sliced
4   tablespoons butter or margarine
½   cup celery, chopped
½   cup onion, chopped
½   cup mayonnaise
6   slices bread, cubed
2   eggs
¾   cup milk
10¾ ounces cream of mushroom soup
    salt and pepper to taste

Preparation

Sauté mushrooms in butter for 4 or 5 minutes. Add onions and celery and sauté another 2 minutes. Stir in mayonnaise. Place ½ of bread cubes in buttered 2-quart casserole. Spread mushroom mixture over bread and cover with remaining bread cubes. Beat eggs lightly with ½ cup milk and pour over mixture. Chill in refrigerator for 1 hour or more. When ready to bake, dilute soup with remaining ¼ cup milk. Add salt and pepper to taste and spread over casserole. Bake in preheated 350° oven for 1 hour.

Mushroom Pie

6 servings

Ingredients

    pastry for 2-crust 8-inch pie
2   medium onions, chopped
1   pound mushrooms, chopped
3   tablespoons butter
1   tablespoon flour
½   cup light cream
1   tablespoon cognac
    salt and pepper to taste

Preparation Line 8-inch glass pie plate with 1 crust. Brown onions and mushrooms in butter. Add flour and stir until thickened. Add cream, cognac, salt and pepper. Stir gently and cook 1 minute more on low heat. Remove from heat and cool. Place in pastry. Cover with top crust, fluting edges. Bake in a preheated 450° oven for 20 minutes.

"Best Way to Have Onions" 6 servings

Ingredients

2 cups water
1 cup dry white wine
½ teaspoon salt
2 pounds fresh small white onions, peeled
¼ cup butter or margarine
¼ cup flour
1 cup light cream
2 tablespoons minced fresh parsley
  salt and pepper to taste
  dash of nutmeg
2 tablespoons grated Parmesan cheese or ½ cup grated Cheddar cheese

Preparation Heat water, wine and salt to boiling. Add onions. Cook uncovered for 20 to 30 minutes or until almost soft. Drain, saving liquid. Melt butter, stir in flour, add cream and 1 cup of onion liquid. (Save the rest for gravy.) Cook until thick, stirring constantly. Add parsley, salt, pepper, nutmeg and onions. Pour into shallow buttered 2-quart casserole. Sprinkle cheese on top. Bake uncovered in preheated 325° oven for 30 minutes.

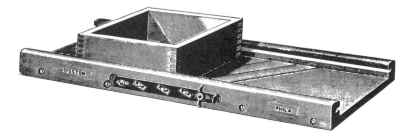

Festive Onions

6 servings

Ingredients

4 cups sliced onions
3 tablespoons butter
2 eggs
1 cup cream
salt and pepper to taste
½ cup freshly grated Parmesan cheese

Preparation

Sauté onions in butter until transparent. Keep warm in 2-quart casserole. Beat eggs until light, then mix with cream, salt and pepper. Pour over onions. Sprinkle cheese on top. Bake uncovered in preheated 425° oven for 15 minutes.

French Peas

6 to 8 servings

Ingredients

2 cups water
1 teaspoon sugar
½ teaspoon salt
20 ounces frozen peas
3 tablespoons butter or margarine
1 cup sliced green onions with some of tops
⅓ pound fresh mushrooms, sliced
1 cup shredded iceberg lettuce
salt and freshly ground pepper to taste
2 tablespoons sliced pimiento

Preparation

Bring water, sugar and salt to a boil. Add peas, separating with a fork. As soon as peas return to a rolling boil, drain and run under cold water. Sauté onions and mushrooms in butter or margarine for 3 minutes. Stir lettuce into onion mixture and sauté for another 3 minutes. Add peas and continue to cook until peas are heated through and lettuce is barely transparent. Add salt and pepper. Garnish with pimiento before serving.

Harvest Potatoes

10 servings

Ingredients

32 ounces frozen hash-brown potatoes
10½ ounces cream of chicken soup
1 cup sour cream
2 cups shredded Cheddar cheese
¾ cup melted butter or margarine
1 onion, diced
2 cups cornflakes, crushed

Preparation

Butter 9 x 13-inch casserole. Combine all ingredients except cornflakes and ¼ cup margarine and place in casserole. Combine cornflakes and margarine and sprinkle on top. Bake in preheated 350° oven for 45 minutes.

Potato Pancakes

6 servings

Serve with applesauce

Ingredients

4 medium potatoes, peeled and grated
1 egg, well beaten
1 teaspoon salt
¼ teaspoon pepper
1 medium onion, grated
1 heaping tablespoon flour
¼ teaspoon baking powder
peanut or corn oil

Preparation

Drain excess moisture from potatoes by pressing in sieve. Combine remaining ingredients with potato and mix well. Drop by heaping tablespoons onto hot skillet lightly greased with peanut or corn oil. Fry until brown and crispy on both sides, about 5 minutes. Add more oil for each pancake and drain on paper towels. Leftover pancakes may be frozen and reheated in 400° oven.

Sweet Potato Casserole

8 to 10 servings

A Southern holiday favorite

Ingredients

3 cups cooked mashed sweet potatoes
½ cup light brown sugar
2 eggs, beaten
½ teaspoon salt
4 tablespoons butter or margarine, melted
½ cup milk or orange juice
1½ teaspoons vanilla extract

Topping:
⅓ cup light brown sugar
⅓ cup flour
1 cup chopped pecans
2 tablespoons margarine or butter, melted

Preparation

Combine all ingredients except topping and spoon into buttered, shallow 2-quart casserole. Combine topping ingredients and sprinkle over potato. Bake in preheated 350° oven for 35 minutes. This may be made ahead and frozen. Thaw, then bake as directed.

Sweet Potato Apple Casserole

6 to 8 servings

Especially nice for a buffet

Ingredients

4 large sweet potatoes
4 Granny Smith Apples, peeled and thinly sliced
½ cup packed dark brown sugar
½ cup chopped pecans
¼ cup melted butter
¼ cup fresh orange juice
  grated rind of 1 orange
1 teaspoon cinnamon
¼ teaspoon mace

Preparation | Pierce potatoes and bake in preheated 450° oven for 40 minutes. Cool. Peel and thinly slice. Alternate layers of apple and potato slices in a buttered shallow baking dish. Sprinkle pecans on top. Combine melted butter, orange juice and rind, cinnamon and mace. Drizzle over top of apple-potato mixture. Cover and bake 40 minutes at 425°.

Spinach Artichoke Casserole 8 servings

Ingredients
20 ounces frozen, chopped spinach
½ cup butter or margarine, melted
8 ounces cream cheese, softened
1 teaspoon lemon juice
⅓ cup plain yogurt
salt and pepper to taste
14 ounces canned artichokes, water packed
18 Ritz crackers, crushed
2 tablespoons butter or margarine

Preparation
Bring spinach to a boil, then drain, squeezing out all liquid. Add melted shortening, cream cheese, lemon juice, yogurt, salt and pepper. Blend well. Cut artichokes into thirds and place in bottom of buttered 1½-quart casserole. Cover with spinach mixture. Top with cracker crumbs and dot with butter or margarine. Bake in preheated 350° oven for 25 to 30 minutes.

Spinach Custard

16 servings

Ingredients

4   medium onions, chopped
2   cloves garlic, minced
½   cup corn or olive oil
40   ounces frozen chopped spinach
12   eggs
2   teaspoons salt
½   teaspoon pepper
4   cups shredded Monterey Jack cheese
2   cups shredded sharp cheese
1   cup cottage cheese
1½   teaspoons Worcestershire sauce and ¾ teaspoon
      thyme, optional

Preparation

Sauté onions and garlic in oil until soft. Add spinach and
cook over low heat until thawed, breaking apart to hasten
heating. Meanwhile, beat eggs until frothy. Season with salt,
pepper and optional seasonings. Stir in cheeses. Combine
with spinach. Turn into two 9 x 13-inch buttered casseroles
and bake, uncovered, in preheated 400° oven for 40 minutes
or until softly set. Stir 4 or 5 times while baking. Recipe
divides easily.

Spinach San Francisco

6 servings

Ingredients

¼   cup butter or margarine
1   medium onion, chopped
1   large clove garlic, minced
3   ounces sliced mushrooms, canned or fresh
      dash of nutmeg or oregano
1   teaspoon salt
¼   teaspoon pepper
20   ounces frozen chopped spinach, thawed and partially
      drained
½   cup sour cream

Preparation   Heat butter or margarine. Add onion and garlic and sauté 2
to 3 minutes. Stir in mushrooms, seasonings and spinach.
Bring to a boil. Cover and reduce heat to simmer, cooking
for about 5 minutes. Drain excess liquid, if any, and stir in
sour cream. Heat gently and serve.

Orange Winter Squash Casserole

4 to 6 servings

A tasty combination

Ingredients   4   cups cooked, mashed winter squash, such as
butternut
2   tablespoons butter or margarine
2   tablespoons cream
salt and pepper to taste
2   large oranges
1   tablespoon cornstarch
⅓   cup light brown sugar
¼   cup butter

Preparation   Mix squash, 2 tablespoons butter, cream, salt and pepper
and pour into buttered 2-quart casserole. Grate rind and
squeeze juice from oranges. Combine juice, rind, cornstarch
and brown sugar, and heat over low heat until thickened.
Stir ¼ cup butter into orange mixture. Pour over squash and
bake in preheated 350° oven for 20 minutes.

Smashing Squash

6 to 8 servings

Ingredients

2   pounds summer squash
1   carrot, grated
1   small onion, grated
½   cup butter or margarine, melted
8   ounces packaged herb stuffing
1   cup sour cream
10¾ ounces cream of chicken soup

Preparation

Slice squash, cook in boiling water for 5 minutes and drain well. Add grated carrot and onion. Add melted butter to stuffing mix. Add half of stuffing mix to vegetables. Stir in sour cream and soup. Spoon into buttered shallow 2-quart casserole and spread remaining stuffing mix on top. Bake in preheated 350° oven for 20 to 30 minutes.

Zucchini Cheese Puff

4 to 6 servings

Great with chicken and rice

Ingredients

2   pounds zucchini
1   cup cottage cheese
1   cup Monterey Jack cheese, shredded
2   eggs, slightly beaten
½   teaspoon dried dill weed
½   teaspoon salt
½   cup dry bread crumbs
2   tablespoons melted butter or margarine

Preparation

Slice zucchini and steam until almost soft. Drain. Combine with cheeses, eggs, dill weed and salt. Spoon into buttered 2-quart casserole and bake in preheated 350° oven for 15 minutes. Sprinkle with bread crumbs mixed with butter. Bake for 15 minutes more.

Zucchini alla Hodgy Podgy   6 servings

A favorite Italian dish from Brunswick's Great Impasta

Ingredients

3   tablespoons olive oil
1   clove garlic, sliced
1 to 2 fresh basil leaves
1   medium onion, chopped
1   pound zucchini, thinly sliced
1   pound yellow summer squash, thinly sliced
1   cup freshly grated Parmesan cheese
4 to 6 slices prosciutto bacon or proscuttini ham, shredded
¾   cup cooked tomato or meat sauce
2   eggs, beaten with 1 tablespoon milk

Preparation

Warm oil over moderate heat. Add garlic, basil, ½ of onion and zucchini. Sauté just until softened. Remove zucchini with a slotted spoon and drain on paper towels. Sauté yellow squash and other ½ onion in same way. Butter 9-inch quiche dish or pie plate from which you can serve. Arrange layer of zucchini on bottom. Sprinkle with handful of cheese and half of meat. Top with half of sauce. Alternate with yellow squash, placing it around edge of plate, creating scalloped edge for pie. Continue layering meat sauce and vegetables, ending with vegetables. Sprinkle with more cheese and pour egg-milk mixture over top. Bake in preheated 375° oven until eggs are set and top is golden, about 15 to 20 minutes.

Zucchini Casserole

6 servings

Ingredients

2 pounds zucchini
1 medium onion
4 tablespoons Bisquick
3 eggs, beaten
¼ teaspoon dried oregano
¼ teaspoon dried basil
  salt and pepper to taste
2 tablespoons butter or margarine
½ cup grated Cheddar cheese
2 tablespoons grated Parmesan cheese

Preparation

Grate zucchini and onion. Add Bisquick, eggs and seasonings. Butter 9 x 13-inch casserole and spoon in zucchini mixture. Dot with butter. Sprinkle cheese over top. Bake in preheated 350° oven for 40 minutes.

Eggs, Cheese, Pasta and Grains

Almond French Toast

8 servings

Ingredients

6 eggs
¼ cup heavy cream
¼ cup amaretto
2 tablespoons maple syrup
½ teaspoon almond extract
  thin sliced French bread (cut diagonally)
  vegetable oil

Topping:
toasted sliced almonds
freshly grated nutmeg
butter
maple syrup

Preparation

Beat eggs, heavy cream, amaretto, maple syrup and almond extract. Dip bread into mixture and grill on hot griddle in vegetable oil. Serve with toasted almonds, fresh nutmeg, butter and maple syrup.

Stuffed French Toast

6 servings

A delicious variation from a Cape Cod inn

Ingredients

8 ounces cream cheese
½ cup chopped walnuts
1 teaspoon vanilla extract
12 slices thin bread
4 eggs, beaten
¾ cup heavy cream
1 teaspoon vanilla
  grated nutmeg
3 large bananas, sliced

Apricot sauce:
12 ounces apricot jam
½ cup orange juice

Preparation

Combine cream cheese, walnuts and vanilla. Spread mixture on 6 slices of bread, covering with remaining slices to make a sandwich. Combine eggs, cream, vanilla and nutmeg to taste. Dip each sandwich into egg mixture and grill in butter, as for French toast.

For sauce, combine jam and juice and heat . To serve, cut toast in points and arrange with bananas. Top with sauce.

Apple Puffed Pancake

6 to 8 servings

A delicious breakfast or brunch dish

Ingredients

6   eggs
1½   cups milk
1   cup flour
3   tablespoons sugar
1   teaspoon vanilla extract
½   teaspoon salt
¼   teaspoon cinnamon
8   tablespoons butter or margarine
2   apples, peeled, cored and thinly sliced
2 to 3 tablespoons light brown sugar

Preparation

Beat eggs, milk, flour, sugar, vanilla, salt and cinnamon in blender or large bowl. Batter may remain slightly lumpy. Preheat oven to 425°. Melt butter in 12-inch quiche dish or 9 x 13-inch baking dish in oven. Add apple slices to baking dish, return to oven, and heat until butter sizzles but does not brown. Immediately pour batter over apples. Sprinkle with brown sugar. Bake for 20 minutes, or until puffed and brown. Serve immediately. Good with sausages.

Bacon Cheese Puff

8 servings

Ingredients

16   slices firm white bread
10   ounces sharp Cheddar cheese, grated
6   eggs, well beaten
1   quart milk
1   teaspoon salt
¼   teaspoon white pepper
¼   teaspoon dry mustard
3   slices bacon
¼   cup chopped fresh parsley

Preparation

Trim crusts from bread and butter each slice. Arrange 8 slices buttered sides down in bottom of buttered 9 x 13-inch baking dish. Cover bread with cheese, reserving ½ cup. Cube remaining 8 slices of bread and place on top of cheese, buttered side up. Combine eggs, milk, salt, pepper and mustard. Pour over bread. Sprinkle remaining cheese on top.

Cover and refrigerate overnight. Bake in pan of water in preheated 350° oven for 1 hour or until puffed and brown. Cook bacon until crisp, crumble and sprinkle over top with parsley. Serve immediately.

California Omelette

1 to 2 servings

*The Chef at Brunswick Omelette Shop says
"practice is the key"*

Ingredients

3   large fresh eggs
½   ripe avocado, pitted, peeled and sliced
2½   ounces cream cheese
4   slices tomato
1   ounce freshly cooked and crumbled bacon
1   tablespoon butter or margarine

Preparation Stir eggs with fork until well blended. Heat butter in 8-inch omelette pan until butter is melted and bubbly. Add egg mixture. When egg starts to cook, stir with wooden spoon until of soft scrambled egg consistency. Wait 30 seconds before removing from burner.

Arrange cream cheese, tomato and avocado evenly over egg and place under hot broiler for 60 seconds. This will heat ingredients and allow omelette to rise. Remove omelette from oven. Add bacon bits and fold onto warm plate.

Chicken Brunch Casserole   8 servings

Equally good prepared with ham

Ingredients
4   large chicken breasts, cooked and deboned, or 16
    slices ham
16 slices thin bread, crusts removed
8   slices Cheddar cheese
6   eggs
    salt to taste
3   cups milk
1   teaspoon dry mustard
1   cup crushed potato chips
½   cup butter or margarine, melted

Preparation Butter 9 x 13-inch baking dish. Arrange 8 slices of bread on bottom. Quarter chicken breasts to make 16 pieces. Layer half of meat over bread. Cover with cheese. Add remaining meat and cover with remaining bread.

Beat eggs, salt, milk and mustard. Pour over casserole. Cover with foil and refrigerate overnight. Before baking, sprinkle with crushed potato chips and melted butter. Bake in preheated 350° oven for 1 hour.

Chili Cheese Bake

6 to 8 servings

Ingredients

2   cups each grated sharp Cheddar and Monterey Jack cheese
14 ounces canned diced green chilies
4   eggs
1½ cups milk

Preparation

Combine cheeses. Sprinkle about ¼ of cheese in bottom of buttered shallow 2-quart baking dish. Top evenly with ⅓ of chilies. Repeat layers two more times, then top with remaining cheese. Beat eggs and add milk. Pour over chilies and cheese. Bake, uncovered, in preheated 350° oven for 35 to 40, minutes or until center appears firm when dish is lightly moved. Let stand about 5 minutes before serving.

Note: Wear rubber gloves to dice chilies.

Mock Soufflé

8 servings

Served at big country breakfasts at a North Bath inn

Ingredients

8 eggs, beaten
2 cups milk
8 tablespoons butter, melted
6 slices homemade white bread, diced
    salt and pepper to taste
1 cup grated sharp Cheddar cheese
1 cup grated or cubed ham
1 small onion, minced
4 tablespoons freshly grated Parmesan cheese
    paprika

Preparation

Beat eggs, milk, butter, salt and pepper. In large, buttered soufflé dish, layer half of bread, cheese, ham and onions. Repeat and pour liquid over all. Sprinkle with Parmesan cheese and paprika. Refrigerate overnight. Bake in preheated 350° oven for 1 hour. Serve at once.

New Pancakes

6 to 8 pancakes

Ingredients

4 eggs, separated
4 tablespoons flour
1 cup small-curd cottage cheese

Preparation

Beat egg whites until stiff and set aside. Beat egg yolks, add flour and cottage cheese, mixing well. Fold egg whites into yolk mixture. Bake on lightly oiled hot griddle, turning once. Serve immediately with favorite syrup.

Puffed Cheese Casserole

6 servings

Ingredients

8 eggs
1 cup cottage cheese
1 cup freshly grated Cheddar cheese
   salt and pepper to taste

Preparation

Mix all ingredients well in blender or food processor. Pour into buttered 2-quart casserole. Bake in preheated 350° oven for 30 to 40 minutes.

Reuben Brunch Casserole

8 servings

Serve with sauerkraut

Ingredients

10 slices rye bread, cut into ¾ inch cubes
1   pound corned beef, sliced thin
2½ cups shredded Swiss cheese
6   eggs, slightly beaten
3   cups milk
¼   teaspoon pepper

Preparation

Butter 9 x 13-inch glass baking dish. Arrange bread cubes on bottom of dish. Coarsely shred corned beef with knife. Layer meat over bread and sprinkle with cheese. Beat eggs, milk and pepper until blended. Pour over beef mixture. Cover with foil and refrigerate overnight. Bake in preheated 350° oven for 45 minutes, or until bubbly and puffed.

Sausage Breakfast Casserole

8 to 10 servings

Ingredients

1   pound ground pork sausage meat
8   slices bread, cubed
2   cups freshly grated Cheddar cheese
4   eggs
¾   teaspoon dry mustard
3   cups milk
10¾ ounces cream of mushroom soup

Preparation

Brown and drain sausage. Spread cubed bread in buttered 9 x 13-inch casserole. Top with sausage. Sprinkle with cheese. Mix eggs, dry mustard and 2½ cups milk, and pour over bread/sausage mixture. Refrigerate overnight, or for at least 3 hours. When ready to bake, mix mushroom soup with ½ cup milk and pour over top of casserole. Bake in preheated 300° oven for 1½ hours.

Spanakopitta

8 servings

*A classic use of phyllo dough from an outstanding
Greek cook*

Ingredients

¾   pound butter, do not substitute
1½ cups virgin first pressed Greek olive oil, do not
      substitute
6   eggs, lightly beaten
20   ounces frozen spinach, defrosted and squeezed dry
1   pound feta cheese
1   pound frozen phyllo dough, defrosted

Preparation

Melt butter with oil on low heat. Mix eggs, spinach and
cheese. Working quickly, unwrap defrosted phyllo and cover
with damp cloth. Using a pastry brush, paint 9 x 13-inch
casserole or roasting pan with butter and oil. Lay in 1 sheet
of dough. Paint with butter and oil, repeating process until
half of dough is used.

Spread with spinach mixture. Layer and paint with butter
and oil the remainder of the dough. Paint top layer well.
Bake in preheated 375° oven for 30 minutes or until brown.
Allow to rest 30 to 40 minutes and serve.

Spanakopitta can be made a day ahead and reheated at 350°
for 15 minutes. Cut with sharp knife. Serves 8 generously
for dinner, 12 for lunch or many as an hors d'oeuvre. May
be frozen. It's easy to do once the technique is mastered.

Variations of a Quiche

4 servings

A different taste using Dijon mustard

Ingredients

Crust:

1⅓ cups flour
½ teaspoon salt
¾ teaspoon sugar
½ cup Crisco
3 to 4 tablespoons water

Filling:

5 large eggs
4 tablespoons sour cream
1 cup half and half
1 cup freshly grated Swiss or Cheddar cheese
1 tablespoon Dijon mustard
  white pepper to taste
¼ cup freshly grated Parmesan cheese, optional

Preparation

For crust, mix flour, salt and sugar. Blend in Crisco. Using fork, add water. Roll out on floured board, place in 8-inch glass pie plate and flute edges.

For filling, beat eggs. Add sour cream and blend in half and half. Add grated cheese, mustard and pepper. Pour into crust. Sprinkle with Parmesan cheese and place in oven carefully.

Bake in preheated 350° oven for 15 minutes; turn down to 325° and bake for 40 to 50 minutes more. Let set for 10 minutes before serving.

Variations: Place any of the following in crust before adding cheese mixture: crisp bacon and sautéed chopped onion; shrimp and crabmeat; sautéed or blanched vegetables; mushrooms sautéed with onions, or ham with a bit more mustard.

Zucchini Basil Fritatta
8 servings

Ingredients

¼ cup virgin Italian olive oil
½ chopped fresh basil or 2 teaspoons dried
3 to 3½ medium zucchini, thinly sliced
12 large eggs
2 cups milk
salt and freshly ground pepper to taste
1 cup freshly grated Gruyere or mozzarella cheese

Preparation

Heat oil and add basil, cooking 30 seconds. Add zucchini. Stir to coat zucchini and sauté 5 minutes. Oil 10-inch quiche dish or oven-proof skillet. Add zucchini. Combine eggs, milk, salt and pepper, beating until foamy. Pour over zucchini.

Bake in preheated 375° oven about 25 minutes or until frittata is nearly solid, but still soft in center. Sprinkle grated cheese over top and return to oven until cheese melts. Cool 5 minutes before serving.

Fettucine Alfredo
4 to 6 servings

Ingredients

1 pound fettucine
¼ cup butter
1½ cups heavy or whipping cream
1 cup freshly grated Parmesan cheese
freshly grated black pepper

Preparation

Cook fettucine as package directs. Drain. While noodles are cooking, prepare sauce. Melt butter with cream. Stir in cheese until melted. Place noodles in warm bowl, add sauce and toss gently. Serve with extra cheese and freshly grated black pepper.

Norfolk Noodles

10 servings

Nice party dish or a meatless meal

Ingredients

12 ounces wide noodles
1   cup fresh parsley, chopped
1   pint large curd cottage cheese
1   pint sour cream
1   tablespoon Worcestershire sauce
    dash of Tabasco sauce
1   bunch green onions, sliced
1   cup freshly grated sharp cheese
½   teaspoon paprika

Preparation

Cook noodles according to package directions and drain. While noodles are hot, mix in other ingredients except sharp cheese and paprika. Place in buttered, shallow 9 x 13-inch baking dish. Top with sharp cheese and paprika. Bake in preheated 350° oven, uncovered, for 40 minutes, or until heated through and cheese is melted.

One-Pot Pasta

6 to 8 servings

Ingredients

12 ounces linguine
½   cup carrots, sliced thin
2   cups fresh broccoli, cut into bite-size pieces
1   cup fresh asparagus, cut into 1-inch pieces
2   cups sliced zucchini
½   cup fresh Chinese snow peas
½   cup frozen green peas, thawed
½   cup half and half
½   cup grated Parmesan cheese
2   tablespoons butter or margarine, melted
    salt and pepper to taste

Preparation   Bring large pot of salted water to boil. Add linguine and
boil 7 minutes, stirring occasionally. Add carrots, broccoli,
and asparagus. Boil 2 minutes. Gradually add zucchini,
snow peas and green peas. Boil 3 minutes longer. Drain
well.

Pour half and half, cheese, butter, salt and pepper into
large bowl. Add vegetables and linguine. Toss well and serve
at once.

Pasta Primavera I   4 servings

Ingredients   7   tablespoons unsalted butter
6   tablespoons good quality olive oil
3   garlic cloves, minced
     any combination of fresh vegetables: broccoli,
     zucchini, mushrooms, green beans, snow peas or
     asparagus
1   cup canned Italian plum tomatoes, crushed
½   cup pine nuts, optional
8   ounces spaghetti or rottini
½   cup light cream
     freshly grated Parmesan cheese

Preparation   Heat 3 tablespoons butter and 3 tablespoons olive oil. Sauté
garlic, tomatoes and pine nuts for 5 minutes. In another
skillet, heat remaining 3 tablespoons olive oil and sauté fresh
vegetables for 3 to 5 minutes. Combine tomato sauce with
vegetables.

Cook pasta according to package directions. Drain well.
Melt remaining 4 tablespoons butter and add to pasta with
cream. Toss lightly. Add sauce and simmer 5 minutes. To
serve, sprinkle with grated cheese.

Pasta Primavera II

6 servings

From New Meadows Inn

Ingredients

1 pound fettucine or linguine
1 cup minced onion
2 garlic cloves, minced
⅓ cup butter (or ½ butter and ½ olive oil)
½ pound mushrooms
1 small carrot, sliced
1 cup whipping cream
2 tablespoons fresh basil, minced, or 2 teaspoons dried
½ pound cauliflower florets
½ pound broccoli florets
1 medium zucchini, sliced
1 cup fresh or frozen peas
1 cup freshly grated Parmesan cheese
  salt and pepper to taste
3 cups diced cooked ham or lightly sautéed Maine shrimp

Preparation

Cook pasta according to package directions. Drain. Sauté onion and garlic in butter until softened. Add mushrooms and carrot and sauté 2 minutes more. Add cream and basil and simmer for another 2 minutes. Add cauliflower, broccoli, zucchini and peas. Simmer again for 5 minutes. Vegetables should still be crisp. Add salt and pepper to taste and Parmesan cheese. Heat until cheese is melted.

Serve over hot pasta and top with ham or shrimp.

Pasta with Creamy Tomato Sauce

4 servings

Ingredients

Tomato Sauce:

3	tablespoons olive oil
1½	pounds ripe tomatoes, coarsely chopped
1	small onion, chopped
1	celery rib, finely chopped
¼	cup chopped fresh parsley
2	tablespoons chopped fresh basil
1	teaspoon sugar
½	teaspoon salt
¼	teaspoon pepper
½	cup heavy or whipping cream

¼	cup olive oil
¼	pound snow peas, halved
1	medium zucchini, chopped
2	ripe plum tomatoes, seeded and coarsely chopped
¼	cup sliced green onions
½	teaspoon salt
8	ounces angel hair pasta
	Parmesan cheese, grated

Preparation

Tomato Sauce: Heat oil and add remaining ingredients except cream. Simmer 30 minutes, stirring occasionally. In blender or food processor, puree sauce, then strain through a sieve to remove skins and seeds. Return to saucepan. Add cream and heat through. Keep warm.

Heat oil and add vegetables and salt. Sauté 5 minutes or until tender-crisp. Set aside.

Cook pasta according to package directions. Drain. Toss with vegetables. Serve with sauce and grated Parmesan cheese.

Pasta with Tomatoes and Basil

6 servings

Ingredients

4	ripe tomatoes, cut into ½ inch cubes
1	pound Brie cheese, rind removed and cut into irregular pieces
1	cup fresh basil leaves, sliced into strips
3	garlic cloves, minced
1	cup plus 1 tablespoon best-quality olive oil
1½	teaspoons salt
1½	pounds linguine or fettucine
½	teaspoon freshly ground black pepper
	freshly grated Parmesan cheese

Preparation

Combine tomatoes, Brie, basil, garlic, 1 cup olive oil, ½ teaspoon salt and pepper, at least 2 hours before serving. Set aside, covered at room temperature.

Add 1 tablespoon olive oil and 1 teaspoon salt to 6 quarts of boiling water. Add linguine or fettucini and cook al dente, 8 to 10 minutes. Drain pasta and immediately toss with tomato sauce. Serve immediately with Parmesan cheese and freshly ground pepper.

Pesto

1½ cups

Ingredients

2	cloves garlic
½	teaspoon salt
2	cups firmly packed fresh basil leaves
¼	cup pine nuts
½	cup good quality olive oil
½	cup freshly grated Parmesan cheese

Preparation

In blender or food processor, finely chop garlic, salt, basil and pine nuts. With processor running, add olive oil in stream. Add cheese and blend well. Serve over hot linguine. Pesto is also delicious served over sautéed fresh garden vegetables or other pastas. Spread on toasted Italian bread for a taste treat.

Tagliolini Al Quattro Formaggi

6 servings

Delicious four cheese fettucini from The Great Impasta

Ingredients

½ cup butter
¼ teaspoon white pepper
   pinch nutmeg
¼ pound fontina cheese, cubed
¼ pound Gorgonzola cheese, crumbled
¼ pound mozzarella cheese, grated
1 cup freshly grated Parmesan cheese
1 cup cream
1½ pounds tagliolini (fettucini)
   freshly ground black pepper

Preparation

Cook tagliolini according to package directions. Melt butter, add pepper and nutmeg. Stir in cheeses and cream with wire whisk. Cook about 5 minutes, or until mixture comes to boil. Remove from heat. Add cooked tagliolini, toss well and serve with freshly ground black pepper.

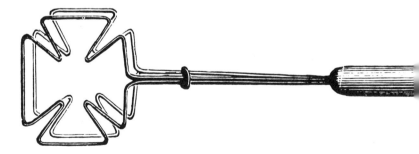

Fresh Tomato Pasta

4 servings

Ingredients

4 large ripe tomatoes, peeled and chopped
2 garlic cloves, minced
20 fresh basil leaves, chopped, about ½ cup lightly packed
⅛ teaspoon dried oregano
1 tablespoon fresh parsley, minced
1 teaspoon salt
pepper to taste
8 ounces mozzarella cheese, grated
8 tablespoon good quality olive oil
8 to 10 ounces pasta of choice

Preparation

Mix all ingredients, except pasta, in glass bowl and let stand at room temperature, at least 1 hour. Cook pasta according to package directions, drain, and immediately combine with tomato sauce. Heat of the pasta will partially melt the cheese.

Western Cheese and Macaroni

4 servings

Ingredients

1 pound link sausage
1 cup diced carrot
1 cup diced onion
1 cup diced celery
1 cup diced green pepper
1 cup elbow macaroni, uncooked
28 ounces canned tomatoes
1 cup grated Cheddar cheese
salt and pepper to taste

Preparation

Slice sausage, if large, and brown. Add other ingredients except cheese and cook, covered, for 35 minutes on low heat. Stir often to prevent sticking. Add cheese and cook until melted.

Curried Rice

6 servings

Ingredients

1⅓ cups white rice
¼ cup vegetable oil
1 onion, finely chopped
2 ribs celery, finely chopped
2 tablespoons minced fresh parsley
1 teaspoon salt
2 teaspoons curry powder, or more
¼ teaspoon thyme
4 cups hot chicken broth

Preparation

Brown rice in oil, stirring constantly. Add onion, celery and parsley, and sauté for 3 minutes. Add seasonings and broth. Cover and simmer 30 minutes, or until liquid is absorbed. Good with creamed shrimp or chicken and chutney.

Parsley Rice

6 servings

An easy company or family dish

Ingredients

1½ cups converted white rice
3⅓ cups beef broth
⅔ cup finely chopped onion
4 tablespoons butter or margarine
4 tablespoons minced fresh parsley
salt and pepper to taste

Preparation

Cook converted rice according to package directions, using beef broth as liquid. Sauté onion in butter until tender. Add to cooked rice and toss with parsley. Season to taste with salt and pepper. Especially good with pork and chicken.

Orange Rice with Almonds   4 servings

Ingredients

½   cup chopped celery
¼   cup chopped green onion
¼   cup butter or margarine
1   cup long-grain rice
1   cup orange juice
1   cup water
1   teaspoon salt
1   teaspoon finely grated orange rind
1   orange, peeled and cut into small pieces
¼   cup slivered almonds

Preparation

Sauté celery and onion in butter until tender, about 4 to 5 minutes. Add rice and brown lightly, stirring frequently, for another 4 to 5 minutes. Add orange juice, water, salt and orange rind. Heat to boiling, cover and simmer 25 minutes, or until rice is tender and liquid is absorbed. Gently stir in orange pieces and almonds.

Polenta   4 to 6 servings

Ingredients

4   cups water
1   teaspoon salt
1   cup yellow cornmeal
1   egg, slightly beaten
½   cup grated Parmesan or Romano cheese
½   cup butter, melted
2   cups good quality tomato sauce

Preparation

Bring 2½ cups water to a boil in top of double boiler. Add salt. Mix cornmeal with remaining water and add to boiling water, stirring. Cook until mixture thickens. Place over boiling water and cook, covered, for 45 minutes, stirring occasionally. Pour into lightly buttered 9 x 9-inch pan, smoothing top. Chill thoroughly.

Using sharp knife, cut polenta into squares, diamonds or rounds. Dip pieces into beaten egg. Coat with grated cheese. Arrange pieces in baking pan and drizzle with butter. Bake in preheated 375° oven for 20 to 25 minutes or until very hot and lightly browned. Serve with heated tomato sauce.

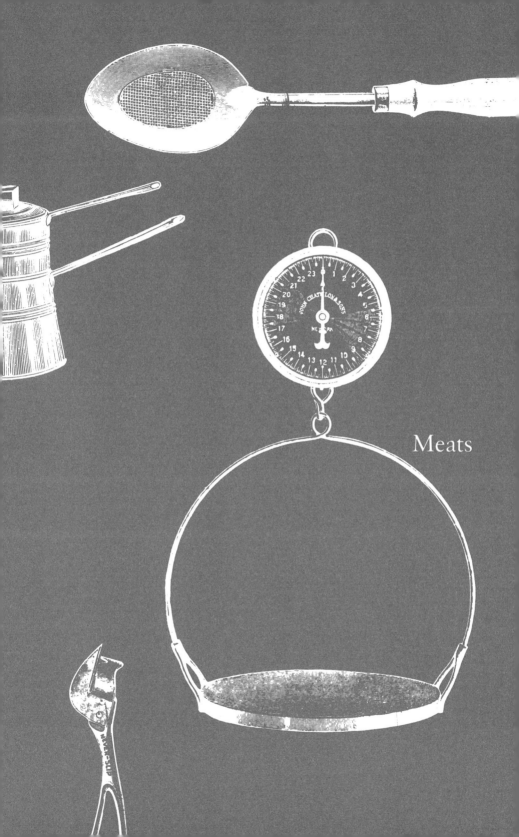

Meats

Beef Tenderloin with Roasted Garlic Potatoes

8 servings

Ingredients

Roast:

1   4 to 4½ pound fillet of beef, fat removed
    salt and pepper to taste
2   tablespoons shallots, minced
3   tablespoons unsalted butter or margarine
1   pound fresh mushrooms, sliced
1   cup dry sherry
    watercress or parsley for garnish

Potatoes:

8   large baking potatoes, peeled and quartered
    salt and freshly ground pepper to taste
2   tablespoons vegetable oil
2   tablespoons unsalted butter or margarine
2   heads of garlic, with cloves lightly crushed, best done
    with flat of knife

Preparation

Remove meat from refrigerator at least 1 hour before roasting. Place meat in large shallow baking pan. Sprinkle with salt and pepper. Roast in preheated 400° oven for 30 minutes.

While meat is roasting, sauté shallots in butter until transparent but not brown. Add mushrooms and sauté until tender but not overcooked.

Remove meat from oven. Reduce temperature to 375°. Spoon mushrooms around beef and pour sherry over meat. Roast 20 to 30 minutes longer, or until meat thermometer inserted in center registers 135° for medium-rare. Baste once or twice with juices in pan.

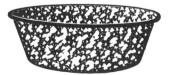

To serve, transfer fillet to large heated platter. Carve most of roast and arrange slices overlapping on platter. Sprinkle lightly with salt and pepper. Arrange mushrooms around meat and spoon pan juices over all. Garnish. Serve with roasted garlic potatoes.

For potatoes, boil in salted water to cover for 2 minutes. Drain and cool. Spread oil and butter over bottom of heavy baking pan in which potatoes will fit in single layer. Add crushed garlic cloves and roll through oil. Roast in preheated 400° oven for 45 to 50 minutes, or until potatoes are golden brown and tender. Remove any garlic that turns dark brown. Turn potatoes carefully several times during baking. Add more oil, if necessary. Season with salt and pepper and spoon garlic over potatoes before serving with roast.

New York Au Poivre Bowdoin Steakhouse

2 servings

Ingredients

2	10-ounce New York sirloin steaks
1	cup flour
½	cup olive oil
4	tablespoons cracked black pepper
3	tablespoons dry red wine
½	cup beef bouillon
3	tablespoons brandy

Preparation

Coat both sides of sirloins in flour, rub down with olive oil and press pepper into both sides. Sauté over high heat to desired degree of doneness (rare, medium etc.). Remove meat to warm serving platter. Add red wine and beef bouillon to pan, reduce by one half over high heat. Add brandy. Ignite, averting face. Flambé until flame burns off. Serve steak with sauce.

Magic Eye Round

4 to 6 servings

Ingredients

1 4½-pound beef eye round roast
8 ounces brown mustard
3 to 4 cups kosher salt

Preparation

Dry roast well. Cover all of roast with entire amount of mustard. This is not easy! Roll roast in plate of salt, covering all mustard thickly. Place roast on rack in roasting pan. Bake in preheated 475° to 500° oven about 40 minutes for medium rare. Test with meat thermometer. Remove salt and mustard coating before serving. The coating seals in the juice.

Steak with Chutney

4 servings

Ingredients

4 1-inch thick tenderloin steaks
4 teaspoons cracked black pepper
1 teaspoon butter or margarine
⅔ cup diced green bell pepper
⅔ cup diced red bell pepper
1 medium onion, diced
1 teaspoon minced garlic
1 teaspoon vegetable oil
¾ cup bottled chutney

Preparation

Trim steaks of excess fat. Sprinkle each side with ½ teaspoon black pepper, pressing pepper firmly into place. Melt butter in large heavy skillet over medium heat. Add bell peppers, onion and garlic. Cook 5 minutes or until tender, stirring once or twice. Remove with slotted spoon. Increase heat to high. Add oil to skillet. When hot, add steaks and cook 2 minutes per side for rare. Remove to heated platter. Reduce heat to low. Add chutney and bell pepper mixture to skillet. Cook only to heat through, about 1 minute. Spoon over steaks.

Betty Stone's Teriyaki Steak   4 servings

Freeze steak/marinade in zip-lock bags for camping or ski trips

Ingredients

⅓   cup soy sauce
⅓   cup cooking oil
1   tablespoon catsup
1   tablespoon vinegar
1   garlic clove, crushed
¼   teaspoon ginger
1   flank steak, 1 to 1½ pounds

Preparation

Combine soy sauce, oil, catsup, vinegar, garlic and ginger. Place steak in flat baking dish and pour marinade over it. Cover and marinate overnight or for several hours, turning once or twice. Steak can also be marinated in zip-lock bag. Remove steak from marinade and broil or barbecue 6 minutes each side. To serve, cut diagonally across grain.

Steak Italienne   4 servings

Ingredients

4   tablespoons vegetable oil
1   garlic clove, chopped fine
     salt and pepper to taste
     juice of one lemon
1 to 1½ pounds round steak, scored and cut into 4 pieces
1   cup dry bread crumbs
3   tablespoons chopped fresh parsley
½   cup freshly grated Parmesan cheese

Preparation

Combine oil, garlic, salt, pepper and lemon juice. Add steak and marinate for 2 hours or longer. Combine bread crumbs, parsley and cheese. Pound into steaks. Lay meat in shallow baking dish, sprinkle with remaining marinade and bake in preheated 500° oven for 15 minutes.

Barbecued Brisket

12 servings

A large crowd recipe

Ingredients

6	pounds beef brisket, whole, trimmed but not rolled
	salt and pepper to taste
2	garlic cloves, minced
2	medium onions, sliced
1	bay leaf
4	cups tomato juice
1	cup catsup
1	cup packed light brown sugar
1	tablespoon dry mustard
1	tablespoon vinegar
1	tablespoon chili powder
2	tablespoons Worcestershire sauce
1	tablespoon onion salt
1	teaspoon celery seed

Preparation

Season brisket with salt and pepper. Place in foil-lined roasting pan. Cover with garlic and onions. Add bay leaf. Cover tightly with foil. Roast in preheated 325° oven until meat feels tender when fork is inserted, about 3 hours. Remove foil and drain off broth. Cool meat.

Meanwhile, prepare barbecue sauce by combining all other ingredients. Simmer over medium heat, uncovered, for 20 minutes, stirring occasionally.

While sauce simmers, slice cooled meat thinly against grain. Return meat to roasting pan. Pour barbecue sauce over meat. Cover and return to 325° oven for about another 1½ hours. Best if made a day in advance. Reheat to serve.

Barbecued Beef

10 to 12 servings

For a summer party, add salads and home baked beans.

Ingredients

1	4-pound chuck or bottom round roast
8	ounces tomato sauce
1	large onion, sliced

Barbecue sauce:
½ cup margarine
3 small onions, chopped
¼ cup vinegar
1½ cups water
¼ cup brown sugar
¼ teaspoon each, dry mustard, pepper, salt, chili powder
   and nutmeg
1 14-ounce bottle catsup
1 12-ounce bottle chili sauce
3 tablespoons Worcestershire sauce

Preparation   Place roast in large oven proof casserole or Dutch oven.
Cover with tomato sauce and onion. Bake in preheated 300°
oven for 3 hours or until meat is very tender. Shred meat
and mix with barbecue sauce. Serve in buns.

For sauce, sauté onions slowly in butter for 20 minutes. Add
rest of ingredients and simmer 40 minutes.

Pot Roast with Prunes   6 to 8 servings

A nice choice for a change-of-pace pot roast

Ingredients   1 4-pound chuck or rump roast
3 tablespoons oil
2 onions, sliced
½ pound uncooked pitted prunes, soaked in water and
   drained
4 whole cloves
   salt and pepper to taste
1 cup water
1 cup apple cider

Preparation   Brown meat on all sides in hot oil in Dutch oven. Add
onions, and when browned, add remaining ingredients.
Reduce heat, cover and simmer slowly until tender—about 3
to 4 hours. Add more water from time to time, if necessary.
Serve with potato pancakes or buttered noodles.

Mexican Style Beef Stew

8 servings

Ingredients

3 pounds boneless beef chuck, cut into 1-inch cubes
3 tablespoons vegetable oil
3 tablespoons butter or margarine
4 medium onions, chopped (about 1½ cups)
½ teaspoon dried thyme leaves
¼ teaspoon cinnamon
⅛ teaspoon cloves
2 tablespoons flour
1 tablespoon catsup
1 bay leaf
2 teaspoons salt
½ teaspoon pepper
1 teaspoon grated lemon peel
1½ cups dry white wine
29 ounces pear halves, packed in own juice
6 medium sweet potatoes, cooked, peeled and halved, or
   1 24-ounce can sweet potatoes in water
3 tablespoons medium raisins
   chopped fresh parsley for garnish

Preparation

Brown beef cubes in hot oil and butter in Dutch oven. Set
meat aside. Add chopped onion, thyme, cinnamon and
cloves to drippings. Sauté, stirring, 5 minutes or until tender.
Remove from heat. Stir in flour, catsup, bay leaf, salt, pepper
and lemon peel. Gradually stir in wine. Drain pears,
reserving 1 cup syrup. Add syrup and browned beef to
mixture in Dutch oven. Simmer, covered, 1 hour and 20
minutes, or until meat is fork-tender. Add sweet potatoes,
pears and raisins. Cook, uncovered, 10 minutes, until heated
through and liquid is slightly thickened. Turn onto heated
serving dish and sprinkle with parsley.

Beef Burgundy
10 to 12 servings

Ingredients

5 pounds chuck roast, cut into large cubes
   flour for dredging
½ cup butter or olive oil
½ pound bacon cut into 1-inch pieces
4 garlic cloves, minced
3 carrots, sliced
4 medium onions, cut into wedges
2 bay leaves
1 teaspoon thyme
   salt to taste
3 cups Burgundy

Preparation

Dredge meat in flour. Brown in butter or oil. Remove meat and set aside. Sauté bacon, garlic, carrots and onions until lightly browned. Place meat and vegetables in large, deep baking dish. Add bay leaves. thyme. salt, wine and water to cover. Bake, uncovered, in preheated 300° oven for 4 to 5 hours or until meat is tender. May also be cooked in crock pot for 6 to 8 hours.

Beefsteak and Vegetables
4 servings

Ingredients

1 pound round steak
½ teaspoon cornstarch
1 teaspoon water
2 tablespoons soy sauce
   pinch of sugar
¼ teaspoon ginger
1 garlic clove, chopped
1 green pepper, cut into chunks
2 medium onions, quartered
2 tomatoes, quartered
4 to 6 fresh mushrooms, sliced thickly

Preparation

Slice meat against grain in very thin slices in 3-inch strips. Moisten cornstarch with water and mix with soy sauce, sugar, ginger and garlic. Marinate meat in this mixture for ½ hour. Sauté meat in small amount oil until half cooked. Remove. Sauté vegetables until tender-crisp, add meat and cook just until meat is cooked through.

15-Minute Beef Stroganoff 5 to 6 servings

Excellent flavor

Ingredients

1   pound round steak, ¼ to ½ inch thick
3   tablespoons butter or margarine
⅔   cup water
3   ounces sliced mushrooms, canned or fresh
1   envelope onion soup mix
1   cup sour cream
2   tablespoons flour

Preparation

Trim fat from meat. Cut meat diagonally across grain in very thin strips. Heat butter or margarine and brown meat quickly. Add water and mushrooms, including liquid, stir in soup mix and heat just to boiling. Blend sour cream and flour together and add to meat mixture. Cook and stir until thickened. Sauce will be thin. Serve over noodles or rice.

Szechuan Beef with Orange Sauce 2 to 3 servings

Ingredients

1   pound flank steak, sliced against grain into ⅛-inch slices
2   tablespoons soy sauce
2   tablespoons dry sherry
2   tablespoons hoisin sauce
3   tablespoons peanut or vegetable oil
1   tablespoon cornstarch
    skin of one orange, orange part only, sliced
3   garlic cloves, crushed
2   slices ginger root, size of quarter
3   dried hot red peppers
2   Chinese black mushrooms, sliced

Preparation

Combine 1 tablespoon each of soy sauce, dry sherry, hoisin sauce, peanut oil and cornstarch. Pour over beef slices and marinate for at least 30 minutes. Combine remaining 1 tablespoon soy sauce, dry sherry and hoisin sauce and set aside. Heat wok or heavy skillet. Add remaining 2 tablespoons oil. Add orange rind, garlic, ginger root, dried hot peppers and mushrooms. Stir-fry about 1 minute until very fragrant. Add beef. Stir-fry until beef is no longer red. Add soy sauce mixture. Stir-fry for 30 seconds longer and serve with rice.

Stoup

4 to 6 servings

Ingredients

1½   pounds round steak or London broil, cubed
2 to 3 tablespoons olive oil
2   ribs celery, chopped
1   large onion, chopped
2   garlic cloves, pressed
    pinch of basil
    freshly ground pepper to taste
2   10¾ ounce cans beef bouillon
1   cup water
¼   cup dry red wine, optional
1   16-ounce can tomatoes, optional
3   large potatoes, cubed
4   carrots, sliced

Preparation

Pat steak cubes dry with paper towels. Heat olive oil and brown meat on all sides. Remove from pan and set aside. Add celery, onion and garlic and sauté until onions are limp. Add basil and pepper and return meat to pan. Cook 1 more minute, stirring constantly. Add bouillon, water and wine. Cover and simmer until meat is almost tender. Add vegetables to pot and cook until done.

Baked Beef Stew

6 to 8 servings

Delicious served on mashed potatoes

Ingredients

2 pounds stew beef, cubed
1 cup sliced carrots
1 cup chopped onions
½ green pepper, diced
1 cup sliced celery
3½ cups stewed tomatoes
3 tablespoons tapioca
3 tablespoons sugar
1½ teaspoons salt
3 tablespoons dry sherry
2 tablespoons dry sherry added at serving time

Preparation

Brown beef in Dutch oven. Add rest of ingredients and bake in preheated 300° oven for 3 hours. Add 2 tablespoons sherry just before serving.

Lucy's Beef Stew

4 to 6 servings

Ingredients

1 garlic clove
  vegetable oil
1½ pounds stew beef, cubed
4 medium onions, quartered
10¾ ounces tomato soup
1 cup dry red wine
½ cup catsup
½ teaspoon basil
¼ teaspoon thyme
½ teaspoon celery salt
  salt and pepper to taste
6 to 8 carrots, peeled and sliced on diagonal into 1-inch chunks
3 celery ribs, cut into 1½-inch chunks
6 medium potatoes, peeled and cut in half
½ pound fresh mushrooms, sliced

Preparation   Sauté garlic in 2 tablespoons oil. Remove and discard. Brown beef in oil, adding more oil if necessary. Add onions, soup and wine. Cook 30 minutes. Add catsup, seasonings, carrots, celery and potatoes. Cover and simmer for about 1½ hours. Add mushrooms last 15 minutes, just before serving.

Texas Style Short Ribs
4 servings

Ingredients
3   pounds beef short ribs
2   teaspoons paprika
1   teaspoon salt
3   tablespoons vegetable oil
1   large onion, sliced
½   cup catsup
⅓   cup vinegar
2   tablespoons water
2   teaspoons chili powder
16   ounces canned baked red kidney beans

Preparation   Dust short ribs with paprika and salt. In pressure cooker, heat oil and brown ribs well. Add sliced onion. Mix catsup, vinegar, water and chili powder and pour over meat. Cover and cook at 15 pounds pressure for 45 minutes. Reduce pressure quickly. Add beans, reheat and serve.

Harriet's Chili

10 to 12 servings

Hot and spicy!

Ingredients

3	pounds lean ground beef
2	large onions, chopped
1	green pepper, chopped
4	garlic cloves, chopped
2	tablespoons oil
28	ounces crushed tomatoes
8	ounces taco sauce (mild, medium or hot)
6	ounces tomato paste
8	ounces chopped green chilies
6	ounces jalapeno relish (optional)
½	cup rum
12	ounces beer
2	tablespoons Worcestershire sauce
1	teaspoon salt
1	teaspoon pepper
2	teaspoons dried oregano
3	teaspoons ground cumin
3	tablespoons chili powder
1	teaspoon crushed red pepper
32	ounces canned red kidney beans

Preparation

Brown beef in oil with onions, green pepper and garlic. Drain off fat. Add remaining ingredients. Stir well and simmer all day. This can be made in large crock pot and cooked on low 8 to 10 hours.

California Casserole

15 servings

Ingredients

2	pounds ground beef
1¼	cups chopped onion
2	garlic cloves
1	cup sour cream
15	ounces tomato sauce

8   ounces medium taco sauce
16   ounces black olives, drained
8   ounces tortilla chips
12   ounces Monterey Jack cheese, grated
     paprika for garnish

Preparation   Brown beef with onion and garlic. Pour off fat. Stir in sour cream, tomato sauce, taco sauce and all but ¼ cup black olives. Place ⅔ of tortilla chips in bottom of greased 9 x 13-inch casserole. Cover with meat mixture. Cover with remaining chips and olives. Top with cheese and sprinkle with paprika. Bake, uncovered, in preheated 375° oven for 30 minutes. For spicier dish, add 1 tablespoon sauce picante to meat mixture.

Mother's Mexicali Spaghetti

6 to 8 servings

Ingredients   1½ pounds lean ground beef
3   garlic cloves, minced
1   large onion, chopped
1   large green pepper, chopped
3½   cups canned tomatoes, cut-up
2 to 3 teaspoons chili powder
1   teaspoon oregano
1   teaspoon Worcestershire sauce
     salt and pepper to taste
1   teaspoon sugar
½   cup chopped black olives
½   pound spaghetti
     freshly grated Parmesan cheese

Preparation   Brown beef in cooking oil-sprayed pan. Add garlic and onion and sauté until partially soft. Add other ingredients and let stand. Cook spaghetti according to package directions, drain, and mix with meat sauce. Place in 3-quart casserole and bake, covered, in preheated 325° oven for 1 hour. Serve with Parmesan cheese.

Saucy Meat Loaf
6 to 8 servings

Ingredients

1 cup soft bread crumbs
1 cup milk
1½ pounds ground beef
1 egg
¼ teaspoon pepper
1 teaspoon Worcestershire sauce
2 tablespoons minced onion
½ cup catsup
3 tablespoons light brown sugar
1 tablespoon prepared mustard
¼ teaspoon salt
½ cup water

Preparation

Soak bread crumbs in milk for few minutes to soften. Mix bread-milk mixture, beef, eggs, pepper, Worcestershire sauce and onion. Shape into loaf and place in 7 x 11-inch baking pan. Combine catsup, brown sugar, mustard, salt and water and pour over meat loaf. Bake in preheated 300° oven for 1 hour and 15 minutes, basting occasionally.

Bowdoinham Escalloped Meat Loaf
4 servings

Ingredients

1 pound ground beef
1 slice soft bread, crumbed
10¾ ounces Campbell's Cheddar cheese soup
¼ teaspoon salt
dash pepper
1 medium onion, chopped
2 medium potatoes, sliced thin
1 to 2 tablespoons butter or margarine
paprika

Preparation   Combine beef, bread crumbs, ½ can soup, salt and pepper. Place mixture in greased 2-quart baking dish. Top with onions, then potatoes. Pour on rest of soup. If soup seems too thick, thin with a little water or milk. Dot with butter and sprinkle with paprika. Bake in preheated 350° oven for 1½ hours.

Spanish Casserole

6 servings

Ingredients
1   pound ground beef
4 to 6 sweet or hot sausages, casings removed
1   medium onion, chopped
¼ to ½ teaspoon garlic powder
18 ounces tomato paste
1   medium green pepper, chopped
4   ounces sliced mushrooms, canned or fresh
1 to 2 tablespoons chili sauce
½   cup green olives, sliced
4   ounces sliced American, mozzarella or provolone cheese
11 ounces corn chips, slightly crushed

Preparation
Brown ground beef, sausage and onion. Sprinkle with garlic powder. Add tomato paste and an almost equal amount of water. Stir well. Add rest of ingredients, except cheese and chips, and simmer 15 minutes. In 2-quart casserole, layer meat, cheese and chips, ending with chips on top. Bake in preheated 350° oven for 30 minutes, or until cheese is melted and casserole bubbles.

Pearl Harbor Italian Spaghetti

6 servings

Brought back to the mainland from Pearl Harbor by Navy wife who survived the bombardment

Ingredients

1   pound ground beef or 1 pound Italian sausage
2   medium onions, sliced
1   medium green pepper, chopped
¼   cup vegetable oil
1½ teaspoons chili powder or to taste
1   teaspoon allspice
     salt to taste
6   ounces tomato paste
10½ ounces tomato soup
2   cups water
1   pound thin spaghetti cooked according to package
     directions
     freshly grated Parmesan or Romano cheese

Preparation

Shape beef into small balls, about 1-inch in diameter, or slice sausage into ½ inch slices. Set aside. Sauté onions and green pepper in oil for 5 minutes. Add meat and brown. Add chili powder and allspice as meat is turned. Salt lightly. Empty tomato paste and soup into mixture, add water, stirring until smooth. Simmer 1 hour, stirring occasionally to prevent scorching. Serve over spaghetti. Pass grated cheese.

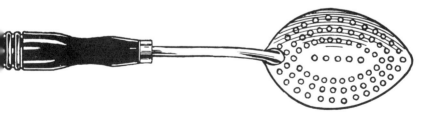

Oriental Meat Balls
8 servings

Ingredients

1   pound ground round and 1 pound lean ground pork
1   egg
1   slice bread softened in ½ cup milk
1   teaspoon salt
¼   teaspoon pepper
    dash garlic salt
2   tablespoons oil for browning

Sauce:
10½ ounces beef bouillon
16   ounces canned pineapple chunks with light syrup
¼   cup red wine vinegar
½   cup shredded green pepper, optional
½   cup sugar
2   tablespoons soy sauce
    salt to taste
2   tablespoons cornstarch moistened in water

Preparation

Mix ingredients for meatballs. Wet fingers, then form meat mixture into walnut-size balls. Brown in oil until done.

Bring sauce ingredients, except cornstarch, to a boil. Add cornstarch, stir and simmer until sauce is thick and clear. Add meatballs to sauce and simmer 15 minutes until heated through. Serve with rice or noodles.

Pork Tenderloins with Orange

4 servings

Ingredients

1½ pounds pork tenderloin, cut into ½ inch thick slices
2   teaspoons dry mustard
½   teaspoon salt
¼   teaspoon freshly ground pepper
2   tablespoons butter
2 to 3 garlic cloves, minced
½   cup dry vermouth
½   cup dry white wine
¾   to 1 cup orange juice
1   tablespoon flour
2   tablespoons water
    minced parsley, zest of orange rind and orange slices
    for garnish

Preparation

Remove all fat from meat. Combine mustard, salt and pepper and lightly rub into meat. Melt butter and add pork and garlic. Brown meat for 3 to 5 minutes on each side. Add vermouth, wine and orange juice. Reduce heat. Simmer, covered, 8 to 10 minutes, or only until tender. Remove meat to warm plate and cover. Make paste of flour and water, stir into pan juices and simmer until thickened. When ready to serve, return meat to sauce in pan to heat through, remove to platter and spoon sauce over meat. Sprinkle with parsley and zest of orange rind. Surround with orange slices.

Apple Stuffed Pork Chops

4 servings

Ingredients

4   thick pork chops
1   medium onion, chopped
1   cup bread crumbs
½   teaspoon salt
¼   teaspoon sage
¼   teaspoon thyme

1   tablespoon minced fresh parsley
2   tart apples, peeled and grated
¼   cup raisins, plumped in hot water for 10 minutes
1   cup apple cider or juice, divided into ½ cup portions
2   tablespoons red currant jelly

Preparation

Trim chops of excess fat and cut pocket in each. Render piece of fat in large skillet and brown chops in it. Set chops aside. Sauté onion in drippings until tender and yellow. Combine onion with bread crumbs, seasonings, apples and raisins. Stuff each chop and lay in flat casserole fitting snugly. Season chops with salt and pepper to taste. Add ½ cup cider or juice to casserole, cover and bake in preheated 350° oven for 30 minutes. Remove foil and cook 20 to 30 minutes longer, until well done. Remove chops to serving platter. Skim excess fat from casserole and add remaining ½ cup cider. Stir in jelly and simmer until slightly thickened, about 5 minutes. Serve sauce over chops.

Chinese Pork Chops
4 servings

Ingredients

1   egg
3   tablespoons soy sauce
1   tablespoon dry sherry or water
⅛   teaspoon ground ginger
½   teaspoon garlic powder
4   tablespoons fine dry bread crumbs
4   lean loin pork chops, well trimmed

Preparation

Spray nonstick jelly roll pan with Pam. Beat egg, soy sauce, sherry, ginger and garlic powder together in pie plate. Sprinkle bread crumbs on sheet of wax paper. Dip chops into egg mixture, then press into bread crumbs, coating evenly on both sides. Arrange in single layer on pan. Bake in preheated 350° oven for 30 minutes. Turn and bake 20 minutes longer, or until chops are tender and show no pink. (Do not overcook.)

Curried Pork and Apple Party Casserole

6 servings

Ingredients

2   pounds lean pork, cut into cubes
1   tablespoon oil
2 to 3 teaspoons curry powder
1   cup water
1   medium onion, chopped
¼   cup raisins
¼   cup chili sauce
2   cups apples, peeled, cored and cubed
¼   cup flour

Preparation

Brown meat in oil. Pour off fat. Sprinkle meat with curry powder, add water, onions, raisins and chili sauce. Stir to combine, cover tightly and cook slowly for 30 minutes. Add apples and continue to cook, covered, another 15 minutes. Thicken cooking liquid with flour blended with a little cold water and cook 2 minutes more. Serve over rice. May be made day ahead and reheated in preheated 350° oven until hot and bubbly.

Pork and Sauerkraut Stew

6 servings

Ingredients

1½ to 2 pounds fresh pork shoulder
1   large onion, chopped
2   tablespoons vegetable oil
1   teaspoon paprika
½   teaspoon salt
1   large can sauerkraut
2   teaspoons flour
1   cup sour cream

Preparation

Cut meat into 1-inch pieces. Sauté onions in oil until yellow. Add meat and sear lightly. Add paprika, salt, sauerkraut and enough water to cover. Cook, stirring occasionally, 45 minutes or until meat is tender. Blend flour with sour cream and add to stew. Simmer for 5 minutes more. Serve with buttered noodles.

Pork Bar-B-Q

8 to 10 servings

Ingredients

1 whole fresh pork butt, about 3 to 4 pounds
15 ounces tomato sauce
2 medium onions, chopped
2 tablespoons catsup
2 tablespoons Worcestershire sauce
2 tablespoons dry mustard
2 tablespoons light brown sugar
1½ tablespoons vinegar
salt, pepper, garlic salt and red pepper to taste

Preparation

Cover pork with water, bring to a boil, then simmer for ½ hour per pound. Let cool, then shred. Combine rest of ingredients and simmer for 1 hour. Mix sauce with pork. Serve on toasted buns.

Barbecue Country Ribs

8 to 10 servings

Simple, but delicious barbecue sauce

Ingredients

8 pounds pork country ribs
15 ounces tomato sauce
6 ounces frozen lemonade concentrate
⅓ cup packed light brown sugar
¼ cup bottled steak sauce
1½ teaspoons salt
2 tablespoons vegetable oil
1 medium onion, quartered

Preparation

Cut meat into 1-rib portions. Arrange meat on rack in open roasting pan. Bake in preheated 350° oven for 1 hour. In blender or food processor, blend tomato sauce, undiluted lemonade concentrate and remaining ingredients until smooth. Brush meat generously with about half of sauce. Bake meat 1 hour longer or until fork-tender, turning and brushing meat occasionally with remaining sauce.

Ham Loaf

4 servings

Ingredients

1 pound ground ham
¾ pound ground fresh pork
1 egg
¾ cup dry bread or cracker crumbs
2 tablespoons grated onion
2 tablespoons chili sauce, optional
   enough milk to make desired consistency

Sauce:
½ cup water or any fruit juice
2 tablespoons vinegar
½ cup light brown sugar
1 teaspoon dry mustard
   salt to taste

Preparation

Combine loaf ingredients and shape into roll. Place in loaf pan and bake in preheated 350° oven for 1½ hours.

Combine sauce ingredients and simmer 5 minutes. Baste ham loaf frequently with sauce while baking.

Tourtière

6 servings

Four generation classic French-Canadian Christmas Eve fare

Ingredients

   pastry for 2-crust, 8-inch pie
1¼ pounds lean ground pork
2 medium onions, chopped
½ cup water
2 crushed common crackers
½ teaspoon poultry seasoning
   dash of allspice
   salt and pepper to taste

Preparation	Cook pork, onions and water over medium heat about 2 hours, until liquid has evaporated. Remove from heat. Add crackers and seasonings. Cool. Line pie plate with pastry, add filling and top with crust. Bake in preheated 350° oven about 45 minutes, or until crust is golden brown. Excellent made ahead, frozen and reheated.

Creton

2 cups

A French breakfast treat when spread on toasted English muffins

Ingredients	1½ pounds ground pork  1 small onion, chopped ½ teaspoon salt ½ teaspoon pepper ¼ teaspoon ground cloves water to cover ground pork
Preparation	Combine all ingredients, except cloves. Stir well, cover and simmer 2 hours or until most of liquid is boiled down. Add cloves. Pour into bowls and refrigerate until ready to use. May be frozen in plastic containers. Serve as spread on toast, English muffins, or as sandwich filling.

Brunch Sausage

8 servings

Ingredients	2 pounds sausage meat 1½ cups crushed Uneeda soda crackers 1 cup diced apple 2 eggs, slightly beaten ¼ cup minced onion ½ cup milk
Preparation	Combine all ingredients and press into greased 16-cup ring mold. Refrigerate overnight. Remove from mold. Place on broiler pan and bake 1 hour in preheated 350° oven. Serve with scrambled eggs or sautéed mushrooms spooned into center ring.

Polish Hunter Stew

4 servings

A real taste treat

Ingredients

4	ounces canned mushrooms in liquid
2	pounds sauerkraut
1	large apple
20	ounces tomatoes
5	peppercorns
1	bay leaf
2	cups diced Polish kielbasa
1	cup coarsely chopped bacon, uncooked

Preparation

Combine all ingredients except meats. Cover and simmer for 1 hour. Add sausage and bacon. Simmer 1 hour longer. Best if made night before and reheated. Serve with steamed potatoes and rye bread.

Jambalaya

12 servings

From way down in Louisiana

Ingredients

½	pound bacon
1	pound smoked sausage
1	pound boneless chicken breast
2	medium onions, chopped
2	ribs celery, chopped
1	cup chopped parsley
1	medium green pepper, chopped
½	cup chopped green onion tops
1	teaspoon garlic powder
1	teaspoon salt, or to taste
	dash red pepper
8	cups water
2	teaspoons Kitchen Bouquet
4	cups long grain rice

Preparation — Brown bacon until crisp and dry. Remove, crumble and set aside. Cut sausage and chicken into bite-size pieces, brown and set aside. Brown onions until dark brown in color. Add celery, parsley, green pepper and green onion, and cook for 10 minutes. Add spices. Add water, Kitchen Bouquet and crumbled bacon. When boiling, add reserved meats and cook for 10 minutes. Add rice, cook 10 minutes more, then stir once. Cover pot and cook until rice is done, about 30 minutes more.

Other meats, such as duck or pork, may be used. Cut into bite-size pieces and brown before adding to jambalaya. Raw shrimp may also be used and added directly to pot without cooking first.

Snow Peas with Lobster Sauce

2 servings

No lobster but delicious served over seafood

Ingredients

2   tablespoons peanut or vegetable oil
1   garlic clove, minced
1   slice ginger root, minced
1   tablespoon fermented black beans, soaked in 1 tablespoon dry sherry
¼   pound ground lean pork
⅓   cup rich chicken broth
    salt to taste
    pinch of sugar
2   teaspoons cornstarch mixed with 1 tablespoon cold water
1   small egg, lightly beaten
1   pound snow peas, cut into 2-inch pieces, blanched

Preparation — Heat wok or large skillet. Add 2 teaspoons oil. When hot, add garlic, ginger and black beans and stir-fry 1 minute. Add ground pork and stir-fry until pork has lost pink color. Add chicken broth, salt and sugar and heat to a simmer.

Add cornstarch mixture. Stir until thickened. Lower heat and gently stir in egg. Cook just until egg is set. Arrange snow peas on platter and pour hot lobster sauce over all. Serve hot.

Chinese Pork Shreds with Lettuce

4 servings

Ingredients

1 pound lean boneless pork, finely shredded
1 tablespoon soy sauce
2 teaspoons cornstarch
1 teaspoon peanut oil
1 small head lettuce, washed and dried
2 tablespoons peanut oil
4 scallions, shredded
1 slice fresh ginger root, minced
4 dried Chinese black mushrooms, soaked in hot water and shredded
½ cup shredded bamboo shoots
2 teaspoons dry sherry
¼ cup chicken broth
1 teaspoon cornstarch mixed with 1 tablespoon cold water
1 teaspoon sesame oil, optional

Preparation

Combine pork shreds, soy sauce, 2 teaspoons cornstarch and 1 teaspoon peanut oil and marinate for 30 minutes. Separate lettuce leaves and arrange on platter.

Heat wok or large skillet. Add 2 tablespoons oil. Add pork shreds and stir-fry for 2 minutes. Remove to platter retaining oil in pan. Stir-fry scallions and ginger root for 30 seconds. Add mushrooms, bamboo shoots and pork shreds. Stir-fry for 1 minute.

Add sherry and chicken broth. Stir in cornstarch mixture and continue stirring until sauce is thickened and glossy. Add sesame oil.

To serve, spoon 2 to 3 tablespoons pork mixture on lettuce leaf, roll up to enclose, and eat with fingers.

Escalopes de Veau Polonaise 6 servings

Ingredients

2   pounds veal scallops, pounded thin
    salt, pepper, flour
6   tablespoons butter
2   onions, chopped
3   medium tomatoes, peeled, seeded and chopped
½   cup dry white wine
2   tablespoons chopped fresh parsley
1   cup sour cream

Preparation

Season veal with salt and pepper, rub with flour and sauté quickly in butter. Remove to serving dish and keep warm. Add onions to pan and sauté until light golden color. Add tomatoes and cook for 5 minutes, then add wine and parsley and simmer for 3 to 4 minutes longer. Finally stir in sour cream, heat but do not let boil, and pour over veal.

Veal Piquant 6 servings

Ingredients

2   pounds veal scallops, pounded very thin
½   cup flour
1   teaspoon salt
½   teaspoon pepper
4   tablespoons olive oil
½   cup butter
¼   cup lemon juice
4   tablespoons minced parsley

Preparation

Dip veal in mixture of flour, salt and pepper. Heat olive oil and ¼ cup butter in large skillet until it sizzles. Lay slices of veal flat in single layer and brown quickly on both sides. Remove from pan. Pour off drippings and add the remaining ¼ cup butter, lemon juice and parsley to pan. When sauce bubbles, return veal to pan and cook briefly, until heated through, stirring to coat veal with sauce. Serve immediately.

Elegant Veal Cutlets

2 servings

Ingredients

2 tablespoons butter
1 garlic clove, cut in half
½ pound thinly sliced veal cutlets
¼ cup flour
1 tablespoon water
½ cup Marsala wine
½ cup sour cream

Preparation

Melt butter in large skillet, brown garlic and remove. Dredge veal with flour and cook in garlic butter until golden. Remove meat to serving dish, set aside, keeping warm. Add water and wine to skillet and boil gently, scraping up browned bits. Stir in sour cream, heat, but do not boil. Pour sauce over meat and serve.

Herbed Veal

6 servings

2 pounds veal cutlets
¼ cup flour
4 tablespoons butter or margarine, melted
2 tablespoons olive oil
¼ teaspoon salt
⅛ teaspoon pepper
2 bunches green onions, chopped
1½ cups chicken broth
1 cup dry white wine
3 garlic cloves, minced
2 tablespoons chopped fresh parsley
1 teaspoon Italian herbs
¼ teaspoon ground cinnamon
hot cooked rice

Preparation   Trim excess fat from veal and cut into 1-inch strips. Dredge in flour. Sauté veal in butter and olive oil until lightly browned. Remove to 9 x 13-inch baking dish. Season with salt and pepper. Sauté onions in pan drippings until tender. Stir in chicken broth, wine, garlic, parsley, herbs and cinnamon. Mix well and pour over veal. Bake, uncovered, in preheated 350° oven for 1 hour. Serve over rice.

Veal Paprika
6 to 8 servings

Ingredients

3   pounds stew veal, cut into ½ inch pieces
    flour
4   tablespoons oil
1   pound fresh mushrooms, sliced
1   cup onions, sliced
3   beef bouillon cubes
1½ cups hot water
½   teaspoon salt, or to taste
2 to 4 tablespoons paprika
    pepper to taste
1   cup sour cream
    paprika and chopped parsley for garnish

Preparation   Roll veal in flour and brown in hot oil. Add sliced mushrooms and onions. Cook 15 minutes, stirring often. Dissolve bouillon cubes in hot water and add with salt, pepper and paprika to meat. Mix well and put in 2½-quart casserole. Cover and bake in preheated 350° oven for 1½ to 2 hours. Just before serving, place sour cream in center. Garnish with paprika and parsley.

Top-of-the-Stove Veal Stew

4 to 6 servings

This stew was cooked on a hot plate in the back of a butcher shop in Connecticut. The aroma was heavenly!

Ingredients

4	strips bacon
2	pounds good quality veal stew meat, cut into 1-inch pieces
12	ounces fresh mushrooms, sliced
3	medium onions, cut into wedges
3	ribs celery with leaves, cut into bite-size pieces
¼	cup chopped parsley
1	garlic clove, minced
2	bay leaves
¼	teaspoon dried thyme
1	teaspoon paprika
	salt and pepper to taste
2	tablespoons Worcestershire sauce
¼	teaspoon celery salt
¼	cup sherry
1	cup beef broth
1	cup sour cream, optional

Preparation

Cook bacon, drain, crumble and set aside. Dry veal pieces well with paper towel, then brown quickly in bacon fat. Drain excess fat. Add bacon and remaining ingredients except sour cream. Cover and simmer 1 to 1½ hours. Add sour cream just before serving if desired. Serve over rice.

Marinated Lamb

6 to 8 servings

Use marinade for kabobs, too

Ingredients

1	small onion, grated
1	garlic clove, crushed
¾	cup dry red wine
¼	cup vegetable oil
½	teaspoon salt
¾	teaspoon rosemary
¾	cup sage, rubbed
⅛	teaspoon pepper
5	pound leg of lamb, boned and butterflied

Preparation

Blend all ingredients well, except lamb. Pour over lamb and marinate for several hours. Cook over hot coals for 45 minutes. To serve, cut diagonally in ¼-inch slices. Lamb should be light pink. May also be cooked in oven under broiler.

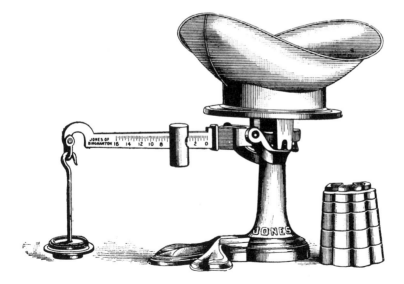

Pot Roast of Lamb

8 to 10 servings

Filled with an aromatic mixture of herbs

Ingredients

5½ pound boned shoulder of lamb
¼ cup lemon juice
1 cup finely chopped onion
½ cup chopped fresh parsley
1½ teaspoons salt
1 teaspoon dried basil leaves
½ teaspoon dried marjoram leaves
2 garlic cloves, crushed
2 tablespoons butter or margarine
10½ ounces condensed beef broth, undiluted
1 bay leaf
2 pounds new potatoes
8 medium onions, peeled
2 tablespoons flour
½ cup chopped fresh mint leaves
lemon slices for garnish

Preparation

Wipe lamb with damp paper towels. Trim excess fat. Spread flat on board and pound with mallet to make even thickness. Pour lemon juice over lamb to cover completely.

For filling, combine chopped onion, parsley, salt, basil, marjoram and garlic. Mix well. Spread evenly over lamb to within 1 inch of edge all around. Starting at short side, roll up. Tie roll with string at 2-inch intervals to secure. If necessary, close ends with trussing pins.

In large Dutch oven, heat butter and brown roast evenly on all sides, about 25 minutes. Spoon off excess fat. Pour beef broth into 2-cup measure. Add enough water to measure 1½ cups. Add to lamb along with bay leaf. Bring to boiling point. Reduce heat, simmer, covered 1½ hours, turning meat at least once. Pare strip around potatoes. Add to lamb with onions. Simmer, covered, 40 minutes, or until lamb and vegetables are tender.

Remove lamb, potatoes and onions to serving platter. Keep
warm. Remove string. Let stand 20 minutes for easier
carving. Skim fat from pan liquid. Measure liquid and add
water to make 1¾ cups. Mix flour with ¼ cup cold water
until smooth. Stir into pan liquid and bring to boil, stirring.
Add chopped mint. Reduce heat and simmer 3 minutes.
Spoon some mint gravy over meat and pass the rest. Garnish
serving platter with lemon slices and mint leaves. if desired.

Lamb Shanks Provençal   6 servings

Ingredients

1	pound dried Great Northern beans, washed
8	cups water
2	tablespoons vegetable oil
1½	cups chopped onion
1	1-pound can tomatoes
2	teaspoons salt
1	teaspoon leaf savory, crumbled
2	garlic cloves, slivered
6	lamb shanks, 3½ to 4 pounds
½	cup water
	parsley for garnish

Preparation

Heat beans to boiling with 8 cups water, and boil 2
minutes. Cover. Remove from heat and let stand 1 hour or
soak beans overnight in water. Heat beans to boiling again
or bring soaked beans to a boil. Reduce heat and cover.
Simmer 1 hour or until tender. Drain, reserving liquid. Place
beans in large, shallow baking dish. In skillet, sauté onion in
oil until golden, about 8 minutes. Add to beans, stir in
tomatoes, salt and savory. Insert garlic slivers in lamb
shanks. Brown lamb shanks on all sides. Arrange on top of
beans. Pour off all fat from skillet, add ½ cup water, heat,
stirring constantly to loosen browned bits and add to beans.
Add enough of reserved liquid to come just to top of beans.
Bake, uncovered, in preheated 350° oven for 2 hours, or
until meat is tender, stirring occasionally with fork. Add
more liquid if needed. Garnish with parsley before serving.

Joshua's Italian Lamb Stew 6 to 8 servings

Ingredients

2 pounds lean cubed lamb
2 tablespoons olive oil
2 medium onions, sliced
1 garlic clove, crushed
32 ounces canned tomatoes
6 ounces tomato paste
1 cup dry red wine
1 bay leaf
salt, pepper and sugar to taste
basil and oregano to taste

Preparation

Brown lamb in hot oil. Remove and set aside. Brown onions in same pan, adding garlic just before done. Return lamb to pan, add remaining ingredients and simmer, uncovered, for 2 hours or until lamb is tender. Serve over spaghetti or linguine.

Poultry

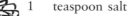

Baked Chicken Soufflé

12 servings

Ingredients

8   slices white bread, crust removed
4   cups cooked chicken, cut into bite-size pieces
½   pound fresh mushrooms, sliced
½   cup butter or margarine
8   ounces water chestnuts, sliced
½   cup mayonnaise
8   ounces very sharp Cheddar cheese, grated
4   eggs, well beaten
1   cup milk
1   teaspoon salt
10¾ ounces cream of mushroom soup
10¾ ounces cream of celery soup
1   jar pimientos, diced
1½ cups buttered bread crumbs

Preparation

Line buttered 9 x 13-inch baking dish with bread and top
with chicken. Sauté mushrooms in butter and layer over
chicken. Top with water chestnuts and spread with
mayonnaise. Sprinkle on cheese. Mix eggs, milk, salt, soups
and pimientos and pour over top. Cover with foil and
refrigerate overnight. Bake, covered, in preheated 350° oven
1 to 1½ hours. Uncover, sprinkle with bread crumbs, bake
15 minutes more.

Cantonese Walnut Chicken · 4 servings

From Jan Wilk, author of "Chinese Cooking"

Ingredients

1¾ cups walnut meats
1 egg, lightly beaten
1 tablespoon dry sherry
2 slices fresh ginger root, smashed to give off juice
salt to taste
2 tablespoons cornstarch
1 large whole chicken breast, boned, skinned and cut into ⅛-inch strips
peanut or vegetable oil
Szechwan pepper-salt optional

Preparation

Dip walnut meats into boiling water for 1 minute. Drain and remove dark skin. Dark outer skin has a slightly bitter taste. Chop walnuts fine. Set aside.

Combine egg, sherry, ginger root, salt and cornstarch. Add chicken slices and marinate for 30 minutes. Coat each slice with walnuts. Heat oil to 375° and deep fry chicken pieces until golden brown. Sprinkle lightly with Szechwan pepper-salt, if desired. Large chicken pieces, pounded until thin, may be prepared the same way.

Although walnuts and chicken are excellent match, roasted peanuts or cashews may be substituted for equally good crunch and taste.

Cheese Stuffed Chicken Breasts

6 servings

Ingredients

¾ cup cream cheese
⅓ cup blue cheese
5 tablespoons butter
   grated nutmeg
¾ cup grated Swiss cheese
3 whole chicken breasts, ¾ pound each, skinned, boned and halved
3 teaspoons Dijon mustard
⅓ cup flour
1 egg, beaten
¼ cup stale bread crumbs
4 tablespoons clarified butter

Preparation

Blend cream cheese, blue cheese, butter and dash of nutmeg. Form into 6 ovals, then roll ovals in Swiss cheese. Chill at least 1 hour.

Flatten each chicken breast slightly between sheets of wax paper. Spread each with ½ teaspoon mustard. Put 1 cheese oval in center of each breast and enclose completely with chicken. Have ready 3 separate bowls containing flour, egg and crumbs. Roll each breast in flour, then egg, then crumbs and chill 1 hour again.

In heavy ovenproof skillet, sear breasts in butter over high heat for 2 to 3 minutes, or until lightly browned. Transfer pan to preheated 400° oven and bake 7 minutes, or until chicken is cooked through.

Chicken à la Felicia

4 servings

Ingredients

¼ cup vegetable oil
1 garlic clove, minced
2 whole chicken breasts, skinned, boned and cubed
½ pound mushrooms, sliced
½ lemon, thinly sliced

¼ cup dry white wine
½ teaspoon each, salt, pepper and oregano
1 tablespoon flour
14 ounces artichoke hearts

Preparation Heat oil and sauté garlic, chicken and mushrooms. Add lemon, wine, salt, pepper, oregano and flour. Simmer 15 minutes. Add artichokes and sauté another 10 minutes. Serve with rice.

Chicken Cacciatore 4 servings

Serve with side dish of pasta

Ingredients
1 small chicken cut into pieces
vegetable oil
1 teaspoon oregano
32 ounces canned tomatoes
salt and pepper to taste
1 garlic clove, chopped
3 green peppers, cut into chunks
2 onions, cut into chunks
3 ounces sliced fresh mushrooms

Preparation Brown chicken well in oil and sprinkle ½ teaspoon oregano over chicken after turning once. Meanwhile stew tomatoes, breaking up pieces. Add ½ teaspoon oregano, salt, pepper and garlic. Add browned chicken to tomatoes and simmer for 1 hour or until chicken is tender. Sauté peppers and onions in small amount of oil until tender, adding mushrooms just before done. Add vegetables to chicken and tomatoes and cook 5 to 10 minutes longer. Transfer to ovenproof casserole. Let sit overnight. Reheat in preheated 350° oven about ½ hour or until heated through.

Chicken in Paper

20 to 24 packages

Fun to make and fun to eat—with chopsticks!

Ingredients

3 to 4 scallions, shredded
1   tablespoon dry sherry
2   tablespoons soy sauce
1   teaspoon sugar
1   teaspoon Hoisin sauce, optional
1   whole chicken breast, skinned, boned and cut into
    1½-inch slices
    sesame oil, optional
20 to 24 squares of wax paper, 6 x 6-inches
3 to 4 sprigs fresh parsley
3 to 4 cups vegetable oil for deep frying

Preparation

Combine scallions, sherry, soy sauce, sugar and Hoisin
sauce. Add chicken slices and marinate for 15 minutes.
Brush each wax paper square with a little sesame or
vegetable oil. With corner facing you, place slice of chicken,
few scallion shreds and piece of parsley on wax paper
square. Fold up corner facing you to cover chicken. Fold
over left corner, then right. Tuck corner on top into fold
near bottom to make tidy package. Heat oil to 375°. Deep
fry packages 1 to 1½ minutes on each side. Drain on
absorbent paper and serve. Beef, shrimp or fish can be
substituted for chicken.

Cold Roast Chicken

6 servings

A French heritage recipe

Ingredients

3   whole 3-pound frying chickens
    salt and freshly ground black pepper to taste
3   garlic cloves
3   bay leaves
    dried thyme
¼   cup butter or margarine

Preparation Sprinkle chickens inside and out with salt and pepper. Place 1 garlic clove, 1 bay leaf and pinch of thyme in cavity of each chicken. Secure cavity.

Melt butter in large oven-proof skillet. Turn chickens to coat in butter. When chickens start to brown, arrange on sides and place skillet in preheated 450° oven. Cook, uncovered, for 15 minutes, basting occasionally. Turn to other side and continue to baste and cook 15 minutes. Place chickens on backs and cook another 30 minutes, or until golden brown. Let stand at room temperature until cool. Chill until ready to serve.

Curried Chicken
4 servings

Ingredients
1	2-pound whole chicken breast, skinned, boned and cut into 1 to 2-inch pieces
4	tablespoons flour
4	tablespoons butter or margarine
½	cup chopped onion
1	small garlic clove, minced
1	tablespoon curry powder
1	teaspoon ground ginger
½	teaspoon salt
1½	cups chicken broth
4	tablespoons raisins
1	large cucumber, peeled and diced

Preparation Coat chicken with flour and sauté in melted butter until browned. Add onion and garlic to chicken and sauté until soft. Add seasonings and broth. Bring to a boil. Add raisins and cucumber. Cover and cook slowly for 30 minutes. Serve over rice.

Dijon Chicken
8 servings

Ingredients

4	large whole chicken breasts, halved
6	tablespoons butter or margarine
4	tablespoons flour
2	cups chicken broth
1	cup half and half
4	tablespoons Dijon mustard
1	tablespoon green peppercorns, optional

Preparation

Sauté chicken in butter until browned. Remove from pan. Add flour and stir until smooth. Add broth, cream and mustard. Simmer chicken in sauce 30 minutes or until done. Add peppercorns just before serving. May be prepared in advance and reheated before serving.

Great Impasta Pollo al Verde (Green Chicken)
6 servings

Ingredients

3	whole chicken breasts, skinned, boned and halved
1	leek, washed, trimmed and cut into rounds
1	bay leaf
	salt and pepper to taste
	juice of ½ lemon

Sauce:

1	cup loosely packed fresh Italian parsley leaves
½	cup loosely packed fresh basil leaves
1	garlic clove
1	tablespoon capers
2 to 3	cornichons or 1 small sour pickle
1	celery rib, coarsely chopped
½	cup virgin olive oil
1	tablespoon red wine vinegar
	juice of ½ lemon
	tomato slices, radishes, red and yellow bell peppers for garnish

Preparation

Add about 1 inch of water to large steamer with rack. Place chicken in 1 layer on rack. Scatter on the leek, bay leaf, salt, pepper and lemon juice. Steam for 30 minutes or until done. Cool. Reserve cooking liquid.

In food processor or blender, combine all sauce ingredients except lemon juice. Purée until very fine. If sauce seems too thick, add few tablespoons cooking liquid. Add lemon juice to suit taste. To serve, discard leeks and bay leaf. Arrange chicken breasts on platter and pour sauce over chicken. Serve at room temperature. Add garnish.

Hungarian Chicken with Cabbage

4 servings

Ingredients

1   3½-pound frying chicken, cut into pieces
1   cup dry white wine
1½ teaspoons salt
1   onion, finely chopped
½   head cabbage, chopped
3   tablespoons vegetable oil
½   teaspoon pepper
1   tablespoon lemon juice

Preparation

Simmer chicken, covered, with wine and salt about 1 hour, or until tender. Brown onion and cabbage in oil. Add to chicken with pepper and lemon juice. Cover tightly and simmer all ingredients 15 minutes. Serve with boiled potatoes or buttered noodles.

Marinated Grilled Chicken
4 servings

1   3-pound chicken, cut into pieces
⅓   cup vegetable oil
⅓   cup vinegar
½   cup lemon juice
1   tablespoon soy sauce

Preparation

Place chicken in 9 x 13-inch baking pan. Mix oil, vinegar, lemon juice and soy sauce. Pour over chicken. Marinate about 2 hours, turning chicken every 15 minutes. Reserve marinade. Cook chicken on outdoor grill, brushing with marinade every time it is turned.

Moroccan Lemon Chicken
8 servings

Ingredients

2   2-pound chickens
2   cups chicken broth or water
¼   cup peanut oil
1   tablespoon olive oil
2   medium onions, sliced
1   garlic clove, minced
1   teaspoon ground ginger or 1-inch piece fresh ginger root
    pinch crushed saffron threads or powder
    salt and freshly ground black pepper to taste
    peel of 1 preserved lemon or 1 whole fresh lemon, quartered
½   cup green olives
    lemon wedges and fresh parsley for garnish

Preparation

Bring chickens, broth, peanut and olive oil, onions, garlic, ginger, saffron, salt and pepper to a boil. Reduce heat and cover. Simmer 40 minutes or until chicken is almost tender. Turn chickens once or twice to cook evenly. Discard fresh ginger. Add lemon peel or fresh lemon. Simmer another 15 minutes. Discard lemon. Add olives and heat through. Garnish with lemon wedges and parsley. Serve with rice.

Oven Barbecued Chicken

8 servings

2   3-pound fryers, quartered
     salt and pepper to taste
3   medium onions, sliced

Sauce:
1½ cups tomato juice
¼   teaspoon cayenne
½   teaspoon salt
¼   teaspoon pepper
¼   teaspoon dry mustard
4½ teaspoons Worcestershire sauce
1   bay leaf
1   teaspoon sugar
¾   cup vinegar
3   garlic cloves, minced
3   tablespoons butter or margarine

Preparation

Place chicken, skin side up, in 9 x 13-inch baking pan. Sprinkle with salt and pepper and add enough water to cover bottom of pan. Cover chicken with onions. Bake in preheated 350° oven for 30 minutes. Turn chicken and bake another 30 minutes. Pour off ¾ cup liquid in pan and discard.

Combine ingredients for sauce and simmer 10 minutes. Pour sauce over chicken and bake ½ hour more, basting frequently. Sauce may be prepared in advance.

Roman Style Chicken and Parmesan Oven Rice

4 servings

Bake in the same oven

Ingredients

2 large whole chicken breasts, skinned, boned and halved
¼ cup flour
4 tablespoons butter or margarine
½ teaspoon salt
½ teaspoon pepper
½ medium onion, diced
1 garlic clove, minced
1 tablespoon cornstarch
⅓ cup dry white wine
2 medium tomatoes, chopped
½ cup ham in julienne strips
¼ teaspoon crushed rosemary

Parmesan Oven Rice
3 tablespoons butter or margarine
⅔ cup rice
1⅔ cups chicken broth
¼ cup freshly grated Parmesan cheese
2 tablespoons minced fresh parsley
½ teaspoon salt
½ teaspoon pepper

Preparation

Coat chicken with flour and brown in 2 tablespoons butter. Place chicken in 2-quart baking dish. Add remaining butter to skillet and sauté onion and garlic until tender. Blend cornstarch with wine. Stir into onion with tomatoes, ham and rosemary. Pour mixture over chicken, cover and bake in preheated 350° oven for 30 minutes. Uncover and bake 20 minutes longer.

Melt butter and add rice. Stir until rice is coated and golden. Remove from heat. Add all other ingredients and pour into 1-quart casserole. Bake covered for 50 minutes in oven with chicken. Stir after 30 minutes.

Sesame Chicken Kabobs

6 servings

Ingredients

2 whole chicken breasts, skinned and boned
¼ cup soy sauce
¼ cup Russian salad dressing
1 tablespoon sesame seeds
2 tablespoons lemon juice
¼ teaspoon ground ginger
¼ teaspoon garlic powder
1 large green pepper, cut into 1-inch pieces
2 medium onions, cut into 8 pieces
3 small zucchini, cut into ¾ inch pieces
1 pint cherry tomatoes

Preparation

Cut chicken into 1-inch pieces. Place in shallow pan. Blend next 6 ingredients well and pour over chicken, cover and marinate in refrigerator 2 hours or overnight. Alternate chicken and vegetables on 6 skewers.

Spray grill with cooking oil. Grill kabobs about 6 inches from coals for 15 to 20 minutes, or until done, turning and basting with marinade.

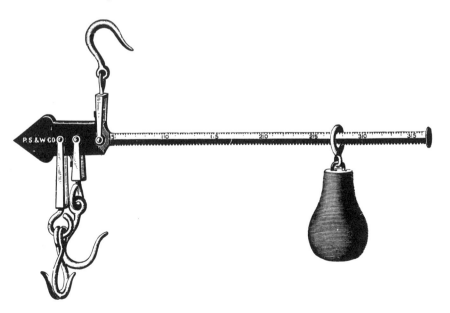

Ski Day Chicken Casserole   8 servings

Actually, good for any day

Ingredients

8   tablespoons butter or margarine
¼   cup flour
1½ cups chicken broth
1   cup sour cream
⅛   teaspoon nutmeg
⅛   teaspoon pepper
    salt to taste
¼   cup dry sherry
½   pound flat egg noodles, cooked and drained
4½ cups cut-up cooked chicken
½   pound mushrooms, sliced and sautéed
1   cup soft bread crumbs
½   cup freshly grated Parmesan cheese

Preparation

Melt 4 tablespoons butter, stir in flour, add broth and sour cream, stirring until thick. Add nutmeg, pepper and salt. Remove from heat and stir in sherry. Arrange noodles in 9 x 13-inch baking dish. Cover with chicken, mushrooms and sauce. Melt remaining 4 tablespoons butter and mix with crumbs. Top casserole with crumbs and cheese. Bake in preheated 350° oven for 30 minutes or until hot and bubbly. May be made day in advance, refrigerated and bake when needed.

Stuffed Chicken Breasts

8 servings

An original from Chuckwagon chef Todd Farrington

Ingredients

8   6-ounce boneless whole butterflied chicken breasts, skinned
8   slices thin ham
5   ounces sharp Cheddar cheese, sliced into 8 pieces
16 ounces chopped frozen broccoli, thawed, or fresh cooked
8   tablespoons butter

Sauce:
2   tablespoons butter
2   tablespoons flour
1   chicken bouillon cube
1   cup water or evaporated milk
1   teaspoon poultry seasoning
    salt and pepper to taste

Preparation

On 1 side of each chicken breast, place slices of ham and cheese and ½ cup broccoli. Fold other side over stuffing and spread 1 tablespoon of butter over top of each breast. Place in buttered 9 x 13-inch baking pan. Bake in preheated 400° oven for 35 to 45 minutes, or until done.

To make sauce, melt butter and add flour. Mix bouillon cube with water or milk. Add liquid to flour and butter and add seasonings. Simmer sauce 10 minutes. To serve, pour sauce over chicken.

Suprêmes de Volaille aux Champignons

6 servings

Ingredients

6   chicken supremes, boned pieces from 3 whole breasts
4   tablespoons butter
1   tablespoon oil
3   tablespoons minced shallots or green onions
½   cup dry white wine
⅔   cup canned beef bouillon
1½ cups whipping cream
½   tablespoon cornstarch, blended with 1 tablespoon water
½   pound fresh mushrooms, sliced
2   tablespoons butter
1   tablespoon oil
    salt and pepper to taste
    chopped parsley and 3 slices prosciutto, diced, for garnish

Preparation

Sauté chicken in 2 tablespoons butter and 1 tablespoon oil. Remove and set aside. Save 2 tablespoons drippings in skillet, or in 2 tablespoons butter, sauté shallots 1 minute. Add wine and bouillon, scraping up brown bits in pan. Boil until reduced to ¼ cup. Mix cream with cornstarch mixture. Add to liquid in skillet and boil several minutes, until cream has reduced and thickened slightly. Remove from heat and season with salt and pepper. Sauté mushrooms in 2 tablespoons butter and 1 tablespoon oil 4 to 5 minutes. Add to cream sauce and simmer 1 minute. Remove from heat and correct seasonings.

Arrange supremes in shallow baking dish, season and cover with cream sauce. Set aside to reheat later or heat in skillet to serve immediately. To serve, reheat in preheated 350° oven until sauce bubbles. Garnish with parsley and diced prosciutto which has been sautéed in butter.

Tarragon Chicken

8 servings

Ingredients

4	whole chicken breasts, skinned, boned and halved
4	tablespoons flour
½	teaspoon salt
	pepper to taste
3	tablespoons butter or margarine
2	small onions, chopped
½	pound mushrooms, sliced
¾	cup white wine or 1 cup chicken broth
½	teaspoon sugar
½	teaspoon dried tarragon, or 1 tablespoon fresh tarragon, crushed
1	cup sour cream
2	green onions, sliced, and ½ teaspoon nutmeg, for garnish

Preparation

Shake chicken with flour, salt and pepper. Set flour aside. Heat butter and add chicken, browning on all sides. Remove from pan and set aside. Sauté onions and mushrooms in same butter until onions are transparent. Return chicken to pan, add wine or broth, sugar and tarragon. Cover and simmer 20 minutes or until chicken is done. Remove chicken and keep warm. Mix 2 tablespoons of flour mixture with sour cream until smooth. Pour into pan drippings. Cook and stir until sauce thickens. Pour over chicken. Garnish with onions and nutmeg. May be prepared day ahead and reheated before serving.

Tender Baked Chicken
4 servings

Ingredients

2 whole breasts, skinned, boned and halved
6 tablespoons butter or margarine
1 tablespoon lemon juice
2 tablespoons White Wine Worchestershire sauce
½ cup flour
1 tablespoon paprika
½ teaspoon curry powder
½ teaspoon dry mustard
¼ teaspoon cinnamon
¼ teaspoon Oriental five spice powder
½ teaspoon ground oregano
¼ teaspoon ground ginger

Preparation

Melt butter or margarine in glass baking dish in oven. Stir in lemon juice and Worchestershire sauce. Shake chicken in bag with flour and spices. Place chicken in baking dish, turn to coat with butter mixture. Bake in preheated 375° oven for 40 minutes.

Tunisian Chicken
4 servings

Ingredients

2 whole chicken breasts, skinned, boned and cut into chunks
¾ teaspoon salt
½ teaspoon pepper
¼ teaspoon ground cumin
4 teaspoons cornstarch
4 teaspoons olive oil
1 egg white, beaten until frothy
6 tablespoons butter
1½ cups minced onion
⅓ cup chopped green olives
¼ cup minced fresh parsley
2 tablespoons lemon juice
2 garlic cloves, minced

½ teaspoon paprika
⅛ teaspoon sugar
⅛ teaspoon hot red pepper
16 whole olives, green or black
½ to 1 cup cashews or peanuts

Preparation   Arrange chicken in shallow baking dish and sprinkle with salt, pepper and cumin. Let stand 20 minutes. Sprinkle with cornstarch and olive oil. Turn to coat and let stand another 20 minutes. Add egg white and let stand another 30 minutes. Remove chicken from marinade and sauté in 4 tablespoons butter until cooked. Transfer to warm dish.

In same pan, sauté onion in 2 tablespoons butter until soft. Add chopped olives, parsley, lemon juice, garlic, paprika, sugar and red pepper. Sauté 3 minutes. Add chicken, olives, nuts and sauté 3 minutes more. Serve with rice pilaf.

Merrymeeting Bourbon Duck 6 servings

Ingredients   6 whole wild duck breasts, skinned and boned
3 tablespoons red currant jelly
8 tablespoons butter
1 tablespoon Worcestershire sauce
1 teaspoon salt
1 teaspoon pepper
⅓ cup dry sherry
⅔ cup bourbon

Preparation   Bring breasts to room temperature. In large iron skillet, melt jelly and butter. Mix in Worcestershire, salt and pepper. Increase heat and add sherry and bourbon. Stir and when mixture comes to a boil, add duck breasts and cook 5 to 8 minutes, depending on size of breasts. Turn occasionally. Do not overcook as meat will toughen. Serve with wild rice and jelly sauce from pan.

Glazed Rock Cornish Hens   4 servings

Ingredients

4   1-pound ready-to-cook Cornish game hens
    salt and pepper to taste
1   cup stuffing mix
⅓   cup butter or margarine, melted
⅓   cup condensed consommé
¼   cup light corn syrup

Preparation

Season hens inside and out with salt and pepper. Stuff each with ¼ cup stuffing mix. Place, breasts up, on rack in shallow roasting pan and brush well with butter. Roast in preheated 400° oven for about 1 hour or until tender. During last 15 minutes, baste several times with mixture of consomme and syrup.

Blue Cheese Buffet Turkey   6 servings

Ingredients

3   tablespoons butter or margarine
3   tablespoons flour
2   teaspoons chicken stock base
    dash each white pepper and nutmeg
1½ cups milk
½   cup cream
2   tablespoons crumbled blue cheese
1   tablespoon dry sherry
1   cup pitted ripe olives, sliced
1¾ cups diced cooked turkey
2   tablespoons chopped pimiento
1   tablespoon finely chopped fresh parsley

Preparation

Melt butter or margarine. Add flour, chicken stock base, pepper and nutmeg. Stir in milk and cream. Cook, stirring, until sauce thickens. Add blue cheese and sherry. Stir in olives, turkey, pimiento and parsley. Heat thoroughly. Serve with rice.

Lea's Turkey Tetrazzini

6 servings

From an Auxilian who raises her own turkeys

Ingredients

6   ounces spaghetti, broken up
¼   cup butter or margarine
½   cup flour
2¾ cups chicken broth
1   cup light cream
¼   cup dry sherry
1   teaspoon salt
     dash of pepper
1   cup sliced mushrooms, fresh or canned
2   cups, or more, diced cooked turkey
¼   cup chopped green pepper
½   cup shredded Swiss or Monterey Jack cheese

Preparation

Cook spaghetti in boiling water until al dente. Drain. Melt butter, blend in flour. Stir broth into flour mixture. Add cream. Heat and stir until mixture thickens and bubbles. Add sherry, salt, pepper, spaghetti, mushrooms, turkey and green pepper. Pour into buttered 7½ x 12-inch baking dish. Sprinkle top with cheese. Bake in preheated 350° oven about 30 minutes. Great do-ahead dish.

Turkey Marengo

6 servings

Low calorie, low salt, low sugar

Ingredients

3   pounds turkey wings, tips removed
1   cup sliced onion
⅓   cup fresh sliced mushrooms
16   ounces tomatoes
½   cup dry white wine or water
2   cups water
     salt to taste
½   teaspoon pepper
1   teaspoon dried oregano

Preparation

Place wings in non-stick Dutch oven and brown without adding oil. Add remaining ingredients, cover and simmer 2 hours. Refrigerate several hours. Before serving, remove fat which has congealed on top and discard.

Reheat turkey, uncovered, simmering 15 minutes or until completely heated. Serve with rice.

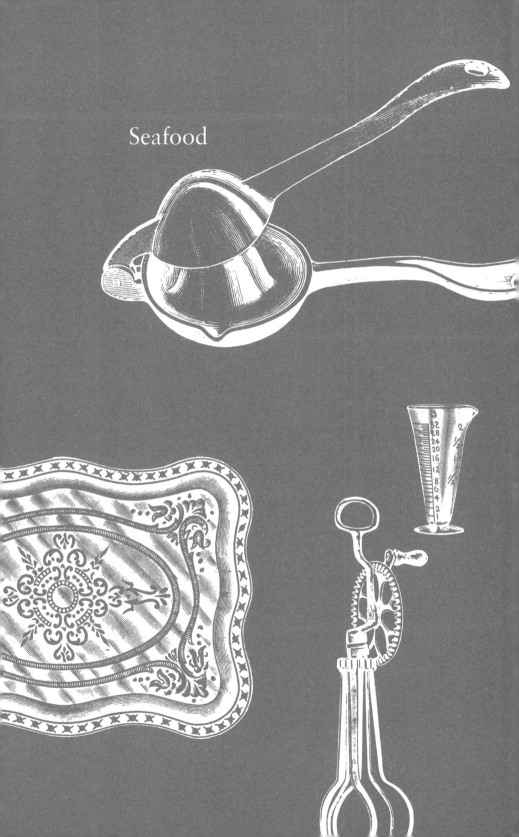

Seafood

Clams in a Snap

4 servings

Ingredients

12 single saltines
1   cup milk
4   tablespoons butter or margarine, melted
7   ounces minced clams
¼   teaspoon Worcestershire sauce
1   teaspoon green pepper, finely chopped
2   teaspoons finely chopped onion
    dash of salt and pepper
2   eggs, beaten

Preparation

Crumble crackers and soak in milk for few minutes. Combine with other ingredients, adding eggs last. Pour into buttered 1-quart casserole and place in shallow pan of water. Bake in preheated 350° oven for 40 minutes.

Favorite Fried Clam Batter

4 servings

Ingredients

1   egg
½   teaspoon soda
2   cups flour
1   teaspoon cream of tartar
12 ounces evaporated milk
    pinch of salt
1   pint fresh clams
    oil for frying

Preparation

Mix all ingredients except clams. Dip clams in batter and fry in deep oil at 375° for 3 to 5 minutes. Hen clams may be cut to size of smaller clams and used, if desired. Batter works well with other seafood also.

Linguine with Clam Sauce

4 servings

Ingredients

3   garlic cloves, minced
4   tablespoons olive oil

4   tablespoons butter or margarine
1   tablespoon chopped fresh parsley
    salt and pepper to taste
7   ounces canned minced clams or 1 cup fresh minced
    clams with liquid
4   ounces sliced mushrooms, drained
    linguine for 4 servings, cooked according to package
    directions
    freshly grated Parmesan cheese

Preparation   Sauté garlic in oil and butter for 5 minutes. Add parsley, salt
and pepper. Stir in clams and clam liquid. Add mushrooms.
Heat until bubbly. Serve over hot linguine and sprinkle
with cheese.

Crab Au Gratin   4 servings

Ingredients   2   tablespoons butter or margarine, melted
¼   cup fine dry bread crumbs
½   cup shredded Swiss cheese
¼   cup sliced almonds, toasted
4   tablespoons butter or margarine
⅓   cup flour
½   teaspoon grated lemon peel
½   teaspoon salt
¼   teaspoon dry mustard
    dash white pepper
2   cups light cream
1   egg, slightly beaten
2½ cups flaked crabmeat
3   tablespoons sliced green onion
    chopped fresh parsley and lemon slices for garnish

Preparation   Melt butter, toss with crumbs, cheese and almonds. Set
aside. Make white sauce of butter, flour, lemon peel, salt,
dry mustard, pepper and cream. Stir 1 cup of cream sauce
into egg, returning to mixture and cooking for several
minutes. Stir in crabmeat and onion. Pour into 4 individual
casseroles or 1½-quart casserole. Top with crumb mixture.
Bake in preheated 350° oven for 25 to 30 minutes; 20
minutes for individual casseroles. Garnish with parsley and
lemon slices.

Crab Imperial

6 servings

Ingredients

2 tablespoons chopped onion
2 tablespoons chopped green pepper
8 tablespoons butter or margarine
2 tablespoons flour
½ teaspoon celery salt
1 cup milk
salt and white pepper to taste
2 tablespoons dry sherry
dash of Tabasco sauce
1 egg, beaten
1 pound crabmeat
1 tablespoon fresh minced parsley
1 pimiento, chopped
⅛ teaspoon grated orange rind
1 cup soft bread crumbs
2 tablespoons butter or margarine, melted
paprika

Preparation

Sauté onion and green pepper in butter. Blend in flour and celery salt. Gradually add milk and cook until thickened. Season with salt, pepper, sherry and Tabasco. Add egg carefully to sauce. Fold in crabmeat, parsley, pimiento and orange rind. Pour into buttered 1½-quart casserole. Top with bread crumbs mixed with melted butter and sprinkle on paprika. Bake in preheated 350° oven for 25 minutes. May also be baked in individual shells for 15 to 20 minutes.

Stuffed Crab

6 to 8 servings

Ingredients

4 cups fresh crabmeat
3 slices white bread, cubed
2 eggs
salt and pepper to taste
2 tablespoons vegetable oil, butter or margarine
½ cup chopped scallions
½ cup chopped fresh parsley

½   cup chopped onion
½   cup bread crumbs
     paprika

Preparation   Combine crabmeat, bread cubes, eggs, salt and pepper. Sauté scallions, parsley and onion in oil or butter. Add to crab mixture, mixing well. Spoon into cleaned crab shells or make "shells" out of heavy foil. Sprinkle with bread crumbs and paprika. Bake in preheated 400° oven for about 20 minutes.

"Died and Gone to Heaven" Baked Stuffed Lobster

6 servings

In the Five Islands style

Ingredients   6   live 1¼ pound lobsters
       meat from 2 cooked cull lobsters (1 claw)
    ½   pound raw shrimp
    ½   pound butter
    ½   pound crabmeat
    ½   pound scallops, cut into pieces
   35   Ritz crackers, crushed
    1   tablespoon Worcestershire sauce
       pepper to taste
       paprika

Preparation   Cook lobsters in boiling salted water for 10 minutes. Remove and let cool. Sauté shrimp in butter. Add meat from cull lobsters, crab and scallops and heat through. Mix in cracker crumbs, Worcestershire sauce and pepper.

Turn lobsters on their backs. Insert knife at head of each and quickly split from head to tail, as far as you can go. Spread open and remove small hard sac just below head by hooking finger under it. Stuff lobsters and sprinkle with paprika. Bake on rimmed cookie sheet in preheated 400° oven for 25 minutes.

Lobster Soufflé

8 servings

Ingredients

2 cups lobster meat, finely chopped
1 cup lobster meat, in larger pieces
salt and pepper to taste
6 tablespoons butter or margarine
6 tablespoons flour
2½ cups hot milk
6 egg yolks, beaten
6 egg whites, beaten until stiff, but not dry
¼ to ½ cup grated cheese
shellfish sauce of choice

Preparation

Season chopped lobster with salt and pepper, keeping fine and large pieces separate. Make sauce of butter, flour and milk, cooking 5 to 10 minutes, stirring constantly until reduced to 2 scant cups. Add chopped lobster quickly. Let cool. Blend in blender until well mixed and return to saucepan.

Gradually add beaten egg yolks and return to heat. Do not boil, but bring mixture to boiling point, stirring constantly. Cool slightly. Fold in large lobster pieces and egg whites. Pour into buttered large soufflé dish. Sprinkle with grated cheese and bake in preheated 350° oven for 50 to 60 minutes until puffed. Serve with any shellfish sauce. Recipe may be baked in 8 individual soufflé dishes for about 30 minutes.

Fried Mussels

4 servings

Ingredients

5½ dozen mussels
4 eggs, beaten
4 cups soft bread crumbs
oil for deep frying
lemon wedges
cocktail or tartar sauce

Preparation

Clean mussels and steam to remove meat from shells. Dip mussel meat in egg, then crumbs. Fry in deep oil at 375° until golden. Drain and serve on hot platter with lemon wedges, cocktail or tartar sauce.

Moules Marinière

4 to 6 servings

Ingredients

1   cup water
1   cup white wine (¾ cup beer may be substituted)
1   tablespoon chopped parsley
2   garlic cloves, finely minced
1   rib celery, diced
2   carrots, finely diced
½   cup minced green onions
1   tablespoon olive oil
2 to 3 tablespoons butter or margarine
8   pounds mussels, scrubbed and debearded

Preparation

Bring water to boil and add wine. Sauté all vegetables in oil and butter until carrots are tender. Add mussels to water and wine. Immediately add vegetable mixture. Cover. Cook over high heat 5 to 8 minutes. Stir once with slotted spoon so mussels cook evenly. Shells will open. Do not overcook. Serve in soup bowls. Allow cooking liquid to settle and serve broth over mussels or for dipping with French bread in individual cups. Mussels may also be dipped in lemon butter.

Mussels with Pasta

4 to 6 servings

From Maine's foremost outdoors cook, Alex Delicata of L.L. Bean

Ingredients

1   quart shucked mussels, with juice
2   tablespoons butter or margarine
½   cup olive oil
1   medium onion, chopped coarsely
2   ribs celery, diced
2   large garlic cloves, minced
1   red sweet pepper, chopped
1   large green pepper, chopped
5   sprigs fresh parsley, chopped
1   tablespoon minced fresh basil leaves
1   teaspoon horseradish or to taste
1   cup tomato juice or crushed tomatoes
¼   cup each freshly grated Parmesan and Romano cheese
8 to 10 ounces spinach pasta twists or spinach noodles

Preparation

Prepare mussels by removing from juice and stir-frying briefly in small amount of butter, until just cooked. Reserve juice. If you have gathered your own mussels, scrub shells well and steam mussels in small amount of water until all shells have opened. Strain juice and save. Pick out mussels and stir-fry briefly in butter.

Heat olive oil, add onion, celery, garlic and peppers, sautéing until soft. Add parsley, basil and horseradish. Add tomato juice and enough mussel liquid to make juicy sauce. Heat through and add mussels at very end, just long enough to warm. Cook pasta al dente, drain. Turn into large shallow casserole. Spoon on mussels and vegetables with sauce and sprinkle with cheeses. Toss and serve. In season, other garden vegetables may be added.

Scalloped Oyster and Corn
6 servings

Ingredients
1   pint shucked oysters
½   pound butter or margarine, melted
2   cups crushed saltine crumbs
16½ ounces cream-style corn
¼   cup light cream
     salt and pepper to taste
¼ to ½ teaspoon liquid hot pepper sauce

Preparation
Drain oysters. Spread on paper towels and cut each oyster in half or thirds, depending on size. Melt butter and combine with crumbs. Combine corn, cream, salt, pepper and hot pepper. Butter 1½-quart casserole. Spread ⅓ crumb mixture on bottom, cover with half of corn mixture. Press half of oysters into corn. Repeat and top with remaining ⅓ crumb mixture. Bake in preheated 350° oven for 45 minutes.

Adora's Scallops
4 servings

From the Penobscot Bay town of Castine

Ingredients
1   pound scallops or more
1½   cups Ritz cracker crumbs
4   tablespoons butter or margarine, melted
½   cup light cream
1   tablespoon dry sherry
     few drops Worcestershire sauce

Preparation
Cut scallops to size of grapes if large. Roll in mixture of crumbs and butter. Arrange in shallow 1½-quart buttered casserole. Mix cream, sherry and Worcestershire and pour over scallops. Cover with remaining crumbs. Bake in preheated 350° oven for 30 minutes.

Baked Scallops in White Clam Sauce

4 servings

Ingredients

1 pound fresh or frozen scallops, halved or quartered if large
16 to 20 small fresh mushrooms
½ cup coarsely grated Swiss cheese
paprika and fresh parsley for garnish

Clam Sauce:
2 tablespoons butter or margarine
2 tablespoons flour
juice of clams and cream to equal 1 cup
2 tablespoons dry white wine
8 ounces chopped or minced clams
Crazy Salt and pepper to taste

Preparation

Melt butter and add flour. Add clam juice and cream, stirring until thickened. Add wine, clams and seasonings, Arrange scallops in 4 small baking dishes or 9 x 9-inch casserole. Place mushrooms on top. Pour cream sauce over scallops and mushrooms. Top with cheese. Bake in preheated 400° oven about 15 minutes, or until hot and bubbly and cheese melts. Garnish with paprika and parsley.

Coquilles St. Jacques

6 servings

Ingredients

½ to 1 pound fresh mushrooms, sliced
juice of 1 lemon
5 tablespoons butter or margarine
1 to 1½ pounds sea scallops, fresh or frozen
1 cup dry white wine
¼ teaspoon ground thyme
1 bay leaf
½ teaspoon salt
⅛ teaspoon pepper
3 tablespoons flour
1 cup light cream
¾ cup buttered soft bread crumbs
2 tablespoons freshly grated Parmesan cheese

Preparation

Sprinkle mushrooms with lemon juice and sauté in 2 tablespoons butter until golden brown. Cut scallops into quarters and simmer with wine and seasonings 5 minutes. Drain, reserving 1 cup broth. Make white sauce with remaining 3 tablespoons butter, flour, broth and cream. Add scallops and mushrooms. Spoon into 6 buttered shells or casserole. Top with cheese and buttered crumbs. Bake in preheated 400° oven for 10 minutes or until brown.

Scallops Provençale

4 servings

Ingredients

3	tablespoons olive oil
3	tablespoons butter or margarine
1	pound scallops, cut into pieces if large
8	shallots, minced, optional
8	green onions, minced
2	garlic cloves, minced
2	teaspoons dried basil
1	teaspoon dried tarragon
¼	teaspoon dried thyme
½	cup dry white wine
4	cups tomatoes, chopped and drained
2	teaspoons sugar
	pasta of choice, cooked and drained

Preparation

Heat olive oil and butter, add scallops and cook several minutes. Remove scallops with slotted spoon. Add shallots and onions and sauté few minutes more. Stir in garlic, herbs and wine. Sauté 1 minute. Stir in tomatoes and cook over medium heat 5 minutes, or until sauce has thickened a bit. Add sugar. Return cooked scallops and gently mix to combine all ingredients. Serve over pasta.

"Jambalayah" Maine Style
6 servings

Ingredients

2 tablespoons butter or margarine
1 tablespoon flour
½ pound cooked ham, coarsely diced
1 large green pepper, diced
2 cups cooked Maine shrimp
2½ cups canned tomatoes
1½ cups water
1 large onion, chopped
½ garlic clove, sliced
1 tablespoon minced fresh parsley
 salt and pepper to taste
1 bay leaf
⅛ teaspoon thyme
¾ cup uncooked rice

Preparation

Preheat electric skillet to 350°. Melt butter, stir in flour, add green pepper and ham. Cook, stirring for 5 minutes. Add shrimp, tomatoes, water, onion, garlic and seasonings. Bring to boiling point. Add rice. Reduce heat to about 200° and simmer 30 minutes or until rice is tender and has absorbed most of moisture. May also be prepared in skillet and then baked in casserole in preheated 325° oven 30 to 40 minutes.

Should there be leftovers, "jambalayah" makes delicious stuffing for green peppers which have been parboiled 6 to 8 minutes. Stuff and top with buttered bread crumbs. Bake at 350° for 30 minutes.

Shrimp Casserole
6 servings

Ingredients

⅓ cup chopped onion
1 tablespoon butter or margarine
2 garlic cloves, minced
2 pounds raw Maine shrimp, shelled
1 cup uncooked rice
28 ounces canned tomatoes

2   cups chicken or beef broth
1   small bay leaf
3   tablespoons chopped fresh parsley
½   teaspoon ground cloves
½   teaspoon marjoram
1   teaspoon chili powder
     dash cayenne pepper
1   teaspoon salt
¼   teaspoon pepper

Preparation   Brown onion in butter with garlic. Add to 2-quart casserole with shrimp, rice, tomatoes, broth and seasonings. Cover tightly and bake in preheated 350° oven for 1½ hours.

Shrimp Curry   8 servings

Ingredients
1¼ cups chopped onion
½   cup chopped celery
1   cup chopped green pepper
3   garlic cloves, minced
8   tablespoons butter or margarine
30 ounces cream of mushroom soup
½   cup raisins, chopped
1   sour apple, chopped, optional
2   tablespoons shredded unsweetened coconut
5   teaspoons curry powder
     salt, pepper and Worcestershire sauce to taste
2   pounds cooked gulf or Maine shrimp
4   tablespoons sour cream
     juice 1 lemon
     condiments: chopped when possible, chutney, onion, raisins, peanuts, hard cooked egg, slivered almonds, coconut, radishes and green pepper

Preparation   Sauté onion, celery, pepper and garlic in butter until tender. Add soup, raisins, apple, coconut, seasonings and shrimp. Heat thoroughly on low heat. Just before serving, add sour cream and lemon juice.

Serve with any or all condiments in individual dishes. Rice is customary accompaniment.

Seafood Pizza

6 servings

Ingredients

Crust:
8 tablespoons cold unsalted butter
1⅔ cups unbleached white flour
⅛ teaspoon freshly ground black pepper
⅛ cup ice water
⅛ cup vinegar

Filling:
½ pound cooked Maine shrimp
½ cup steamed and shucked clams
12 to 16 steamed and shucked mussels
2 tablespoons butter or margarine
1 large garlic clove, minced
1 cup freshly grated mozzarella or Gruyere cheese
1 egg, lightly beaten
2 cups sour cream
½ cup chopped fresh dill
  pinch of salt
1 purple onion, sliced
  fresh dill and lemon wedges for garnish

Preparation

For crust, cut cold butter into flour or process 10 seconds in food processor. Add pepper, blend in water and vinegar to make ball, or process only until dough forms ball. Roll dough to 12-inch circle. Grease 9-inch removable-bottom tart pan or 9-inch layer cake pan. Fit dough into pan, doubling edges. Bake in preheated 375° oven for 10 minutes.

For filling, sauté seafood with butter and garlic and add cheese. Add egg, salt, dill, sour cream and mix well. Pour into crust, spreading evenly. Separate onion slices into rings and press into top, making a pretty design. Bake at 375° for 20 minutes, or until crust is golden and top is bubbly. Let stand 5 minutes before serving. Garnish with dill and lemon wedges.

Seafood Tetrazzini

8 to 10 servings

From New Meadows Inn, home of the Maine shore dinner

Ingredients

4 cups medium white sauce
1 pound sharp Cheddar Wispride cheese
1 pound broad noodles, cooked according to package directions
½ pound scallops, cooked and cut into bite-size pieces
½ pound Maine shrimp, cooked and shelled
meat from 1 or more cooked lobsters
½ cup dry sherry
½ teaspoon white pepper
dash Worcestershire sauce
dash Tabasco sauce

Preparation

Blend white sauce and cheese. Add rest of ingredients and pour into 9 x 13-inch buttered casserole. Bake in preheated 350° oven for 30 minutes.

Grilled Marinated Bluefish

4 servings

Ingredients

4 garlic cloves, minced
1 cup vegetable oil
½ cup lemon juice
salt and pepper to taste
1 teaspoon oregano
2 pounds bluefish steaks, 1-inch thick

Ingredients

Combine garlic, oil, lemon juice and seasonings. Pour over fish and marinate at least 1 hour. Cook fish on grill basting with marinade, about 10 minutes on each side, or until fish flakes easily when tested with fork.

Orange Broiled Bluefish

6 servings

Preparation

2 bluefish fillets, about 1¼ pounds each
  juice from 1 lemon or lime
½ cup frozen orange juice concentrate, thawed
4 tablespoons butter or margarine, melted
¼ cup soy sauce
1 tablespoon grated orange rind
  dash of powdered ginger

Preparation

Sprinkle cleaned and dried fillets with lemon or lime juice 30 minutes before cooking. Make orange sauce by mixing remaining ingredients. Place fillets, skin side down, on rack of broiler pan and baste generously with orange sauce. Broil 3 to 4 inches from heat or further away from heat if fish is quite thick. For very thick fish, turn oven to 350° after topping has become brown and bake another 10 minutes. Baste fish often. It is not necessary to turn fish. Start testing for doneness after 10 minutes.

Stuffed Bluefish

6 servings

Ingredients

1 medium-sized whole bluefish, dressed
1½ cup bread crumbs
¼ cup milk
1 to 2 teaspoons grated raw onion or onion soup mix
½ teaspoon salt
¼ teaspoon grated lemon rind
1 teaspoon melted butter or margarine
  lemon wedges for garnish

Preparation

Mix crumbs, milk, onion, salt, lemon rind and margarine. Stuff fish and place in shallow baking pan, using foil as liner. Bake in preheated 350° oven for 1 hour, or until fish flakes easily when tested with fork. Garnish with lemon wedges.

Gingered Cod

3 servings

Ingredients

1 pound cod fish cheeks or fillets
1 cup flour
1 teaspoon fresh chopped dill or other herbs
  salt and pepper to taste
4 tablespoons butter or margarine
  freshly grated ginger root

Preparation

Cut fish into uniform size pieces, about 1½-inches. Coat with flour and seasonings. Pan fry in margarine. Garnish with freshly grated ginger.

Amy's Easy Fish 'n Cheese

3 servings

Ingredients

1 pound haddock fillets
⅓ cup mayonnaise
¼ cup freshly grated Parmesan cheese
2 tablespoons fine dry bread crumbs

Preparation

Wash and pat fillets dry. Brush with mayonnaise. Mix cheese and crumbs. Roll fish in mixture and place in buttered 8 x 10-inch baking dish. Top with any remaining crumbs. Bake in preheated 375° oven for 20 to 30 minutes, or until fish is lightly browned.

Cape Cod Haddock

6 servings

Ingredients

1 small onion, sliced
½ pound mushrooms, sliced
1 tablespoon chopped parsley
1 teaspoon vegetable oil
1 teaspoon salt
⅛ teaspoon pepper
½ cup milk
2 pounds haddock fillets
¼ cup freshly grated Parmesan cheese
lemon for garnish

Preparation

Sauté onions, mushrooms and parsley in oil for 15 minutes. Slowly stir in salt, pepper and milk, and heat. Place fish in buttered 7 x 11-inch baking dish. Pour contents of skillet over fish and sprinkle with cheese. Bake in preheated 350° oven for 35 to 45 minutes, or until fish flakes easily. Serve with lemon wedges.

Fast Fish

6 servings

Ingredients

2 pounds haddock fillets, or other lean white fish fillets
2 cups Italian bread crumbs or other style
juice of 2 lemons
8 tablespoons butter or margarine, melted

Preparation

Arrange fish in one layer in buttered 8 x 10-inch casserole. Cover liberally with crumbs. Combine lemon juice and butter. Pour over all crumbs so they are moistened. Bake in preheated 350° oven for 25 minutes, or until fish flakes easily.

Poor Man's Lobster

6 servings

The age of this recipe may indicate that haddock was once "poor man's lobster", but the price of haddock today indicates that it is, alas, no longer, "poor man's fare".

Ingredients

2   pounds haddock fillets
1½   teaspoons vinegar
2   teaspoons salt
8   tablespoons butter or margarine, melted

Preparation

Cover fillets with cold water and add vinegar and salt. Bring to a boil and boil only 10 minutes. Serve with melted butter. Fish may be placed under broiler 1 to 2 minutes to brown.

Impossible Salmon Pie

6 servings

Ingredients

15½ ounces canned salmon, drained with skin and bones removed
1   medium onion, chopped
1   small green pepper, chopped
½   cup shredded Swiss cheese
1½   cups milk
¾   cup Bisquick
3   eggs
½   teaspoon dried tarragon
½   teaspoon salt
⅛   teaspoon pepper

Preparation

Sprinkle salmon, onion, green pepper and cheese evenly over lightly buttered 10-inch pie plate. Beat remaining ingredients until smooth. Pour into pie plate. At this point, pie may be stored, covered, for up to 24 hours in refrigerator. When ready, bake in preheated 400° oven about 35 minutes, or until knife inserted in center comes out clean.

Salmon Fettuccine

6 servings

Ingredients

15½ ounces canned salmon and liquid
 milk
1½ cups sliced fresh mushrooms
¼ cup finely chopped onion
1 small garlic clove, minced (optional)
3 tablespoons butter or margarine
¼ cup flour
¼ cup dry white wine, or ¼ cup milk
¼ cup freshly grated Parmesan cheese
2 tablespoons minced fresh parsley
⅛ teaspoon dill weed
⅛ teaspoon pepper
 salt to taste
10 ounces spinach or egg fettuccine noodles, cooked
 and drained
 additional Parmesan cheese

Preparation

Drain salmon, reserving liquid. Break into chunks, removing bones and skin. Add milk to make 1¾ cups salmon liquid. Sauté mushrooms, onion and garlic in butter until onion is tender. Add flour and stir until blended. Add milk mixture and wine. Heat and stir until mixture comes to boil. Simmer 5 minutes. Carefully stir in salmon, Parmesan cheese, dill and pepper. Salt to taste. Cook gently another 2 minutes. Serve over hot fettuccine. Pass additional Parmesan cheese.

Marinated Salmon Steaks

4 servings

Ingredients

4 fresh or frozen salmon steaks, cut 1-inch thick, about
 2 pounds
¼ cup vegetable oil
¼ cup dry white wine
1 teaspoon finely grated lime peel
2 tablespoons lime juice
2 garlic cloves, minced
¼ teaspoon white pepper

Preparation Thaw salmon if frozen. Mix oil, wine, lime peel and juice, garlic and pepper. Spread fish in non-metal dish. Coat with marinade and cover. Refrigerate 6 hours or overnight, turning salmon occasionally. Before grilling, wipe moisture from fish with paper towels. Grill on medium hot coals or on unheated rack of broiler pan, 4 inches from heat, for 7 minutes on each side. Turn at least once. Baste frequently with marinade. Fish should flake easily when done.

Fish Birds

8 servings

Ingredients
⅓   cup lemon juice
5⅓ tablespoons butter or margarine, melted
¼   teaspoon salt
¼   teaspoon pepper
1⅓ cups cooked rice
1   cup shredded Cheddar cheese
10 ounces frozen chopped broccoli, thawed, or equal amount blanched fresh broccoli
2   pounds or 8 fillets of sole, about same size
    paprika

Preparation
Mix lemon juice, butter, salt and pepper. Combine rice, cheese, broccoli and ⅓ of lemon butter. Divide among 8 fillets, roll up, placing seam side down in 7 x 11-inch buttered baking dish. Top with rest of lemon butter. Sprinkle with paprika. Bake in preheated 375° oven for 25 minutes or until fish flakes easily. If prepared ahead and refrigerated, reserve lemon butter and add when ready to bake. Add 5 minutes to baking time.

Easy Baked Fillets of Sole   4 to 6 servings

Ingredients

1   package Stove Top mushroom and onion stuffing mix,
    prepared according to package directions
6   ounces fresh crabmeat
¼   cup sour cream
1½ pounds fillet of sole
4   tablespoons butter or margarine, melted
1   tablespoon lemon juice
    freshly ground pepper to taste
¼   cup chopped fresh parsley

Preparation

Mix stuffing, crabmeat and sour cream. Spread in buttered
8 x 12-inch baking dish. Cover with fish. Drizzle with butter
and lemon juice. Sprinkle with pepper and parsley. Bake in
preheated 350° oven for 15 to 20 minutes or until fish flakes.

Shrimp Stuffed Sole   6 servings

Ingredients

1½ pounds fillet of sole
    salt and pepper to taste
    butter
½   pound cooked Maine shrimp or 6½ ounces canned
    shrimp drained and rinsed
10½ ounces cream of shrimp or cream of mushroom soup
⅓   cup dry sherry, white wine or milk
2   tablespoons lemon juice
¼   cup freshly grated Parmesan cheese
    paprika
    fresh parsley

Preparation

Season each fillet with salt and pepper, dot with butter.
Spoon shrimp to center of each and roll up, securing with
toothpicks. Place in buttered 9 x 9-inch baking dish.
Combine soup, sherry and lemon juice and pour over fish.
Sprinkle with cheese and paprika. Bake in preheated 350°
oven for 20 minutes or until fish flakes easily. Garnish with
parsley.

Broiled Swordfish

2 to 3 servings

Ingredients

1   pound swordfish
1   tablespoon fresh lemon juice
2   teaspoons fresh crushed thyme or ½ teaspoon dried
1   teaspoon fresh dill weed or ¼ teaspoon dried
     freshly ground black pepper to taste
2   tablespoons sauterne or white table wine
2   teaspoons minced parsley and lemon wedges for garnish

Preparation

Fish may be cut into portions or broiled in whole slice.
Wipe with damp cloth and pierce with fork. Sprinkle with
lemon juice, thyme, dill and pepper. Drip wine over steaks.
Broil fish about 2 inches from heat, 15 to 20 minutes, or
until tender and still moist. Garnish with parsley and lemon.

Tuna Broccoli Divan

6 to 8 servings

Ingredients

3   tablespoons butter or margarine
3   tablespoons flour
1½   cups milk
     salt and pepper to taste
¼   cup dry sherry, optional
1½   cups egg noodles, cooked according to package
     directions, drained
1½   cups broccoli, cooked
12   ounces canned tuna or pilchards, drained
½   cup dry bread crumbs
½   cup freshly grated Parmesan cheese or 1 cup grated
     Cheddar cheese or more

Preparation

Make white sauce of butter, flour, milk, salt and pepper.
Add sherry. In buttered 2-quart casserole, layer half of
noodles, cheese, half of broccoli, 1 can tuna, half of sauce.
Repeat. Top with crumbs and cheese. Bake in preheated
350° oven for 30 minutes.

Portuguese Style Marinated Fish

10 servings

Tuna recommended but good with bluefish

Ingredients

3   cups wine or cider vinegar
4   cups water
5   garlic cloves, sliced
1   tablespoon chopped red pepper or other hot pepper to taste
4   tablespoons salt
1   tablespoon pickling spice in spice bag
3 to 4 pounds thick tuna or bluefish

Preparation

Mix all ingredients except fish in large glass bowl. Place fish in bowl so that it is completely covered. Refrigerate at least 24 hours or up to 1 week. Turn and stir occasionally.

Remove fish and pat dry. Pan fry in small amount of oil or grill on single piece of foil, which has been pierced. Turn. Cook until flakes easily when tested with fork.

Variation: Marinade may also be used for 4 to 5 pounds cubed pork meat. When ready to cook, fry in ¼ cup oil for 1 hour over low heat. Turn occasionally until meat is falling apart. Spoon into hard rolls.

Trout and Fiddleheads

4 to 6 servings

Alex Delicata likes this combination

Ingredients

4 to 6 10-inch trout
¼ cup flour
¼ cup corn flour
¼ teaspoon salt
¼ teaspoon pepper
¼ teaspoon garlic powder
¼ teaspoon rosemary
½ cup vegetable oil
fiddleheads, amount your choice
4 quarts water
butter

Preparation

Clean fish well in cold water. Blend flours and spices. Shake fish in paper bag with flours and spices. Fry trout in hot oil, turning once when skins begin to crisp, 4 to 5 minutes.

Drop fiddleheads into boiling water and boil for 3 minutes only. Drain. Fiddleheads will be crunchy but cooked. Dot with butter. Serve with fish. If you can't find fresh fiddleheads in the spring, canned ones are available year-around from L.L. Bean.

One Dish Fish
6 servings

Ingredients

vegetable oil
2   pounds white fish fillets
1   tablespoon fresh dill
1   teaspoon thyme
2   tablespoons fresh lemon juice

Preparation

Generously coat 8 x 10-inch casserole with oil. Add spices and lemon juice. Coat fish in casserole by turning to cover both sides. Bake in preheated 300° oven for 30 minutes or until fish flakes.

Pan Fried Fish
3 to 4 servings

Ingredients

1   pound fresh or frozen fish fillets, thawed, cut into 3 or 4 pieces
½   cup yellow corn meal
½   cup flour
½   teaspoon dill weed or chili powder, optional
½   teaspoon salt, optional
⅛   teaspoon pepper
1   egg
2   tablespoons water
2   tablespoons margarine
2   tablespoons vegetable oil
    lemon wedges or tartar sauce for garnish

Preparation

Combine dry ingredients and coat fish. Combine egg and water. Dip fish in egg wash and coat again in dry ingredients. Pan fry in melted margarine and oil until fish flakes easily. Drain on paper towel. Serve with lemon wedges or tartar sauce.

Puffy Broiled Fillets

4 servings

Ingredients

1 pound fish fillets
freshly ground black pepper
2 tablespoons butter or margarine, melted
¼ cup tartar sauce or 1 to 2 tablespoons mustard
1 egg white, beaten stiff

Preparation

Place fillets in oiled 8 x 10-inch baking pan. Season with pepper and brush with margarine. Broil 10 minutes 3 to 4 inches from heat. Gently fold tartar sauce or mustard into egg white. When fish flakes easily, spread mixture over it and broil 2 minutes or until topping is golden.

To microwave, place fish in baking dish. Season with pepper but no margarine. Gently fold tartar sauce into egg white and spread over fish. Microwave 5 to 6 minutes on HIGH.

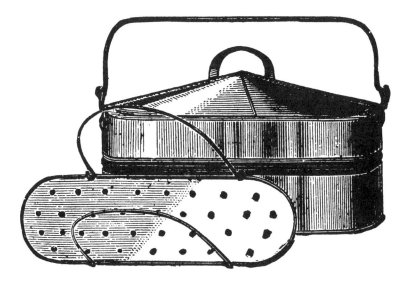

Tomato Fish Rolls
6 servings

Ingredients

¼ cup chopped celery
2 tablespoons minced onion
1 cup chopped fresh mushrooms or 1 4-ounce can, drained
2 tablespoons butter or margarine
⅓ cup water
1 cup Pepperidge Farm stuffing mix
salt to taste
6 fish fillets
8 ounces seasoned tomato sauce

Preparation

Sauté celery, onion and mushrooms in butter until golden. Add water and stuffing mix. Salt each fillet. Divide stuffing and place on fish. Roll up and place seam side down in buttered 9 x 9-inch baking dish. Pour tomato sauce over fish, cover with foil and bake in preheated 350° oven for 10 minutes. Remove foil and bake 15 minutes more, or until fish flakes easily when tested with fork.

Desserts

Allie's Mama's Filled Cookies

2½ dozen

This is the story of these old-fashioned cookies. Ada Holbrook, who was Allie's Mama to Marjorie Holbrook Standish growing up in Brunswick, kept one drawer of her Hoosier kitchen cabinet always filled with these cookies. The Hoosier cabinet was the first Marjorie ever saw and these cookies were her favorite. After the death of her husband, Ada brought up 7 children on their rambling New Meadows River farm. Many of her descendants continue to live in Brunswick.

Ingredients

Dough:
8   tablespoons margarine
½   teaspoon salt
1   teaspoon vanilla extract
1   cup sugar
1   egg
2½ cups sifted flour
2   teaspoons cream of tartar
1   teaspoon soda
½   cup milk

Filling:
1   cup chopped raisins
1   teaspoon flour
½   teaspoon salt
1   cup cold water

Preparation

Cream shortening, adding salt and vanilla. Add sugar gradually. Add unbeaten egg, creaming mixture until light and fluffy. Sift flour with cream of tartar and soda. Add to creamed mixture alternately with milk. Roll cookie dough on floured board. Use 3-inch cookie cutter to make about 60 cookies. Using wide spatula, lift ½ of cookies and place on greased cookie sheets. Place 1 teaspoon raisin filling on each, top with another cookie. Lightly press tops in place. Bake in preheated 400° oven for 8 to 10 minutes, or until lightly browned.

For filling, combine raisins, flour and salt. Add water. Cook over low heat until thickened. Cool.

Almond Buttons

8 dozen

Ingredients

2 cups blanched almonds
2 cups flour
¾ cup confectioners' sugar
¼ teaspoon salt
1 cup and 1½ tablespoons butter, softened
1 teaspoon vanilla extract
¼ teaspoon almond extract
3 ounces semi-sweet chocolate

Preparation

Finely grind 1 cup almonds in food processor or blender. Add flour, sugar and salt. Thoroughly work in 1 cup butter, vanilla and almond extracts by hand until soft dough forms. Dough should not crumble. Chill. Shape into ½ inch balls. Place 1 inch apart on ungreased cookie sheets, pressing centers with finger. Bake in preheated 350° oven for 15 minutes. Cookies will only color slightly. Remove to wire rack. Cool.

Melt chocolate and remaining butter. With spoon, drizzle small amount of chocolate into center of each cookie. Top with remaining almonds.

Apricot Nut Balls

4 dozen

Ingredients

2 eggs, slightly beaten
1 cup sugar
1 cup sweetened flaked coconut
1 cup chopped walnuts, pecans or almonds
1 cup chopped dried apricots
½ cup chopped dates
1 teaspoon vanilla extract
½ teaspoon almond extract

Preparation

Beat eggs, mix in sugar and add coconut, nuts, apricots and dates. Cook over medium heat for 10 to 15 minutes, stirring constantly. Add vanilla and almond extracts. Cool completely.

Form mixture into 1-inch balls, roll and press in granulated sugar to coat evenly. Let stand to set. Store in covered container in refrigerator.

Aunt Dot's Sugar Cookies   3 dozen

Ingredients

1   cup butter or margarine
1½   cups powdered sugar
1   egg
1½   teaspoons vanilla extract
2½   cups flour
1   teaspoon baking soda
1   teaspoon cream of tartar

Preparation

Cream butter with sugar. Beat in egg and vanilla. Sift flour, baking soda and cream of tartar, add and mix well. Chill. Roll into walnut-size balls. Place on lightly greased cookie sheet, 2 inches apart. Flatten balls with spatula dipped in milk and sprinkle with sugar. Bake in preheated 375° oven for 8 to 10 minutes.

Aunt Lu's Brownies   15 servings

From 1920's — still a RMH Coffee Shop favorite

Ingredients

½   cup butter or margarine, melted
1   cup sugar
2   eggs
½   cup flour
2   ounces unsweetened chocolate
1   teaspoon vanilla extract
1   cup large walnut pieces

Preparation

Combine butter and sugar. Beat eggs and add to mixture. Stir in flour. Melt chocolate and stir in well. Add vanilla and nuts. Pour into greased 7 x 11-inch pan. Bake in preheated 400° oven for 20 to 22 minutes. May use 8 x 8-inch pan, adjusting baking time to 25 minutes. A crusty top makes these brownies special.

Canadian Bars

40 bars

A delicious no-bake bar

Ingredients

Crust:
½ cup butter or margarine, melted
¼ cup sugar
⅓ cup cocoa
1 teaspoon vanilla extract
1 egg
2 cups graham cracker crumbs
1 cup shredded coconut
½ cup chopped pecans

Topping:
¼ cup butter or margarine, softened
2 tablespoons vanilla instant pudding powder
3 tablespoons milk
2 cups sifted confectioners' sugar

Glaze:
3 ounces semi-sweet chocolate chips
1 tablespoon butter or margarine

Preparation

Combine melted butter and remaining ingredients for crust. Mix well. Press into greased 9 x 13-inch pan. Blend topping ingredients together. Beat until creamy and smooth. Spread over crumb layer. Chill well. Melt chocolate and butter over hot water. Spread over chilled mixture. Chill until set. Remove and let stand 10 minutes for ease in cutting. Cut into finger-size bars. Will keep many days in the refrigerator or can be frozen.

Chess Bars

3 dozen

Good to take on the boat

Ingredients

Pastry:
½ cup margarine
2 tablespoons sugar
1 cup flour

Filling:
2 eggs
1½ cups brown sugar
2 tablespoons flour
1 teaspoon baking powder
1 tablespoon grated lemon rind
1 cup chopped pecans

Preparation

Cream margarine and 2 tablespoons sugar until light and fluffy. Add 1 cup flour, mixing well. Pat dough firmly into bottom of 9-inch square baking pan. Bake in preheated 350° oven for 10 minutes.

For filling, beat eggs well, add brown sugar, flour, baking powder and lemon rind. Blend well. Stir in pecans and pour over partially baked pastry layer. Bake at 350° for 25 minutes. When slightly cooled, cut into small bars.

Rocks

4 dozen

Ingredients

¾ cup light brown sugar
¾ cup white sugar
1 cup shortening
2 eggs
3 cups flour
1 teaspoon salt
1 teaspoon baking soda
1½ teaspoons cinnamon
1½ teaspoons nutmeg
2 tablespoons milk

1   pound pitted dates, coarsely chopped
1   cup coarsely chopped nuts

Preparation   Cream sugars and shortening. Add eggs and beat well. Stir in dry ingredients and milk. Add dates and nuts. Drop by generous tablespoon onto greased cookie sheets. Flatten with spatula dipped in milk. Bake in preheated 375° oven for 8 to 10 minutes, or until brown.

French Squares   4 dozen

Ingredients

Crust:
½   cup butter or margarine
½   cup light brown sugar
1   cup flour

Topping:
1   cup light brown sugar
2   eggs, beaten
1   teaspoon vanilla extract
½   cup sweetened flaked coconut
1   tablespoon flour
½   teaspoon baking powder
1   cup nuts, coarsely chopped
    confectioners' sugar

Preparation   Prepare crust by mixing butter and sugar until creamy. Add flour and blend well. Press evenly into bottom of greased 8 x 12-inch baking pan. Bake in preheated 300° oven for 20 minutes or until golden. Cool.

Prepare topping by mixing ingredients. Spread gently over cooled base. Bake at 350° for 20 minutes. Cool. Cut into desired size squares and sprinkle with confectioners' sugar.

Fudge Nut Oatmeal Squares   3 dozen

Ingredients

Oatmeal layer:
½ cup margarine, softened
1 cup light brown sugar, firmly packed
1 egg
½ teaspoon vanilla extract
¾ cup flour
½ teaspoon baking soda
½ teaspoon salt
2 cups rolled oats
½ cup coconut
½ cup chopped nuts

Fudge layer:
1 cup semi-sweet chocolate pieces
1 tablespoon margarine
⅓ cup sweetened condensed milk
½ cup chopped nuts
1 teaspoon vanilla extract

Preparation

Beat margarine and sugar until light and fluffy. Add egg and vanilla, beating well. Sift flour, baking soda and salt into sugar mixture. Mix well. Stir in oats, coconut and nuts. Reserve 1 cup of oatmeal mixture for topping. Press rest of mixture into greased 9 x 9-inch baking pan.

For fudge layer, combine chocolate, margarine and milk in saucepan. Cook, stirring, over low heat until chocolate and margarine melt. Remove from heat. Stir in nuts and vanilla. Spread over oatmeal layer. Sprinkle top with reserved mixture. Bake in preheated 350° oven for 25 minutes or until top is lightly browned. Cool before cutting into 1½-inch squares.

Ginger Snap Cookies   6 dozen

Ingredients

2 cups sifted flour
2 teaspoons baking soda
2 teaspoons ginger

½ teaspoon salt
¾ cup shortening
1 cup sugar
1 egg
¼ cup molasses
1 teaspoon vanilla extract

Preparation Sift flour, baking soda, ginger and salt. Cream shortening and sugar. Add egg and beat. Add molasses and vanilla. Beat until fluffy. Stir in flour mixture. Chill overnight. Roll into 1-inch balls and dip in sugar. Bake on greased cookie sheet in preheated 350° oven for 8 to 10 minutes or until done. Cookies should be crisp when cool.

Gourmet Chocolate Chip Cookies

2 dozen

The ultimate taste treat for chocolate chip cookie lovers

Ingredients
1 cup unsalted butter, softened
1 cup light brown sugar, firmly packed
1 cup dark brown sugar, firmly packed
2 large eggs
1 tablespoon vanilla extract
2½ cups flour
2 teaspoons salt
1 teaspoon baking powder
4 cups walnuts, chopped
3 cups semi-sweet chocolate bits

Preparation Beat butter and sugars until light and creamy. Beat in eggs, 1 at a time. Add vanilla and mix well. Combine flour, salt and baking powder. Add to mixture and stir well. Add nuts and mix in evenly. Carefully add chocolate bits. Chill dough 1 hour.

Drop dough by ¼ cup measure on greased baking sheet, making sure to place portions 3 inches apart to allow for spreading. Bake in preheated 375° oven for 12 to 15 minutes or until light golden brown. Let cool on baking sheet before removing to wire rack. Store in airtight container if they last that long.

Joe Froggers

2 dozen

A much-loved big old-fashioned molasses cookie

Ingredients

½ cup shortening
1 cup sugar
1 cup dark molasses
½ cup water
4 cups flour
1½ teaspoons salt
1 teaspoon baking soda
1½ teaspoons ginger
½ teaspoon cloves
½ teaspoon nutmeg
¼ teaspoon allspice

Preparation

Cream shortening and sugar until light. Stir in molasses and water. Sift dry ingredients and blend into shortening mixture. Chill several hours or overnight. Roll dough ¼ inch thick on floured board. Cut into 3-inch circles. Sprinkle with sugar and place on well-buttered cookie sheet. Bake in preheated 375° oven for 10 to 12 minutes. Leave on cookie sheet for few minutes before removing, to prevent breaking. Store in covered container.

Lemon Wafers

2 dozen

Crisp, light cookie with refreshing lemon flavor

Ingredients

½ cup butter or margarine
¾ cup sugar
1 egg
2 teaspoons freshly grated lemon rind
1½ cups sifted flour
½ teaspoon salt
½ teaspoon baking soda
1 tablespoon lemon juice

Preparation   Cream butter and sugar together. Add egg and lemon rind,
                 beating well. Sift flour, salt and baking soda together. Slowly
                 beat in flour mixture, a little at a time, then add lemon
                 juice. Chill dough at least 1 hour. Shape dough by
                 tablespoons (or teaspoons for smaller cookies) into balls.
                 Roll in sugar until coated. Place 2 inches apart on greased
                 cookie sheets. With fork, press to flatten. Bake in preheated
                 375° oven for 10 to 12 minutes or until golden. Remove to
                 rack to cool.

Mocha Nut Tarts   4 dozen

Ingredients   *Crust:*
                  1¾ cups flour
                  ⅓   cup cocoa
                  ¼   cup sugar
                  ¾   cup chilled butter or unsalted margarine, cut into
                      pieces.
                  ⅓ to ½ cup strong coffee, chilled

                  Filling:
                  1   12-ounce package semi-sweet chocolate chips, melted
                  ⅔   cup sugar
                  2   tablespoons butter or margarine, melted
                  2   tablespoons milk
                  1   tablespoon coffee liqueur
                  2   eggs, room temperature
                  ½   cup finely chopped walnuts

Preparation   Sift flour, cocoa and sugar. Add butter and cut in until
                  consistency of coarse meal. Mix in coffee gradually until
                  soft dough forms. Wrap and chill several hours or overnight.
                  Lightly grease miniature muffin pans. Cut dough into
                  quarters and each quarter into 12 pieces. Press each piece
                  into muffin tins to form cups.

                  For filling, combine melted chips, sugar, butter, milk, and
                  coffee liqueur. Blend well. Add eggs, beating until smooth.
                  Stir in nuts. Place 1 rounded teaspoon filling in each pastry
                  lined muffin cup. Bake in preheated 350° oven for 20 to 25
                  minutes, or until filling is set. Cool in pans 15 minutes, then
                  transfer to racks to cool completely.

Orange Walnut Tea Cookies 3 dozen

Low in sugar

Ingredients

½ cup butter
¼ cup sugar
1 large egg, separated
   finely grated rind of 1 orange
   finely grated rind of 1 lemon
1 teaspoon fresh lemon juice
1 cup flour
1½ teaspoons water
1 cup walnuts, finely chopped

Preparation

Cream butter and sugar. Beat in egg yolk, orange and lemon rinds and lemon juice. Gently blend in flour. Cover dough and chill until firm enough to handle. Shape dough into balls, using generous ½ tablespoon for each. Beat egg white and water. Dip each ball into egg white mixture, then roll lightly in walnuts.

Bake, 1-inch apart, on greased cookie sheet in preheated 325° oven for 20 to 25 minutes or until bottoms are lightly browned. Remove to rack to cool. Store in airtight container.

Quick and Easy Oatmeal Cookies 3 to 4 dozen

A quick energy, wholesome snack

Ingredients

1 cup light brown sugar
1 cup white sugar
1 cup Crisco
2 eggs
1 teaspoon vanilla extract
1½ cups flour
1 teaspoon salt
1 teaspoon baking soda
3 cups rolled oats
   raisins or chopped nuts, if desired

Preparation   Cream sugars and Crisco until light. Beat in eggs and
vanilla. Sift flour, salt and baking soda and add to creamed
mixture. Stir in oatmeal and raisins or nuts. Drop by
heaping teaspoons onto ungreased cookie sheet. Bake in
preheated 350° oven for 10 minutes. Cool on rack before
storing.

Very Orange Date Nut Bars   3 dozen

Ingredients   3   eggs
6   ounces frozen orange juice concentrate, thawed
1   cup sugar
2   cups graham cracker crumbs
1   teaspoon baking powder
¼   teaspoon salt
1   cup walnuts or pecans, finely chopped
8   ounces pitted dates, chopped
1   teaspoon vanilla extract

Glaze:
1¼   cups confectioners' sugar
2½   tablespoons orange juice

Preparation   Beat eggs until light and fluffy. Beat in orange juice. Blend
in remaining ingredients. Mix well. Spread in greased and
lightly floured 9-inch square pan. Bake in preheated 350°
oven for 50 minutes. Beat confectioners' sugar and orange
juice until smooth and spread glaze over bars. Cut into
1½-inch squares.

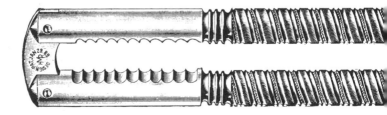

Chocolate Chiffon Pie

6 to 8 servings

A rich chocolate-flavored pie

Ingredients

Crust:
1½ cups graham crackers, finely rolled
¼ cup butter or margarine, softened
¼ cup sugar
½ cup finely chopped nuts

Filling:
1 envelope unflavored gelatin
¼ cup cold water
½ cup boiling water
2 ounces unsweetened chocolate
3 eggs, separated
⅓ cup sugar
¼ teaspoon salt
1 teaspoon vanilla extract
½ cup sugar
1 cup heavy cream, whipped, with 2 tablespoons sugar

Syrup:
1½ tablespoons light corn syrup
½ ounce unsweetened chocolate

Preparation

Mix crust ingredients and press evenly on sides and bottom of 9-inch pie plate. Bake in preheated 375° oven for 8 minutes. Chill.

Soften gelatin in cold water. Combine boiling water and chocolate, and stir over low heat until blended. Remove from heat and add softened gelatin. Stir until dissolved. Beat egg yolks until thick and light. Gradually beat in ⅓ cup sugar, salt and vanilla. Stir in chocolate mixture. Be sure not to curdle egg yolks. Chill until mixture mounds when spooned.

Beat egg whites to soft peaks. Gradually add ½ cup sugar, and continue beating until stiff peaks form. Gently fold in chocolate mixture. Pile into crust. Chill until firm. Top with whipped cream. Make syrup by stirring corn syrup and chocolate over low heat to blend. Drizzle over whipped cream.

4th of July Pecan Cheese Pie 8 servings

A wonderful way to celebrate America's birthday

Ingredients

1   10-inch unbaked pie shell

Cheese layer:
8   ounces cream cheese, softened
1   egg
⅓   cup sugar
1   teaspoon vanilla extract
1¼   cups pecans, coarsely chopped

Pecan filling:
3   eggs
1   cup light corn syrup
¼   cup sugar
¼   teaspoon salt
1   teaspoon vanilla extract
     whipped cream and pecan halves for garnish

Preparation

Beat cream cheese, 1 egg, ⅓ cup sugar and 1 teaspoon vanilla until smooth. Spread over bottom of unbaked pie shell. Sprinkle with 1¼ cups pecans. For filling, beat remaining eggs until foamy. Add corn syrup, sugar, salt and vanilla. Beat to blend well. Pour over pecans. Bake in preheated 375° oven for 40 minutes, or until knife inserted halfway between center and edge comes out clean. Cool and garnish with whipped cream and pecan halves.

Frozen Crunchy Strawberry Pie

6 to 8 servings

Ingredients

Buttercrunch crust:
½ cup butter or margarine
¼ cup light brown sugar
1   cup flour
½ cup chopped pecans

Filling:
2   cups fresh strawberries, mashed, or 1 10-ounce package frozen strawberries, thawed
1   egg white, unbeaten
½ cup sugar
2   tablespoons lemon juice
½ cup heavy cream
fresh strawberries for garnish

Preparation

Mix crust ingredients. Pour into 9 x 13-inch baking pan and spread evenly. Bake in preheated 400° oven for 15 minutes. Stir with fork occasionally to brown evenly. Cool. Remove and reserve ½ cup for topping. Press remainder into 9-inch pie plate and chill.

Beat strawberries, egg white, sugar and lemon juice until thick, about 5 minutes. Beat heavy cream until thick and fold into strawberry mixture. Pour into crumb-lined pie plate. Top with reserved crumbs. Freeze for 3 hours before serving. Garnish with strawberries.

Georgetown Blueberry Pie

6 to 8 servings

Fresh blueberries at their best

Ingredients

1   9-inch baked pie shell

Filling:
4   cups fresh Maine blueberries
1   cup sugar

1   cup water
3   tablespoons flour
¼   teaspoon salt
     whipped cream and big blueberries for garnish

Preparation   Cook 1 cup blueberries, 1 cup sugar and ¾ cup water until soft. Make paste of flour, ¼ cup water and salt. Add to blueberry mixture, stirring constantly, and cook until thick. Gently fold in remaining 3 cups blueberries. Mix well and pour into pie shell. Chill for 3 hours. Serve with whipped cream dusted with cinnamon. Garnish with blueberries.

High Head Blueberry Pie   6 to 8 servings

Ingredients   1   9-inch unbaked pie shell

Filling:
4   cups fresh blueberries
⅔   cup sugar
¼   cup flour
½   teaspoon cinnamon
¼   teaspoon salt
¼   cup milk
¼   cup heavy or whipping cream
     whipped cream or ice cream for garnish

Preparation   Pour blueberries into pie shell. Combine sugar, flour, cinnamon and salt. Stir in milk and cream with whisk and mix well. Pour over blueberries. Liquid will not completely cover blueberries but try to distribute evenly. Bake in preheated 400° oven for 45 minutes. Cool and refrigerate. Serve with whipped cream or ice cream.

Heavenly Pie

8 servings

Ingredients

1   9-inch baked pie shell

Filling:
4   eggs, separated
1   cup sugar
½   cup orange juice, strained
¼   cup lemon juice, strained
1   envelope unflavored gelatin, softened in ¼ cup cold water
1   banana, mashed
    grated rind 1 orange
    orange and banana slices for garnish

Preparation

Beat egg yolks with ½ cup sugar, add orange and lemon juices. Cook mixture, stirring constantly, over hot water until thick and creamy. Remove from heat and add softened gelatin. Cool. Add banana and orange rind. Beat egg whites until stiff but not dry. Gradually add ½ cup sugar. Blend well. Fold into fruited custard mixture. Pour into pie shell. Chill well before serving. Garnish with orange and banana slices. Make no more than 1 day in advance.

Luscious Pineapple Cheese Pie

6 to 8 servings

Ingredients

1   9-inch unbaked pie shell

Filling:
⅓   cup sugar
1   tablespoon cornstarch
1   9-ounce can crushed pineapple, undrained

Cheese topping:
8   ounces cream cheese, softened
½   cup sugar
2   eggs
½   cup milk
½   teaspoon vanilla extract
¼   cup finely chopped pecans

Preparation

Blend sugar with cornstarch. Add pineapple. Cook, stirring constantly, until mixture is thick and clear. Cool.

Beat cream cheese with sugar. Add eggs, 1 at a time, beating well after each addition. Blend in milk and vanilla. Spread cooled pineapple filling over bottom of unbaked pie shell. Cover with cream cheese mixture. Sprinkle with pecans. Bake in preheated 400° oven for 10 minutes. Reduce heat to 325° and continue baking for 40 minutes. Cool well before serving.

Mocha Fudge Mud Pie

10 servings

Pure elegance and "do ahead" at that

Ingredients

Crust:
8½ ounces chocolate wafers
½ cup butter or margarine

Filling:
1 quart coffee ice cream, softened

Sauce:
⅓ cup cocoa
⅔ cup sugar
⅓ cup heavy cream
3 tablespoons butter or margarine
1 teaspoon vanilla extract

Topping:
1 cup heavy cream
2 tablespoons sugar
1 teaspoon vanilla extract
2 ounces semi-sweet chocolate for garnish

Preparation

In blender or food processor, blend chocolate wafers to fine crumbs. Melt butter and add to crumbs, mixing well. Press mixture to bottom and sides of 9-inch pie plate. Bake in preheated 375° oven for 10 minutes. Cool completely.

Carefully spread softened coffee ice cream in crust. Freeze until firm, about 1½ hours.

For sauce, combine cocoa, sugar, cream and butter, and cook until mixture is smooth and boils. Remove from heat and stir in vanilla. Cool. Pour over ice cream and return pie to freezer. Freeze until firm.

Whip heavy cream with sugar and vanilla. Beat until soft peaks form. Spread whipped cream over pie. Pie may be served at this point or returned to freezer to freeze whipped cream layer. Garnish with curls made from semi-sweet chocolate.

Pennellville Red Raspberry Pie

6 to 8 servings

Ingredients

pastry for 2-crust 9-inch pie

Filling:
4   cups fresh raspberries
1   cup sugar
⅓   cup black currant liqueur
4   tablespoons cornstarch
1   tablespoon fresh lemon juice
    pinch of salt
2   tablespoons unsalted butter
4   very thin lemon slices

Preparation

Gently toss raspberries and sugar. Whisk liqueur and cornstarch together, adding lemon juice and salt. Stir into berries.

Roll out ⅔ of pastry and line pie plate. Leave edges untrimmed. Spoon in berries, dot with butter and arrange lemon slices overlapping slightly in center of berries. Roll out remaining pastry into 10-inch round. Cut into ½ inch strips. Arrange over berries in lattice pattern. Trim overhanging pastry. Bring edge of lower crust over lattice and crimp edge.

Bake in preheated 425° oven for 15 minutes. Lower heat to 350° and bake for another 30 to 40 minutes, or until crust is golden brown and filling is bubbling.

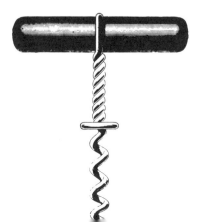

Rhubarb Cheesecake Pie

6 to 8 servings

A nice combination of tastes

Ingredients

1   9-inch unbaked pie shell

Filling:
3   cups rhubarb, cut into ½ inch pieces
½   cup sugar
1   tablespoon flour

Cheese topping:
2   eggs
1   cup sugar
8   ounces cream cheese, softened

Preparation

Toss rhubarb with ½ cup sugar and flour. Add to pie shell. Bake in preheated 425° oven for 15 to 20 minutes.

Beat eggs with 1 cup sugar and cream cheese until smooth. Pour over rhubarb. Reduce heat to 350° and continue baking for 30 minutes. Cool before serving.

Sour Cream Lime Pie

6 servings

Ingredients

1   9-inch baked pie shell

Filling:
1   cup sugar
3   tablespoons cornstarch
¼   cup butter
2 to 4 teaspoons grated lime rind
⅓   cup lime juice
1   cup light cream
1   cup sour cream

Whipped sour cream topping:
1   cup heavy cream
1   tablespoon confectioners' sugar
1   cup sour cream
    thin slices of lime for garnish

Preparation   Combine sugar, cornstarch, butter, lime rind, lime juice and light cream in saucepan. Bring slowly to a boil, stirring constantly. Cook until thickened and smooth. Remove from heat. Cool. Fold in sour cream. Pour mixture into pie shell.

Whip heavy cream. Fold in sugar and sour cream. Spoon over pie. Sprinkle with more grated rind, if desired. Garnish with thin slices of lime. Chill before serving.

Tart Lemony Pie
6 to 8 servings

Ingredients   1   9-inch baked pie shell or 1 graham cracker pie shell

Filling:
½   cup freshly squeezed lemon juice
1½   teaspoons grated lemon rind
14   ounces condensed milk
2   eggs and 1 egg white
¼   teaspoon cream of tartar
4   tablespoons sugar

Preparation   Combine lemon juice and rind. Gradually stir into condensed milk. Separate eggs. Add yolks to mixture and blend well. Pour into baked shell. Add cream of tartar to egg whites. Beat to soft peaks. Add sugar while beating and continue until stiff peaks form. Pile lightly on filling, spreading to edge of crust. Bake in preheated 325° oven until meringue is lightly browned.

Alabama Pound Cake   20 servings

A large fine-textured cake that improves with age

Ingredients

1   cup butter, softened
2¾ cups sugar
6   large eggs
3   cups sifted flour
½   teaspoon salt
¼   teaspoon baking soda
1   cup sour cream
1½ teaspoons vanilla extract

Preparation

Cream butter and sugar, beating until light and fluffy. Add eggs, 1 at a time, beating well after each addition. Sift dry ingredients and add alternately with sour cream to creamed mixture. Beat until smooth. Blend in vanilla.

Pour batter into greased and floured 9-inch tube pan. Bake in preheated 350° oven for 1 hour and 20 minutes, or until tests done. Remove from oven and let stand in pan 10 minutes. Turn out on rack to cool. Frost with Elegant Icing, if desired.

Elegant Icing

Ingredients

½   cup butter
½   cup evaporated milk
2   cups sugar
¼   cup white corn syrup
⅛   teaspoon salt
1   teaspoon vanilla extract

Preparation

Combine all ingredients, except vanilla. Cook, stirring, over medium heat until mixture comes to a boil. Boil 2 minutes. Remove from heat and add vanilla. Beat until consistency to spread on cake.

Blackberry Jam Cake

10 to 12 servings

Ingredients

¾   cup butter or margarine, softened
1   cup sugar
3   eggs
1   cup buttermilk
3   cups cake flour, sifted
1   teaspoon cinnamon
1   teaspoon mace
1   teaspoon nutmeg
1½ teaspoons baking soda dissolved in 1 teaspoon hot
     water
1   cup blackberry jam
     butter icing, recipe of choice

Preparation

Cream butter and sugar. Add eggs and beat thoroughly. Add baking soda and water to buttermilk. Sift dry ingredients and add to creamed mixture alternately with buttermilk. Fold in jam and mix well. Pour into 2 well-greased and floured 9-inch round cake pans. Bake in preheated 350° oven for 30 to 40 minutes. Remove from oven and cool 5 minutes before removing from pans. When cool, frost with butter icing of choice.

Chocolate Truffle Cake

10 servings

For the chocoholic's birthday

Ingredients

16 ounces semi-sweet chocolate
½ cup unsalted butter
1½ teaspoons flour
1½ teaspoons sugar
1 teaspoon hot water
4 eggs, separated
1 cup whipping cream
confectioners' sugar
rum or vanilla extract
chocolate leaves for garnish

Preparation

Melt chocolate and butter in top of double boiler. Add flour, sugar and water. Blend well. Remove from heat. Add egg yolks, one at a time, beating until smooth each time. Beat egg whites until stiff but not dry. Carefully fold whites into chocolate mixture. Grease bottom only of 8-inch springform pan. Pour in batter. Spread evenly. Bake in preheated 425° oven for 15 minutes.

Cake will look unbaked in center. Let cool completely in pan before serving, chilling if necessary. Whip cream and sweeten with confectioners' sugar to taste. Flavor with rum or vanilla. Spread over center of cake. Garnish with chocolate leaves.

Chocolate Leaves

Create a masterpiece that delights the eye as well as the palate

Ingredients

8 ounces semi-sweet chocolate
1 tablespoon vegetable shortening
small waxy green leaves, such as begonia, ivy or violet

Preparation   Melt chocolate and shortening in double boiler over hot
water. Using spoon or brush, generously coat undersides of
leaves. Chill until firm. Loosen carefully and peel away green
leaf. Keep chilled until used as garnish.

Downeast Raspberry Cake   12 servings

Excellent picnic fare

Ingredients   ⅓   cup butter or margarine
1   cup sugar
1   egg
3   teaspoons baking powder
½   teaspoon salt
2   cups sifted flour
1   cup milk
1   teaspoon vanilla extract
1   pint fresh raspberries

Glaze:
1½   cups sifted confectioners' sugar
1   teaspoon butter, melted
3   tablespoons heavy cream

Preparation   Cream margarine and sugar. Add egg and beat. Sift dry
ingredients. Add milk and vanilla alternately with dry
ingredients to creamed mixture. Mix until smooth. Pour
batter into greased and floured 9 x 13-inch baking pan.
Sprinkle raspberries evenly over batter. Bake in preheated
375° oven for 30 minutes.

Mix confectioners' sugar, butter and heavy cream for glaze.
Frost in pan while still warm.

Elegant Jelly Roll

12 servings

Ingredients

5   eggs, separated
¾   cup sugar
1   tablespoon grated fresh lemon rind
2   tablespoons fresh lemon juice
1   cup sifted cake flour
¼   teaspoon salt
     confectioners' sugar, sifted
1   cup apricot, raspberry or strawberry jam or jelly, or
1   cup lemon curd

Preparation

Beat egg whites until stiff but not dry. Add ½ cup sugar slowly, beating constantly. Set aside. Beat egg yolks separately until thick and lemon colored. Add ¼ cup sugar gradually, continuing to beat until stiff enough to hold soft peaks. Add lemon juice and rind. Fold this mixture gently into egg whites. Combine flour and salt and fold quickly but lightly into egg mixture.

Line greased 11 x 16-inch jelly roll pan with wax paper. Grease wax paper. Pour in batter. Bake in preheated 350° oven for 14 minutes. Be careful not to overbake. Turn onto clean tea towel well sprinkled with confectioners' sugar. Remove wax paper. Trim edges. Place clean sheet of wax paper on cake while still warm. Roll, lifting widest side of towel, to form long roll. Wrap in towel until cool. Unroll carefully to prevent breaking cake. Remove wax paper. Spread with whipped or softened jelly, jam or curd. Roll up. Top may be sprinkled with more confectioners' sugar. Slice and serve.

Fern's Nut Cake

9 servings

No egg yolks or dairy products

Ingredients

½   cup vegetable shortening
1½ cups sugar
3   teaspoons baking powder
¼   teaspoon salt
2   cups flour

1   teaspoon vanilla extract
⅔   cup water
4   egg whites
1   cup ground walnuts or pecans

Preparation   Cream shortening and sugar. Sift dry ingredients 4 times. Add vanilla to water and add alternately with flour mixture to creamed mixture. Beat egg whites to soft peaks and fold in with nuts. Pour into greased and floured 9 x 9-inch pan. Bake in preheated 350° oven for 35 to 40 minutes. Delicious served plain or with frosting of choice.

Howard's Blueberry Cake   9 servings

Ingredients   ⅓   cup butter or margarine
½   cup light brown sugar
½   cup white sugar
1   egg
1¾   cups sifted flour
2   teaspoons baking powder
¼   teaspoon each, salt, cinnamon and nutmeg
¾   cup milk
1   teaspoon grated lemon rind
1   cup fresh blueberries

Icing:
1   tablespoon butter
2   tablespoons fresh lemon juice
1   cup confectioners' sugar, or enough to make thin icing

Preparation   Cream butter and sugars. Add egg and beat thoroughly. Sift dry ingredients several times and add alternately with milk into cream mixture. Mix well after each addition. Stir in grated lemon rind and fold in blueberries carefully. Pour batter into 9 x 9-inch or 7 x 11-inch baking pan, leveling top and filling corners. Bake in preheated 350° oven for 45 minutes, or until tests done.

Mix icing ingredients and spread over warm cake.

Knobby Apple Cake

9 servings

From the Massachusetts Extension Service about 50 years ago

Ingredients

2   tablespoons butter or margarine
1   cup sugar
1   egg
1   teaspoon vanilla extract
3   cups peeled and chopped apples
½   teaspoon cinnamon
½   teaspoon nutmeg
½   teaspoon salt
1   teaspoon baking soda
1   cup sifted flour
½   cup chopped walnuts

Preparation

Cream margarine and sugar. Add beaten egg and vanilla. Mix well. Stir in apples. Sift dry ingredients and add to apple mixture. Blend well and add nuts. Pour into greased and floured 8 x 8-inch baking pan. Bake in preheated 350° oven for 35 to 40 minutes. Serve warm from pan or let cool. May be served with whipped cream or vanilla ice cream. If baked in 9 x 13-inch pan, cake is thinner and can be cut into bars. Adjust baking time if using larger pan.

Maine Blueberry Bundt Cake

10 to 12 servings

Ingredients

3 cups flour
1½ teaspoons baking powder
¾ teaspoon baking soda
¼ teaspoon salt
¾ cup butter or margarine, softened
1½ cups sugar
4 eggs
1½ teaspoons vanilla extract
1 cup sour cream or plain yogurt
2 cups blueberries

Streusel filling:
¼ cup light brown sugar
1 tablespoon flour
½ teaspoon cinnamon

Icing:
1 cup sifted confectioners' sugar
2 tablespoons milk or cream

Preparation

Sift flour, baking powder, baking soda and salt. Cream butter and sugar until light and fluffy. Add eggs 1 at a time, beating well after each addition. Add vanilla. Add sour cream or yogurt alternately with flour mixture, ending with flour mixture. Mix well. Grease and flour 10-inch tube or bundt pan.

Mix streusel filling. Pour ½ batter into prepared pan. Sprinkle 1 cup blueberries over batter. Evenly sprinkle streusel over blueberries. Add rest of batter. Sprinkle remaining blueberries on top. Blueberries will sink into batter and distribute evenly throughout cake.

Bake in preheated 375° oven for 1 hour or until tests done. Cool in pan for 20 minutes. Gently turn out. Combine sugar and milk for icing and drizzle over cake.

Maine Blueberry Gingerbread

9 to 12 servings

From the Maine Department of Agriculture

Ingredients

½ cup shortening
1 cup sugar
1 egg
2 cups sifted flour
½ teaspoon ginger
1 teaspoon cinnamon
½ teaspoon salt
1 cup sour milk or buttermilk
1 teaspoon baking soda
3 tablespoons molasses
1 cup blueberries, fresh or frozen
3 tablespoons sugar

Preparation

Cream shortening and sugar. Add egg and mix well. Mix and sift together flour, ginger, cinnamon and salt. Add to creamed mixture alternately with sour milk, in which soda has been dissolved. Add molasses. Carefully fold in blueberries and pour batter into greased and floured 9 x 9-inch pan. Sprinkle 3 tablespoons of sugar over batter. Bake in preheated 350° oven for 50 minutes to 1 hour. Sugar makes sweet, crusty topping when cake is baked.

Molasses Gingerbread

8 servings

Handed down from Mother

Ingredients

½ cup shortening
½ cup sugar
1 egg
1 cup molasses
1 teaspoon baking soda
½ teaspoon salt
1 teaspoon ginger
2½ cups flour
1 cup boiling water

Preparation   Cream shortening and sugar. Add egg and beat until light
and fluffy. Beat in molasses. Sift dry ingredients and add
alternately with water. Mix to smooth batter. Pour into
greased and floured 9 x 9-inch pan. Bake in preheated 350°
oven for 50 minutes or until tests done.

Serve with sweetened whipped cream or for delicious
change, try Pumpkin Cream Topping.

Pumpkin Cream Topping   8 servings

Ingredients   1   cup chilled whipping cream
¼   cup sifted confectioners' sugar
¾   teaspoon pumpkin pie spice
½   cup cooked and puréed pumpkin

Preparation   Combine cream, confectioners' sugar and pumpkin pie spice
in chilled mixing bowl. Beat until stiff peaks form. Fold
chilled pumpkin into flavored cream. Serve as topping on
gingerbread.

Quick Raised Cake

12 servings

For afternoon tea

Ingredients

½   cup shortening
1   cup sugar
1   egg
1   teaspoon lemon extract
1   cup milk, scalded and cooled
2¼ cups flour
½   teaspoon baking soda
1   teaspoon cream of tartar
½   teaspoon salt
½   teaspoon nutmeg
½   cup each raisins and citron
½   package dry yeast dissolved in 2 tablespoons water

Preparation

Cream shortening, sugar and egg. Add lemon extract and milk alternately with sifted dry ingredients. Mix in raisins and citron. Add dissolved yeast last, blending in evenly. Pour batter into greased and floured 9 x 3-inch round cake pan. Bake in preheated 325° oven for 1 hour or until tests done. Mixed candied fruit may be substituted for citron.

Snow Cake

9 servings

For children on "no school" snow days

Ingredients

⅓   cup butter or margarine
1   cup sugar
1   teaspoon vanilla or lemon extract
1¾ cups flour
2   teaspoons baking powder
½   teaspoon salt
½   cup milk
2   cups freshly fallen snow
    thin chocolate icing of choice

Preparation Cream margarine and sugar. Add vanilla or lemon extract. Add flour, baking powder and salt to creamed mixture alternately with milk, beginning and ending with flour mixture. Beat after each addition. Fold in snow.

Bake in greased and floured 8 x 8-inch baking pan in preheated 350° oven for about 30 minutes or until tests done. Cool and frost with thin chocolate icing of choice.

Texas Cake   24 servings

Dessert for a crowd

Ingredients
2   cups flour
2   cups sugar
½   teaspoon salt
1   teaspoon baking soda
2   eggs, beaten
½   cup sour cream or buttermilk
1   teaspoon vanilla extract
1   cup water
1   cup butter or margarine
4   tablespoons cocoa

Frosting:
8   tablespoons butter or margarine
6   tablespoons milk
4   tablespoons cocoa
1   cup chopped walnuts or pecans
1   teaspoon vanilla extract
1   pound sifted confectioners' sugar

Preparation Sift flour, sugar, salt and baking soda. Add eggs, sour cream and vanilla, blending well. Bring water to a boil, add butter and cocoa. While still hot, add dry ingredients. Mix well and pour into greased jelly roll pan. Bake in preheated 375° oven for 20 minutes.

While cake is baking, heat frosting ingredients, mixing well. Pour over cake while both are hot. Cut into squares. Serve warm or cold.

Apricot Almond Cheese Cake

12 to 14 servings

Ingredients

Crust:
4 tablespoons butter or margarine, softened
2 tablespoons sugar
½ teaspoon vanilla extract
½ cup flour

Apricot filling:
¾ cup dried apricots
2 tablespoons sugar
½ cup water
2 tablespoons Amaretto liqueur
1 teaspoon lemon juice

Cream cheese filling:
⅔ cup sugar
2 tablespoons flour
⅛ teaspoon salt
1½ pounds cream cheese, softened
2 eggs, at room temperature
¼ cup Amaretto liqueur
1 tablespoon vanilla extract
1 cup heavy or whipping cream

Preparation

To prepare crust, beat butter and sugar until light and fluffy. Add vanilla, then stir in flour. With floured fingertips, press dough evenly onto bottom of ungreased 9-inch springform pan. Bake in preheated 400° oven 10 to 12 minutes or until golden. Cool completely.

Combine all ingredients for apricot filling and bring to a boil while stirring. Simmer 5 minutes. Remove from heat and purée. Cool to room temperature.

For cream cheese filling, combine sugar, flour and salt. Add cream cheese and beat until smooth and well-blended. Add eggs, Amaretto and vanilla. Beat again just until well-blended. Stir in heavy cream. Pour cream cheese filling on top of crust in pan. Drop apricot filling by teaspoonfuls onto cheese filling. Press down lightly so apricot filling is covered. Bake in preheated 375° oven for 55 minutes. Center will be slightly soft. Remove from oven and immediately run spatula around edge of cake to loosen from pan which helps to prevent cracking. Cool on wire rack 1 hour, then cover and chill 4 to 5 hours before cutting.

Mocha Chocolate Chip Cheesecake

10 to 12 servings

Ingredients

Crust:
1½ cups chocolate wafer crumbs
6 tablespoons butter or margarine, room temperature
⅓ cup sugar

Filling:
1½ pounds cream cheese, room temperature
1 cup sugar
4 eggs
⅓ cup whipping cream
1 tablespoon instant coffee powder
1 teaspoon vanilla extract
1 cup miniature semi-sweet chocolate chips

Preparation

Butter bottom and sides of 10-inch springform pan. Combine crumbs, butter and sugar, mixing well. Pat crumbs evenly onto sides and bottom of prepared pan. Set aside.

Beat cream cheese until fluffy. Blend in sugar. Add eggs, one at a time, beating well after each addition. Add cream, coffee and vanilla. Beat 2 minutes. Pour into crust. Sprinkle with chocolate chips and swirl through batter. Set pan on baking sheet. Bake in preheated 350° oven for 1 hour or until center tests done. Cake will appear soft. Cool completely on rack and then chill thoroughly before serving.

Milwaukee Cheesecake   10 to 14 servings

Refreshingly light and eggless

Ingredients

Crust:
18 pieces Zwieback
¼ cup sugar
¾ teaspoon cinnamon
¼ cup butter or margarine, melted

Filling:
1 3-ounce package lemon-flavored gelatin
1 cup boiling water
1 8-ounce package cream cheese, softened
1 cup sugar
2 teaspoons vanilla extract
1 pint heavy cream
   thin lemon slices, fresh mint sprigs or Zwieback crumbs for garnish

Preparation

Roll Zwieback into crumbs. Combine with sugar, cinnamon and melted butter. Press firmly and evenly onto bottom and sides of 10-inch springform pan.

For filling, mix gelatin and boiling water, stirring to dissolve. Chill until consistency of egg whites. Beat cream cheese, sugar and vanilla until smooth. Blend in gelatin evenly. In separate chilled bowl, whip heavy cream until very stiff. Gently fold into filling mixture. Pour into prepared pan. Refrigerate for 16 to 24 hours. Garnish with thin lemon slices, fresh mint sprigs or Zwieback crumbs before serving.

Sour Cream Cheesecake   12 servings

Ingredients

Crust:
1¾ cups graham cracker crumbs
½ teaspoon cinnamon
½ cup butter or margarine, melted

Filling:
3 eggs
1 cup sugar
¼ teaspoon salt
2 teaspoons vanilla extract
½ teaspoon almond extract
20 ounces cream cheese, softened
3 cups sour cream

Fruit topping:
21 ounces canned cherry pie filling
2 teaspoons lemon juice
½ teaspoon almond extract
¼ teaspoon vanilla extract

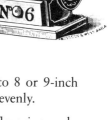

Preparation

Mix crumbs, cinnamon and butter. Press into 8 or 9-inch springform pan, covering bottom and sides evenly.

For filling, beat eggs well. Add sugar, salt, flavoring and cream cheese. Beat until smooth. Blend in sour cream. Pour into prepared pan. Bake in preheated 375° oven for 40 to 50 minutes. Center will be slightly soft when done. Remove and cool before adding topping.

Combine topping ingredients, mixing well. Spread evenly over cooled cheesecake. Chill before serving.

Brandied Fruit

10 servings

Ingredients

32 ounces canned bing cherries
16 ounces canned apricot halves
16 ounces canned sliced peaches
16 ounces canned pineapple chunks
1 cup brown sugar
grated rind of 1 lemon and 1 orange
½ cup brandy

Preparation

Drain all fruits well and place in 3-quart glass casserole dish with sugar and rinds. Bake in preheated 325° oven for 2 hours, stirring once or twice. After two thirds of baking time, add brandy and stir fruit. Serve warm over vanilla ice cream.

Honey Almond Pears

6 servings

Superior dessert with little effort

Ingredients		
	6	fresh pears
		lemon juice
	⅔	cup sugar
	4	tablespoons honey
	4	tablespoons butter or margarine
	2	tablespoons milk
	1	cup unblanched almonds, sliced

Preparation

Peel, halve and core pears. Coat with lemon juice. Place rounded side up in 9 x 13-inch baking dish. Combine sugar, honey, butter and milk. Boil 4 minutes. Stir to prevent burning. Stir in almonds and pour over pears. Bake in preheated 350° oven 15 minutes or longer, depending on ripeness of pears. Serve hot or cold.

Banana Freeze

6 servings

Ingredients		
	½	cup very ripe mashed banana
		dash of salt
	1	tablespoon sugar
	1	egg white

Preparation

Beat ingredients until very stiff and fluffy, using an electric mixer. Freeze. Serve as light dessert or as topping for fresh fruit. Seasonal fresh fruits may be substituted for bananas. May be frozen in popsicle forms for children.

Black Bottom Ice Cream Dessert

15 to 20 servings

Ingredients

1   package Nabisco Mystic Mint cookies, chilled or frozen
1   cup butter or margarine
3   cups confectioners' sugar, sifted
4   eggs, beaten
3   ounces unsweetened chocolate, melted
½   gallon ice cream, flavor of your choice

Preparation

Crush cookies in blender, 4 at a time. Reserve ¾ cup cookie crumbs. Pat rest of crumbs into bottom of greased 9 x 13-inch baking pan.

Cream butter and sugar. Add eggs and blend well. Stir in chocolate. Pour on top of crumbs. Freeze until firm. Soften ice cream and spread over chocolate layer. Sprinkle with reserved crumbs. Freeze. Cut into squares and serve. For a special touch, serve with green creme de menthe liqueur.

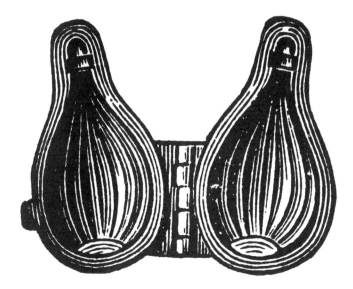

Bowdoin Logs

18 to 20 logs

An elegant original from the Bowdoin College Wentworth Hall Dining Service

Ingredients

Logs:

2 boxes Nabisco Famous Chocolate Wafers
1 cup sliced almonds
1 half-gallon block ice cream, flavor of choice

Chocolate sauce:

8   tablespoons butter or margarine
1   pound confectioners' sugar
12 ounces evaporated milk
8   ounces unsweetened chocolate
⅛   teaspoon salt
1   teaspoon vanilla extract

Preparation

For logs, blend chocolate wafers in food processor or blender until fine and smooth. Toast almonds on cookie sheet in preheated 350° oven for 5 to 10 minutes. Remove and cool. Cut ice cream into 18 to 24 equal size rectangular blocks. Place several scoops of wafer crumbs on flat surface and, working quickly, roll a block of ice cream back and forth on crumbs while pressing down lightly until it is shaped into log. Freeze immediately. Repeat with remaining blocks and crumbs.

For sauce, combine all ingredients in double boiler over medium or low heat. Cook until thick and smooth, ½ hour or longer. Set aside until needed. Reheat over warm water.

To serve, cut ends off each log. Put dab of chocolate sauce on dessert plate and place a log on sauce. Add another dab of sauce on center of log. Garnish with almonds.

Coffee Soufflé

6 to 8 servings

An old Brunswick family recipe

Ingredients

1½ cups strong coffee
½ cup milk
⅔ cup sugar
1 tablespoon unflavored gelatin
¼ teaspoon salt
3 eggs, separated
½ teaspoon vanilla extract
whipped cream and grated chocolate for garnish

Preparation

Heat coffee, milk, ⅓ cup sugar and gelatin in double boiler. In separate bowl, beat egg yolks slightly and add remaining sugar and salt. Add coffee mixture and return to double boiler. Cook until mixture coats spoon, stirring constantly. Remove from heat. Beat egg whites until stiff. Gently fold egg whites into coffee mixture. Pour into 6 to 8 stemmed glasses. Chill and serve. Top with whipped cream and garnish with grated chocolate if desired.

Frozen Chocolate Mousse Torte

12 to 16 servings

Ingredients

7 ounces almond paste
5 eggs
1 tablespoon cocoa
6 ounces semi-sweet chocolate
2 teaspoons instant coffee
1 tablespoon dark rum or water
2 tablespoons sugar
½ cup whipping cream
semi-sweet chocolate bar for garnish

Preparation

Break almond paste into small pieces in bowl of food processor. Add 2 eggs and cocoa. Whirl until smooth. Pour into greased and floured 10-inch springform pan. Bake in preheated 375° oven 15 minutes or until cake springs back when lightly touched. Cool on wire rack.

Separate 2 of remaining eggs. Set aside whites. Melt chocolate in double-boiler over hot water. Beat egg yolks with remaining whole egg. Beat in coffee, rum and melted chocolate.

Beat egg whites until foamy. Gradually add sugar and beat until moist, stiff peaks form. Fold into chocolate mixture. Whip cream and fold in. Spread evenly over cooled cake and freeze until firm, at least 3 hours.

To serve, remove sides of pan and thaw torte about 10 minutes. Garnish with curls made from chocolate bar.

Mocha Rum Mousse
4 servings

Ingredients

8 ounces sweet cooking chocolate
¼ cup coffee
5 eggs, separated
1 teaspoon rum
   sweetened whipped cream for garnish

Preparation

Melt chocolate in coffee in top of double boiler. Stir constantly. Cool. Beat in egg yolks one at a time. Stir in rum. Beat egg whites until stiff but not dry. Fold gently into cooled chocolate mixture. Pile lightly into individual souffle dishes or glasses. Chill, preferably 8 hours. Serve with dab of whipped cream.

Rhubarb Cream
6 to 8 servings

Ingredients

1 pound rhubarb, diced
1½ cups water
1 cup sugar
1 teaspoon grated lemon rind
2 envelopes unflavored gelatin
½ cup heavy cream, whipped

Preparation

Mix rhubarb, 1 cup water, sugar and lemon rind. Cover and bring to boil. Simmer until tender. Sprinkle gelatin over ½ cup water. Let stand 5 minutes to soften. Stir into rhubarb mixture. Cook 5 minutes. Mash rhubarb. Pour into bowl and chill until mixture holds shape, 1½ to 2 hours. Fold in whipped cream to form smooth sauce. Chill before serving.

Alaskan Rhubarb Crunch
8 servings

Delicious with ice cream

Ingredients

1 cup sifted flour
¾ cup rolled oats
1 cup light brown sugar, firmly packed
½ cup butter, melted
1 teaspoon cinnamon
4 cups rhubarb, diced
1 cup white sugar
2 tablespoons cornstarch
1 cup water
1 teaspoon vanilla extract

Preparation

Mix flour, oats, brown sugar, butter and cinnamon until crumbly. Press half of mixture into 9 x 9-inch pan. Cover crumb layer with rhubarb. Combine white sugar, cornstarch, water and vanilla in saucepan. Cook, stirring constantly, until thick and clear. Pour sauce over rhubarb. Top with remaining crumbs. Bake in preheated 350° oven for 50 to 60 minutes, or until the top is lightly browned and rhubarb tender. Serve hot or cold.

Cranberry Apple Crisp
9 servings

Ingredients

3 cups tart apples, peeled, cored and chopped
2 cups cranberries
1 cup sugar

Topping:
1½ cups rolled oats
8 tablespoons butter or margarine, melted
½ cup light brown sugar
½ cup nuts, chopped
⅓ cup flour
vanilla ice cream or whipped cream for garnish

Preparation   Combine apples, cranberries and sugar. Cook over medium heat until cranberries pop. Spread evenly in lightly buttered 9 x 9-inch baking pan. Combine topping ingredients and spread over fruit layer. Bake in preheated 350° oven for 30 minutes or until topping is lightly browned and fruit mixture bubbles. Serve warm with vanilla ice cream or whipped cream.

Creamy Grapenut Pudding   6 servings

Ingredients
1   cup grapenuts
1   quart milk
2   eggs
⅔   cup sugar
⅛   teaspoon salt
1   teaspoon vanilla extract
1   tablespoon butter

Preparation   Cook grapenuts in milk until soft. Cool slightly. Beat eggs, sugar and salt. Warm eggs with little milk mixture before adding to remainder of milk and grapenuts. Add vanilla. Pour into greased 2-quart glass baking dish. Float small pieces of butter on top. Bake in preheated 375° oven 1 hour. Serve warm or chilled.

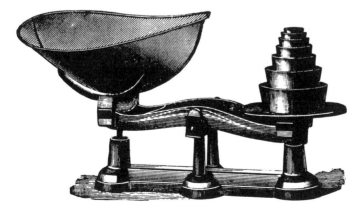

Danish Apple Squares

12 to 14 servings

Serve with Cheddar cheese or French vanilla ice cream

Preparation

Dough:
2½ cups flour
½ teaspoon salt
1 cup butter or margarine
1 egg, separated
⅔ cup milk

Filling:
8 cups apples, peeled, cored and sliced
1½ cups crushed cornflakes
1 cup sugar
1½ teaspoons cinnamon

Icing:
1 cup confectioners' sugar, sifted
1 tablespoon butter
¼ teaspoon almond extract
  milk

Preparation

Mix flour and salt. Cut in butter to form coarse crumbs.
Beat egg yolk and milk together. Add to flour mixture.
Divide dough in half and roll out to fit 9 x 15-inch baking
pan. Sprinkle with cornflakes. Spread apples evenly over
cornflakes. Sprinkle sugar and cinnamon over apples. Roll
out remaining dough. Cover and seal edges. Beat reserved
egg white and brush on pastry crust. Bake in preheated
350° oven for 50 to 60 minutes. Cool.

Mix icing ingredients with enough milk to form thin glaze.
Drizzle over top. Cut into squares.

Linzer Torte

8 to 10 servings

Ingredients

Crust:
1 cup flour
½ teaspoon cinnamon
⅛ teaspoon ground cloves

⅛ teaspoon ground ginger
1 cup chilled butter (do not substitute)
½ cup sugar
2 cups finely ground almonds
1 egg plus 1 egg yolk
1 teaspoon freshly grated lemon peel

Filling:
¾ cup tart jam or jelly, preferably red currant

Preparation Combine flour, cinnamon, cloves and ginger. Cut in butter until mixture resembles coarse crumbs. Stir in sugar and ground almonds. Separate egg and set aside white. Mix yolks slightly and add to dough with lemon peel. Work dough slightly with hands. Form into ball, cover and chill thoroughly.

Grease 9-inch round cake pan. Line bottom with greased paper. Line sides and bottom with half of rolled dough. Spread jam. Make lattice work with strips of remaining dough. Brush with reserved egg white. Bake in preheated 300° oven for 1 hour. Cool and let "ripen" for 1 to 2 days at room temperature before serving.

Marmalade Soufflé   4 servings

Ingredients
4 large egg whites
3½ tablespoons sugar
2½ tablespoons English-type orange marmalade
1¼ teaspoons orange extract
¼ cup finely chopped nuts
   sweetened whipped cream, flavored with brandy, cream sherry or rum

Preparation Beat egg whites until stiff, about 10 minutes. Mix sugar, marmalade and extract with small amount of beaten whites, then fold into rest of whites. Pour into well-buttered top of 2-quart double boiler. Use only 1½ inches water in bottom of boiler. Cook, covered, over low heat for 1 hour, 10 minutes. Do not lift lid for at least 1 hour. Turn onto warm platter and sprinkle with chopped nuts. Serve with sweetened whipped cream.

"Slump" and "Grunt"

6 servings

Maine folklore credits the name of this recipe to the known fact that men folks on the farm, when served this dessert at noon, were inclined to "slump" into a porch chair and "grunt" instead of returning to complete their chores!

Ingredients

4   cups blueberries, fresh or frozen
½   cup water
¾   cup sugar
2   tablespoons butter
1   cup flour
2   teaspoons baking powder
½   teaspoon salt
¼   cup sugar
½   cup milk
     fresh cream, sour cream or ice cream for garnish

Preparation

For "slump", combine blueberries, water, ¾ cup sugar and butter, in 2 to 3-quart covered sauce pan. Bring to a boil and simmer. Mix remaining ingredients to make stiff batter. Spoon over hot mixture as for dumplings. Cover tightly and simmer 12 minutes. Do not uncover during cooking. Serve hot with fresh cream or sour cream.

For "grunt", combine blueberries, water, ¾ cup sugar and add to greased 2-quart casserole. Bake in preheated 400° oven until mixture simmers. Make topping by blending dry ingredients, cutting in butter and adding milk. Spoon over hot berries. Bake for 20 minutes. Serve hot with fresh cream or ice cream. Sprinkle with cinnamon or nutmeg if desired.

Steamed Cranberry Pudding

6 to 8 servings

Excellent for reduced cholesterol diets

Ingredients

Pudding:
2   teaspoons baking soda
½   cup molasses
½   cup boiling water
1   teaspoon baking powder
1⅓ cups sifted flour
1   cup fresh cranberries

Sauce:
½   cup sugar
¼   cup butter
½   cup all-purpose cream

Preparation

Add baking soda to molasses and stir in boiling water. Sift flour with baking powder. Combine flour mixture with molasses mixture. Lightly flour cranberries. Add to mixture, folding in gently. Butter 1-quart mold or 1-pound coffee can. Pour batter into prepared mold, cover tightly and steam 2 hours. Unmold and serve warm with warm sauce.

For sauce, combine sugar, butter and cream in top of double boiler. Stir and cook over boiling water 15 minutes.

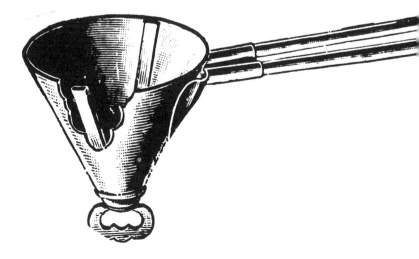

Strawberry Rhubarb Kuchen 9 servings

A tasty and different way to serve tender spring rhubarb

Ingredients

Crust:
1   cup sifted flour
1   tablespoon sugar
1½ teaspoons baking powder
⅛   teaspoon salt
2   tablespoons butter or margarine
1   egg
2   tablespoons milk

Filling:
1   3-ounce package strawberry-flavored gelatin
⅓   cup sugar
3   tablespoons flour
1½ pounds rhubarb, sliced (5 cups)

Topping:
⅔   cup sugar
⅓   cup flour
3   tablespoons butter or margarine

Preparation

For crust, combine flour, sugar, baking powder and salt. Cut in butter to form coarse crumbs. Beat egg and milk and add. Stir until dry ingredients are moistened. Pat dough evenly on bottom and 1 inch of sides of 9 x 9-inch pan.

Combine gelatin, sugar, flour and rhubarb, mixing well. Pour into crust-lined pan.

Combine topping ingredients, cutting in butter until crumbly. Sprinkle evenly over rhubarb filling. Bake in preheated 375° oven for 45 minutes or until rhubarb is tender and topping is lightly browned. Cool and cut into squares. Serve with vanilla ice cream.

Potpourri

Blueberry Butter

¾ cup

Ingredients

8   tablespoons unsalted butter
¼   cup blueberries
2   teaspoons dark brown sugar
    pinch of salt

Preparation

Combine all ingredients in bowl of food processor and blend for 1 minute.

Strawberries or raspberries may be substituted for blueberries. Serve blueberry butter with blueberry muffins or scones, raspberry butter with raspberry muffins, etc.

English Toffee

1½ pounds

Ingredients

1   cup butter
1   cup sugar
⅓   cup slivered almonds
4   ounces plain Hershey's chocolate bar, cut into small
    pieces
½   cup chopped pecans

Preparation

Melt butter. Add sugar and almonds. Cook over medium heat, stirring constantly, 10 minutes until golden brown. If butter starts to separate from sugar, turn up heat. Pour quickly into buttered 9 x 13-inch baking pan. Spread chocolate over toffee and smooth carefully. Sprinkle pecans over top. Cool and break up candy with sharp knife.

Mamie Eisenhower Chocolate Fudge

3 pounds

From the famous fudge ladies at RMH Christmas fair

Ingredients

4½ cups sugar
      pinch of salt
2   tablespoons butter
12   ounces evaporated milk
12   ounces German's sweet chocolate, cut into pieces
8   ounces Marshmallow Fluff
1½ cups chopped nuts

Preparation

Boil sugar, salt, butter and milk 8 minutes. Add chocolate, marshmallow and nuts. Pour into 9 x 13-inch buttered baking pan. Cool and cut lines through when set. Invert onto wax paper. Wrap each piece in plastic wrap.

Sour Cream Fudge

3 pounds

Ingredients

2   cups white sugar
4   cups light brown sugar
3   cups sour cream
1 to 2 cups Marshmallow Fluff
1   teaspoon vanilla extract
1   cup chopped nuts

Preparation

Combine white and brown sugars and sour cream. Cook to soft ball stage, 240°. Remove from heat and add marshmallow, vanilla and nuts. Beat until creamy and pour into 6 x 9½-inch buttered pan. Cool and cut lines through when set. Invert onto wax paper. Wrap each piece in plastic wrap.

Wonderful Peanut Butter Balls · 8 dozen

Ingredients

½ cup margarine
2 cups peanut butter
1 pound confectioners' sugar
3 cups Rice Krispies
8 ounces Hershey's milk chocolate bar
6 ounces semi-sweet chocolate chips
½ cake, 2½ by 2½ inches, paraffin wax

Preparation

Blend margarine, peanut butter and sugar. Mix in rice cereal. Roll into ¾ inch balls. Melt chocolate bar, chocolate chips and wax in double boiler. Dip balls into chocolate mixture and place on wax paper.

Peanut Brittle · 2 pounds

Ingredients

1 pound raw peanuts
2 cups sugar
¾ cup light corn syrup
¼ cup water
⅛ teaspoon salt
1 teaspoon baking soda

Preparation

Mix all ingredients, except baking soda, in electric fry pan. Turn heat to high and cook, stirring constantly to prevent scorching. When candy turns light golden brown, turn off heat, add baking soda and turn onto large buttered cookie sheet. Cool and break into pieces.

Texas Pralines

1¼ pounds

Enjoy in any climate

Ingredients

2　cups sugar
¾　cup milk
½　teaspoon baking soda
1　teaspoon butter
1　teaspoon vanilla extract
1¼　cups pecan halves

Preparation

Combine sugar, milk, baking soda and butter. Cook slowly, stirring constantly, until candy becomes a golden brown, 238° on candy thermometer, or forms soft ball when dropped in cold water. Remove from heat, add vanilla and beat until it begins to thicken. Add pecans and beat until creamy. Drop by teaspoonfuls on salted wax paper. Servings should be small as candy is very rich.

Spiced Peaches

3 pints

A nice gift from your kitchen

Ingredients

¾　cup brown sugar
⅓　cup vinegar
1　cup peach juice from canned peaches
1　teaspoon whole cloves
2　3-inch cinnamon sticks
1　teaspoon whole allspice, optional
2　29-ounce cans peaches, halves or slices, drained

Preparation

Bring all ingredients except peaches to a rolling boil for 1 minute. Add peaches to sterilized jars. Pour mixture over them. Include cinnamon sticks in jars, if desired.

Apple Chutney
6 pints

Ingredients

3   pounds Red Delicious or Granny Smith apples, pared,
    cored and coarsely chopped
4   large onions, chopped
2   large green tomatoes, coarsely chopped
2   pounds light brown sugar
24 ounces raisins
3   cups cider vinegar
3   tablespoons cinnamon
1   teaspoon nutmeg
2   teaspoons curry powder
4   shakes Tabasco sauce

Preparation

Combine all ingredients and bring to a boil. Reduce heat
and simmer, covered, stirring frequently, for 1 hour. Cool
slightly and spoon into hot sterilized jars. Seal immediately.

Orange Cranberry Chutney
3 pints

Ingredients

4   medium seedless oranges
½   cup fresh orange juice
1   pound fresh or frozen cranberries
2   cups sugar
½   cup raisins
¼   cup diced candied ginger
¾   teaspoon curry powder
½   teaspoon liquid red pepper
1   whole cinnamon stick
1   small garlic clove, diced

Preparation   Remove outer rind from 2 or more oranges. Cut rind in thin slivers to make ⅓ cup. Remove all membrane and skin from remaining oranges. Cut oranges crosswise in slices about ¼ inch thick. Cut these in sixths. Combine slivered rind, juice, cranberries, sugar, raisins, ginger, curry powder, liquid pepper, cinnamon and garlic. Cook over medium heat, stirring, until sugar dissolves. Continue to cook, uncovered, until berries pop. Remove from heat and discard cinnamon stick. Add oranges and blend lightly but well. May be stored in refrigerator about 6 to 8 weeks or sealed in sterilized jars for longer period.

Mango Chutney   4 cups

Ingredients   3   cups mangos, about 3 medium fruit, slightly underripe, preferably Hayden's, available in June and July, peeled, seeded and cut into ½ inch strips
2   cups light brown sugar
1   cup malt or white vinegar
1   cup fresh lime juice
1½   cups seedless raisins, half dark and half white
½   cup fresh ginger, peeled and cut into 1¼-inch strips
1   cup chopped onion
1   tablespoon salt
1   large garlic clove, crushed
2   tablespoons mustard seed
2   teaspoons hot red pepper flakes
2   whole cloves
1   1-inch cinnamon stick, broken up

Preparation   Combine all ingredients except spices. Tie mustard seed, pepper flakes, cloves and cinnamon in cheesecloth bag. Add to mixture. Bring to a boil. Simmer 15 minutes, covered. Let cool and stand overnight to plump fruit. Next day, cook gently another 15 minutes. Let cool again, stirring from time to time. Discard cheesecloth bag. Pour into hot sterilized jars and seal. Refrigerate.

Rhubarb Relish

8 cups

Ingredients

4   cups rhubarb, peeled and diced
4   cups thinly sliced onions
2   cups vinegar
3   cups brown sugar, packed
1   teaspoon salt
1   teaspoon cinnamon
1   teaspoon allspice
½   teaspoon pepper
½   teaspoon cloves
1   garlic clove, optional

Preparation

Mix all ingredients. Boil 1 hour, stirring often to prevent scorching. Pour into sterilized jars and seal.

Apple Marmalade

8 cups

Ingredients

5   pounds tart apples, peeled, cored and thinly sliced
2   oranges
2   lemons
5   pounds sugar
2½ cups water

Preparation

Squeeze juice from oranges and lemons and cut peel into thin strips. Combine sugar and water and boil to make sugar syrup. Add fruits and juices and simmer very slowly until thick. Pour into hot sterilized jars and seal at once.

Cantaloupe Jam

6 cups

Ingredients

3½ cups diced cantaloupe
1   orange, seeded and ground
1   lemon, seeded and ground
2½ cups peeled and diced peaches
1   cup mashed banana
4   cups sugar
½   teaspoon salt

Preparation	Combine cantaloupe, orange and lemon. Slowly bring to a boil, stirring frequently. Simmer 10 minutes. Add peaches, banana, sugar and salt. Boil vigorously for 20 minutes, or until thick, stirring constantly to prevent scorching. Pour into hot sterilized jars and seal.

Cinnamon Cider Jelly
7 cups

Ingredients	4 cups sweet cider 2 tablespoons cinnamon candies 1¾ ounces powdered fruit pectin 4½ cups sugar
Preparation	Combine cider, candy and pectin. Stir over high heat until mixture reaches a rolling boil. Add sugar all at once. Bring to a full boil again and boil hard 1 minute, stirring constantly. Cool 5 minutes, stirring occasionally. Skim off any foam. Pour into hot sterilized jars and seal with paraffin wax. Beautiful color.

Pepper Jelly
8 cups

Ingredients	½ cup jalapeno peppers, chopped 1½ cups green pepper 6½ cups sugar 1½ cups cider vinegar 1 bottle Certo green food coloring, if desired
Preparation	Put peppers in blender with ½ cup of vinegar. Blend and add rest of vinegar. Add to sugar. Bring to a boil. Boil 3 minutes, skim, add Certo and boil 1 minute. Remove from heat. Add 2 or 3 drops of green food coloring until right color. Pour into sterilized jars and cover. This makes hot pepper jelly. For sweet jelly, omit jalapeno and increase amount of green peppers. Good served over cream cheese on crackers for hors d'oeuvre.

Lime Zucchini Marmalade   8 cups

A refreshing flavor

Ingredients

4   cups coarsely grated zucchini
2   cups water
½   cup fresh lime juice, 3 to 4 limes
1¾   ounces powdered fruit pectin
5   cups sugar
3   tablespoons grated lime rind

Preparation

Grate lime rind before squeezing juice from limes. Combine zucchini, water and lime juice. Bring to a boil and boil gently for 10 minutes. Stir in fruit pectin and return to a boil. Stir in sugar and lime rind. Return to hard rolling boil that cannot be stirred down. Boil, stirring constantly, for 2 minutes. Remove from heat and stir 5 minutes. Ladle into hot sterilized jars and seal with paraffin wax. Store in cool place.

Chili Sauce   13 cups

Neither sweet nor sour—just very good

Ingredients

24   large ripe tomatoes
6   medium onions
4   green peppers
2   cups sugar
2   cups cider vinegar
4   teaspoons salt
1   teaspoon ground allspice
1   teaspoon ground clove

Preparation

Process vegetables in food processor or grind in meat grinder. Mix all ingredients and boil slowly 3 hours, or until thick. Stir to prevent sticking. Seal in hot sterilized jars.

Dilly Carrots

6 pints

Ingredients

6   garlic cloves
6   large fresh dill tops
5   pounds carrots, peeled and cut into sticks
4½ cups water
4   cups white vinegar
½   cup pickling salt
    few drops Tabasco sauce

Preparation

Put 1 garlic clove and 1 dill top in bottom of each pint jar. Pack carrots into jars. Boil water, vinegar, salt and Tabasco. Pour over carrots. Seal and process in boiling water bath 20 minutes. Three pounds green beans, tips removed, may be substituted for carrots.

Harvest Relish

8 to 10 pints

Good with baked beans

Ingredients

4   onions, ground
4   cups chopped cabbage
4   cups chopped green tomatoes
12 green peppers, chopped
6   red peppers, chopped
½   cup salt
6   cups sugar
1   tablespoon celery seed
2   tablespoons mustard seed
2   teaspoons turmeric
4   cups vinegar
2   cups water

Preparation

Combine vegetables and salt and let set overnight. In morning, rinse vegetables and drain. Combine remaining ingredients and pour over vegetables. Bring to a boil. Simmer 3 minutes stirring frequently. Pack into hot sterilized pint jars and process in boiling water 10 minutes.

Mustard Sandwich Pickles   8 to 10 pints

Ingredients

4   pounds pickling cucumbers, sliced
6   medium white onions, thinly sliced
1   cup pickling salt
3½ cups sugar
¾   cup flour
½   cup dry mustard
1½ teaspoons turmeric
1   teaspoon celery seed
4   cups cider vinegar

Preparation

Layer cucumbers, onions and salt in very large non-metal
bowl. Cover with cold water. Let stand overnight. Drain and
rinse well with cold water. In large kettle, mix sugar, flour,
mustard, turmeric and celery seed. Gradually add vinegar.
Cook and stir constantly until mixture boils. Add vegetables
and bring to a boil, stirring constantly to prevent scorching.
Pack immediately into 8 to 10 hot sterilized jars. Process in
boiling water bath 5 minutes.

Hanscom Sour Pickles   2 gallons

Ingredients

2   gallons pickling cucumbers
1   gallon cider vinegar
1   cup sugar
1   cup pickling salt
1   cup dry mustard

Preparation

Wash cucumbers and pack into glass gallon jars. Mix other
ingredients and shake well. Pour over cucumbers. Seal jars.
Refrigerate. Shake every few days. Ready to eat in about 2
weeks. Quart jars may also be used.

Quick Bread and Butter Pickles

1 gallon

Ingredients

9 cups thinly sliced cucumbers
1 cup thinly sliced onions
2 cups sugar
1 cup cider vinegar
2 tablespoons salt
1 tablespoon celery seed

Preparation

Layer cucumbers and onion in glass gallon jar. Mix other ingredients and add to jar. Refrigerate, shaking pickles every day. Ready to eat in 5 days. Store in refrigerator.

Hoosier Mincemeat

10 quarts

Ingredients

9 pounds apples, diced
3 pounds raisins
2 pounds currants
1 pound white sugar
1 pound brown sugar
2 quarts cider
1 quart dark Karo corn syrup
1½ pounds ground suet
4 pounds beef, roasted and ground
2 quarts tart cherries
2 lemons, juice and grated rind
3 teaspoons cloves
10 teaspoons cinnamon
5 teaspoons nutmeg
3 tablespoons salt

Preparation

Mix all ingredients and simmer for 3 to 4 hours, or until thick. May be frozen. Venison may be substituted for beef.

Bowdoin Wassail

20 cups

Served on Sunday afternoons to Bowdoin College freshmen at the President's House from 1952 to 1967

Ingredients

1   gallon apple cider
6   ounces frozen lemonade
6   ounces frozen orange juice
18 ounces water
½   teaspoon nutmeg
1   teaspoon cloves
1   teaspoon allspice
2   cinnamon sticks
    orange and lemon slices for garnish

Preparation

Simmer cider, juices and water. Add spices. Simmer for 30 minutes. Serve hot. Garnish with thin slices of orange and lemon. Rum to taste may be added.

Hot Mulled Cider

16 cups

Sip by the fire on snowy evenings

Ingredients

1   gallon cider
2   long cinnamon sticks, broken in half
2   teaspoons whole cloves
2   teaspoons whole allspice

Preparation

Heat cider in crockpot or in large pot on wood stove. Add cinnamon sticks. Tie cloves and allspice in cheesecloth bag and add. Simmer for at least 30 minutes before serving. Rum to taste may be added.

Acknowledgements

The Regional Memorial Hospital Auxiliary sincerely thanks the following people for their efforts and interests in preparing this book.

Doris Allen
Marie Almy
Allen Andraski
Jo Atlass
Geri Aylward
Flossie Baldwin
Barbara Bard
Roderick Bard
Ann Barry
Alice Baxter
Dorothy Bayer
Gerald Beals
Erika Beckwith
Robert Beckwith
Caroline Below
Lois Berge
Betty Bibber
Charlotte Billings
Lorraine Bisson
Karen Black
Janet Bodwell
Bowdoin College,
    Wentworth Hall
    Dining Service
Judy Brennan
Frank Brockman
Mary Brown
Merton Brown
Timmy Browne
Christine Bulick
Ruth Burt
Virginia Buttle
Helen Buzzell
Lucy Bygrave
Lindsey Cadot
Ron Campbell
Celina Caouette
Lucille Caron
Mary Carpenter
Sandra Carter
Adelaide Cass
Frances Caswell
Kay Charles
Chuck Wagon Restaurant
Ana-Maria Ciampa
Jacquelyn Clark

Linda Clement
Patricia Clockedile
Alisa Coffin
Christine Coffin
June Coffin
Linda Coldwell
Eleanor Cole
Margaret Cole
Martha Reed Coles
Commissioned Officers'
    Mess, NASB
Margit Cook
Anna Cooper
Bette Copeland
Elise Copeland
Pamela Cormier
The Corsican Restaurant
Carol Cossar
Muriel Cox
Edith Coxe
Robert Crandall
Joan Creswell
Jane Crichton
Lindsay Crosby
Loraine Crosby
Jeannette Cross
Josephine Cunningham
Ella Curtis
Shirley Curtis
Henry D'Alessandris
Louise Dartnell
Betsy Davis
Marguerite Davis
Marion Davis
Virginia Davis
Mary Day
Ruth Deane
Alex Delicata
Ann-Marie Dill
Linda Donahue
Pat Doore
Marian Downing
Roberta Doyle
Carol Dube
Gabrielle Dubois
Robin Dudley

Jane Dugan
Lucille Dumais
MaLeRoy Dunlap
Marjorie Dunning
Zoé Durrell
Honour Edgerton
Lucille Ericson
Jennifer Ertner
Peg Estes
Lori Fairservice
M'Lou Fales
Todd Farrington
Lea Favreau
Jean Fay
Gloria Fife
Helen Fish
Betty Fitzjarrald
Barbara Fleming
Margery Follansbee
Teen Foshay
Dorothy Fredrickson
Margot Freeman
Doris Gallagher
JoAnne Gallo
Judy Gardiner
Sandra Garson
Kathye Geary
Kim Gilbert
Jeanne Gilliam
Ernestine Gillis
Karen Giustra
Deborah Gleason
Richard Gnauck
Barbara Gordon
Haffy Gould
Grane's Fairhaven Inn
Joan Granger
Sally Gray
Deborah Greeley
Betty Green
Greenery at Senter's
Barbara Griffin
Susan Gullett
Michelle Guptill
Hazel Guyler
Kay Haggerty

Sara Hammond
Susan Handforth
Maria Hanley
Anne Hannaford-Oceretko
Helen Hanscom
Jan Harris
Lori Harris
Stephen Harris
Patty Hartigan
Jean Hathaway
J. Hathaway's Restaurant
Becky Hawkins
Cara Hayes
Mary Hayes
Jane Hazelton
Louise Helmreich
Linda Henderson
Betty Hentz
Gail Hodsdon
Bernice Holbrook
Benjamin Holden
Elsie Holt
Elizabeth Horton
Dottie Hunter
Helen Hunter
Margaret Hutchins
Gerry Hyde
Carol Jackson
Esther Jackson
Clara Jacobs
Dora Jordan
Joshua's Restaurant
Judy Kamin
McGee Kanwit
Edith Kelby
Lynda Kelly
Nancy Kerner
Barbara Killion
Wilhelmina Kimball
Zona King
Karen Kiraly
Joyce Kittredge
Linda Knowles
Suzanne Labree
Alice Lachance
Dan Lambert
Barbara Landry
Kathy Larson
Barbara Laughlin
Joan Laughlin
Kenneth Laughlin

Claudia Lavigne
Viviane Lebel
Helen Leo
Marjorie Libby
Sally Light
Phyllis Little
Priscilla Little
Anne Locke
Gwen Locke
Janet Logan
Rebecca Longley
Gerard Lord
Lorraine Maloney
Linda Marquis
Bertha Marshall
Phyllis McGraves
Eleanor Means
Mary Lou Meisenbach
Susan Melrose
Rolande Menard
Betsy Merrill
Helen Merrill
Clara Merriman
Juliette Messier
Marjorie Meyer
Ellen Miller
Peggy Miller
Grace Mitchell
Hati Modr
Faith Moll
Teresa Monahan
Betty Moody
Jane Moody
JoAnne Moore
Jeannette Morin
Priscilla Morris
Anita Morse
Dolly Morse
New Meadows Inn
Priscilla Newgarden
Elfriede Nicholson
Frances Nicita
Betsy Niven
Helen Norton
Linda Nunn
Ellen Nyhus
Omelette Shop
Oriental Restaurant
Jerry Ouellette
Joan Ouellette
Betty Page

Harriet Pankratz
Harriet Paris
Pamela Parker
Audrey Parkinson
Marie Peabody
Natalie Pendleton
Tina Perow
Sandra Peters
Joan Phillips
Larry Pinette
Mary Pitt
Elizabeth Porter
Joan Poulin
Gertrude Powers
Jeannine Powers
Jean Principe
Walter Pushard
Sue Ranger
Loretta Reddy
Leon Richardson
Margaret Richardson
Dorothy Roberts
Adele Robinson
Pat Robinson
Patricia Robinson
Winifred Rose
Janice Roy
Lydia Rubin
Lucy Ruiter
Elsie Ryan
Christine Sanborn
Valeda Sawyer
Deborah Schall
Narcissa Schall
Carmel Schinck
Helen Schlaack
Betsy Schmidt
Linda Schwab
Marilyn Scott
Lynne Shapiro
Brenda Shaw
Joan Shepherd
Dorothy Skelton
Marybeth Skillings
Georgie Skolfield
Bettina Smith
Gwyeth Smith
Mary Smith
Priscilla Smith
Rosamond Smith
Heidi Sproul

Marjorie Standish
Natalie Stanwood
Dorothy Stetson
Millie Stewart
Lucy Stinson
Betty Stone
Stowe House
Glenna Sullivan
Eleanor Sumner
Dorothy Sylvester
Hazel Thayer
The Bowdoin Steakhouse
The Great Impasta
Patti Thibodeau
Dorothy Thompson
Joan Thompson
Patricia Thorburn
Andy Torrey
Anita Tracy
Marilyn True
Mary Jane Turcotte
Twenty-Two Lincoln
Mary Ellen Van Lunen
Marilyn VanderSchaaf
Robin Wade
Margaret Warming
Ruth Weeks
Marge West
Betty White
Dorothy White
Judy White
Mary Baxter White
Susan White
Elizabeth Whitman
Barbara Whitney
Lois Widmer
Janet Wilk
Alice Willard-Michael
Doris Williams
Marita Williams
Dorothy Wilson
Eleanor Wilson
Joan Wilson
Mary Wilson
Mary Lou Wilson
Marion Winkelbauer
Jean Wise
Vivian Wixom
Anne Yancey
Eleanor Yanok
Sarah Zeitler

Index

ORDER FORM

Merrymeeting Merry Eating
Mid Coast Hospital / Brunswick Auxiliary
58 Baribeau Drive
Brunswick, Maine 04011

Please send me _____ copies of *Merrymeeting Merry Eating* at $15.95 per copy plus $3 shipping and handling (Maine residents also add 96¢ sales tax). Please make check or money order payable to *Merrymeeting Merry Eating*.

Name _____

Address _____

City _____ State _____ Zip _____

All proceeds from books sales benefit Mid Coast Hospital.

- -

ORDER FORM

Merrymeeting Merry Eating
Mid Coast Hospital / Brunswick Auxiliary
58 Baribeau Drive
Brunswick, Maine 04011

Please send me _____ copies of *Merrymeeting Merry Eating* at $15.95 per copy plus $3 shipping and handling (Maine residents also add 96¢ sales tax). Please make check or money order payable to *Merrymeeting Merry Eating*.

Name _____

Address _____

City _____ State _____ Zip _____

All proceeds from books sales benefit Mid Coast Hospital.